THE MEMOIRS OF
WILLIAM JENNINGS BRYAN

A

WILLIAM JENNINGS BRYAN
From the painting by Irving R. Wiles in the State Department at Washington.

THE MEMOIRS OF
WILLIAM JENNINGS BRYAN

BY HIMSELF AND HIS WIFE
MARY BAIRD BRYAN

𝔍𝔩𝔩𝔲𝔰𝔱𝔯𝔞𝔱𝔢𝔡

THE JOHN C. WINSTON COMPANY

CHICAGO   PHILADELPHIA   TORONTO

INTRODUCTION

By Mary Baird Bryan

IT has fallen to me to take up the pen which Mr. Bryan laid down.

In justice to him, it should be borne in mind that his chapters are in the first draft; he had no opportunity to revise or polish them.

While I am willing to carry out his ideas, the fact remains that it is impossible for me, or for anyone else, to do this work as he had planned it. The intimate knowledge of people and of small happenings has passed with him.

However, from his private correspondence, from his documents, and from my diary, I hope to bring to light the truth on several controversial questions.

I wish, too, to give a careful and just analysis of his character. His dominant traits will explain his course of action in several crises.

In this work I have been assisted in research and collation by our children, by other members of the family, by faithful friends, and by the competent staff which was furnished me by the Publishers.

Mary B. Bryan

CONTENTS

CONTENTS

PART I

PREFACE

By William J. Bryan

IN giving the public the story of my life I trust I may be credited with something more than a desire to acquaint the public with myself. The time has passed when I could have any ulterior motive in a heart-to-heart talk with the American people. Whatever ambition I have had has been more than gratified; I feel that I have received more than I have deserved and been abundantly repaid for the efforts I have made in behalf of the American people.

It is my purpose to show that in my own case good fortune has had more to do with such success as I may have achieved than any efforts of my own. Success in politics—and, to a large extent in other lines of activity—is the conjunction of opportunity and the preparedness to meet it. Opportunity comes independently of one's own efforts; and his preparedness to meet opportunity is due, as I shall show, largely to others. The facts as I present them will prove that I have been wonderfully fortunate in the opportunities that have come to me and that I am indebted to a multitude of individuals known and unknown for such preparation as I have had to improve the opportunities as they came.

My second purpose is to show the goodness of the American people, their patriotism, their moral courage, their high ideals, their willingness to sacrifice for their convictions—the virtues that not only make popular government possible but insure its success. No man in public life has ever been in a better position to record these virtues of the people or under deeper obligation to give them the credit they deserve.

I trust that with the two purposes in view I may be able so to shift the accent from "I" to "they" as to purge my Memoirs of every trace of egotism or self-assertion. I shall relate my own connection with individuals, measures, and events, but I shall endeavor so to interweave the actions of others with my own acts as to make the results appear as the result of a joint effort in which I have played but a part, and often but an inconsequential part.

In politics as in the army, the generals receive the glory while the enlisted men die in the trenches. The names that are prominent become household words, while the multitude who bear the burden are nameless in history.

That which was called Bryanism in derision by many, represented a group of substantial reforms; it was not an individual thing but rather the result of united effort of some six and a half millions of American voters. I was but one of the millions, but because I was in a position of leadership I received the glory and the censure, while others equally earnest and often with more sacrifice labored and died unknown to fame.

To begin the story of my good fortune. I was born in the greatest of all ages. No golden ages of the past offered any such opportunity for large service and, therefore, for the enjoyment that comes from consciousness that one has been helpful.

I was born a member of the greatest of all the races— the Caucasian Race, and had mingled in my veins the blood of English, Irish, and Scotch. One has only to consider the limitations upon one's opportunities imposed by race to understand the incalculable benefit of having the way opened between the child and the stars.

I was born a citizen of the greatest of all lands. So far as my power to prevent was concerned, I might have been born in the darkest of the continents and among the most backward of earth's peoples. It was a gift of priceless value to see the light in beloved America, and to live under the greatest of the republics of history.

And I was equally fortunate, as I shall show, in my family environment. I cannot trace my ancestry beyond

PREFACE

the fourth generation and there is not among them, so far as I know, one of great wealth or great political or social prominence, but so far as I have been able to learn, they were honest, industrious, Christian, moral, religious people —not a black sheep in the flock, not a drunkard, not one for whose life I would have to utter an apology. The environment in which my youth was spent was as ideal as any that I know.

At the age of fourteen I became a member of the Church, as the result of a spiritual awakening that took place in the little town in which I was born. I shall elaborate upon it in the proper place in my story; I mention it now because it has had more influence in my life for good than any other experience, and I have been increasingly grateful for the circumstances that led me to take a stand on religion before I left home for college. It was of incalculable value to me during the period of questioning that seems unavoidable in the life of students. The influences of the Church, the Sunday school, the prayer meeting and the Y. M. C. A. were about me and sustained me until my feet were upon the Solid Rock and my faith built upon an enduring foundation.

I have often been reminded of one of the concluding verses of the Twenty-third Psalm: "Thou preparest a table before me in the presence of mine enemies." And still more frequently do I recall that wonderfully expressive description of superlative blessings: "My cup runneth over." If judging the future by the past can be made the basis of a firm hope, I can say, "Surely goodness and mercy shall follow me all the days of my life."

No one has been the recipient of as large a measure of unselfish devotion; no one is in better position to record with grateful appreciation the kindnesses received. I have never been in a position to repay friends in a political way. During my first term in Congress, the Republicans were in control of the national administration, so that I had no patronage at my command. During my second term in Congress, I was not in harmony with President Cleveland on the money question and soon ceased to be influential in the securing of appointments. Thus, during the four years in office in the earlier part of my life, I was unable to pay my debts with lucrative positions or to secure support by the hope of appointments. Even when I was Secretary of State, as I shall later relate, I was not able to reward any considerable number of political friends. My debts were larger and, in an appointive way, my assets smaller than those of any other cabinet member. All of the clerical force of the State Department is under the Civil Service, as are also the Consular offices. There are but a handful of assistants in the whole office who hold appointing power. Our ambassadors and ministers are largely chosen upon recommendation of the United States Senators.

And yet, while during the six years and three months of my official life I was practically powerless to reward those who had contributed to my success, I am sure that no one in this country—probably no one who ever lived—has had more friends, kept them for a longer period or received from them greater loyalty or more constant support. I have reason to know that the masses are patriotic and incorruptible. They cannot be purchased and they cannot be terrified. No matter how they may err or be led astray, the American people are sound at heart. They have solved successfully all problems that confronted them during the momentous years of our nation's history and there is not the slightest reason to doubt that they will meet every emergency, rise to every responsibility and prove that their capacity for self-government is as undeniable as their right to self-government.

The story of my life is but an account of opportunities improved and of circumstances of which I have taken advantage, but for the wisdom to see opportunities and the ability to take advantage of circumstances, I am indebted

PREFACE

to others more largely than to myself. In tracing my life from the beginning up to the time of the completion of this volume, I am simply showing what anyone, equally fortunate and with equal opportunities, can accomplish in this favored land of ours in this golden age.

If to the encouragement that my words may bring to the young men of our land I can add a moral, it is this: Truth, being of God, is omnipotent. It has within itself the power to propagate itself. Man may delay, but cannot prevent its triumph. Man borrows more strength from a great truth than he gives to it. It is of little importance to truth whether any individual espouses it, but to the individual it is of vital importance that he shall know the truth and, knowing it, adhere to it.

Jefferson said that he had learned that firm adherence to principle was the best handmaiden, even unto ambition.

If my Memoirs prove of benefit to others they will pay in part the debt I owe to those who in the past have contributed to the spread of the Christian religion, the safeguarding of society, and the establishing of popular government—the causes to which the mature years of my life have been dedicated.

"HE BELONGS TO THE AGES"

"The message of Mr. Bryan was not alone to the men of his day, but to the men of the ages."

CHAPTER I

In the Beginning

I WAS born on the nineteenth day of March, 1860, at Salem, Illinois. A picture of my birthplace to be found among the illustrations shows the house in which I first saw the light. The house stood on Broadway about halfway between the public square and the Baltimore and Ohio Railroad—prior to 1872 called the Ohio and Mississippi. It had never been materially changed from the time when it was built in 1852. My father, then a young lawyer just starting in at the practice, helped to hew the timbers to build the house. Being thus doubly attached to the homestead, I purchased it and gave it to the city of Salem, moving it a few feet to the west in order to give room for the erection of the Bryan Bennett Library, to which reference will be made in another chapter.

I do not know the hour of my birth, because the hour never became material until after the death of my parents. As soon as I was nominated for the Presidency, astrologists made their appearance and offered to consult my horoscope with a view to ascertaining whether I would be elected. I never had any faith in their calculations but, complying with my general rule, gave the specialists along various lines such information as I could furnish. I remember that one astrologer wrote a letter which my wife answered in my absence. He asked for the hour of the birth both of Mrs. Bryan and myself. She responded giving the day of my birth and the day and hour of her birth. Her parents were then residing with us and she was able to secure the information desired. The astrologer cast my horoscope, based upon such facts as he had, and declared that it indicated my election. He was very much mortified at my defeat— seemingly more than I was myself—and hastened to explain to Mrs. Bryan that his failure was due wholly to the fact that she did not give the exact hour of my birth. Having the hour of her birth, he had, since the election, cast her horoscope and felt sure that I would be yet elected for the Presidency. My wife enjoyed the humor of it and informed me that if I would stick to her she would land me in the White House yet. I responded, expressing my appreciation but admitting it was a little mortifying for a Presidential candidate to keep his horoscope in his wife's name.

I did not, until after the Chicago convention, hear much about the incidents of my childhood. I only know that I was blessed with as happy an environment as a child could hope for or ask. The two older children, John and Virginia, had died before the third child was born. As she was a daughter, I became the oldest son and had all the care that a mother could bestow upon a child and all the interest that a father could feel. A letter written just after my birth conveyed to the distant relative at whose home I lived while in college the fact of my birth. My father, who was suffering from a serious attack of diabetes, wrote to this relative that the birth of a son had increased his desire to live.

After my nomination, I met a Salem friend who told me that he had visited our home when I was just beginning to walk. It was evening and they were getting me ready for bed. According to this friend, my father stood me up before the visitor, and boastingly remarked, "He will be President some day." As my father never divulged to me any such expectations, I will be pardoned for considering the remark apocryphal.

The first thing that I can recollect is the younger child, Harry, crawling upon the floor. As he died when less than a year old, I could not have been more than three. My next recollection is of looking at the corpse of a neighbor who was a minister. They lifted me up so that I could see his face.

IN THE BEGINNING

According to family tradition, I was not a perfect child by any means, unless the word "perfect" is used to describe a boy with all the natural inclinations to mischief. Tradition has it that I used to disobey the injunctions of my mother and slip away from home to play with other children. Our yard was enclosed with the old-fashioned paling fence with a baseboard about a foot deep. By crawling close to the ground, I could conceal myself behind this broad board and thus get to the side of the fence without being noticed. More than once I was brought back and chastised and tied to the bed-post as a punishment.

My Ambitions Before Six

Three ambitions entered into my life before I was six years old—I fix the age at six because one of the first things to stay in my memory is the removal to our farm home which occurred in the summer of 1866. The incidents of my boyhood are roughly classified as having occurred while we lived in town or after we moved to the country. That is the way I know of these three early ambitions. The first was to be a Baptist preacher—due doubtless to the fact that my father was a member of that church. Of course, I was too young to have any distinct recollection of either this ambition or its abandonment, but the record as given by my parents is that my father took me to an immersion one night during a protracted meeting held in a Christian Church. I saw the convert going down into the pool of water to be baptized. I evidently watched the ceremony with great interest and was deeply impressed by it. On my return home, I asked my father whether it would be necessary for me to go down into the pool of water in order to be a Baptist preacher. He answered in the affirmative, and after that they never could get me to say that I was "going to be a Baptist preacher." I do not know that any conclusion can be drawn from this incident unless it be that at this early age my parents had impressed upon me the virtue of truthfulness and that therefore I was not willing to avow an ambition from which I had been turned by fear of water.

My second ambition was to be a farmer and raise pumpkins. This did not last long, but long enough to be a matter of remark in the family. It may have been due to the plans we were making to remove to the country. I remember that a young lady by the name of Hester, daughter of Brother Williams, the much beloved pastor of the Christian Church, came into my life about that time and promised to wait for me. She was a very handsome girl, nearly grown, and encouraged me in my taste for agricultural pursuits. When I shortly afterwards decided to be a lawyer, she gave my change of plans as an excuse for refusing to look forward to a life partnership, and married a farmer cousin of mine.

My third ambition was probably due to the fact that my father was a lawyer, and at that time a circuit judge. I used to go down to the courthouse and sit upon the steps leading up to the bench and listen to the trial of cases. This ambition was more permanent than the ones which it succeeded. It remained with me during my school days and my college days, as the reader will see if he follows this narrative.

My Ancestry

Ancestry counts. We inherit more than we ourselves can add. It means much to be borne of a race with centuries of civilization back of it. Blood, if it be good, inspires one to great effort—if it be bad it may paralyze ambition and fix the boundary to one's possibilities. I am speaking of the rule, not of the rare exceptions; many have become degenerate in spite of inheriting the stimulus to better things, and a few have, to a degree, overcome handicaps of their life and early environment.

If one is tempted to boast that he is self-made, a few reflections will puncture his pride. Let him analyze himself, separate all that has come to him into three factors: one representing that which has come to him by inheritance; another representing that which has entered his life through environment; and the third representing what he can fairly credit to himself—that which is not based upon either inheritance or environment—and the third factor will not be large enough to flatter his vanity.

The child comes into the world without its own volition, containing within himself capacities and weaknesses for which he is in no way responsible; he finds himself in an environment which he did not choose and cannot control. His first impressions come to him with breath and his life is largely moulded for him before he has intelligence to choose or standards by which to measure effort.

It is a consciousness of the helplessness of the new-born babe and of his dependence upon an unknown past and upon surroundings that he cannot comprehend that makes me increasingly grateful for the parentage with which the Heavenly Father blessed me and for the home in which my life began.

My father, Silas Lillard Bryan, was of Irish extraction. I do not know from what part of Ireland his ancestors came, nor when they crossed the ocean. I learned this since his death from a biographical sketch which I have reason to believe was written by him or submitted to him for his approval. William Bryan is the most remote forefather of whom I have knowledge. He lived in what was then a part of Culpeper (now Rappahannock) County and near the town of Sperryville, Virginia. He owned a tract of timber land in the Blue Ridge Mountains of which we learned when I was a young man because of a ninety-nine-year lease which expired about that time. We knew nothing of William Bryan's parents, brothers, or sisters. He belonged to the Baptist Church in that neighborhood, which was known as the Bryan Meeting House.

I digress at this point long enough to relate the experience which I have had with my name. I had scarcely entered upon the practice of law when my business brought me into acquaintance with a number of people of Irish birth who frequently addressed me as "Mr. O'Brien." I was at first in doubt as to whether I should correct the mistake or allow it to pass unnoticed, but, deciding that honesty was the best policy, I said to a very typical son of the Emerald Isle, "My name is not O'Brien, but Bryan."

"It's all the same," he replied. "When Bryan Boru became king his descendants put on the 'O.' The Bryans are the same stock, but just common people."

I have had frequent occasion to use this explanation. The most notable opportunity was a dinner in Ireland tendered me by the Mayor of Dublin in 1903. One of the speakers jestingly called upon me to tell when I had dropped the "O." I replied by asking whether any of them ever knew of an O'Brien prior to the line of King Bryan Boru. When no one could name an earlier O'Brien, I explained to them that Bryan was the original name and that the "O" had been *added* by them, not eliminated by my ancestors.

After the campaign of 1896 I received a letter from a man in California named Bryan. He sent me an interview which he had given to the newspapers.

It seems that some one had claimed to have seen my name printed as "O'Brien" when I began the practice of law at Jacksonville, Illinois. My correspondent had given out an interview denying that there had been any change in my name and saying that he was a relative of mine. He explained to me that he was not a relative, but added that it was a poor friend that could not lie for another.

We know nothing of the parents, brothers, or sisters of William Bryan, my great-grandfather, and therefore have been unable to answer a multitude of questions which have been asked from time to time, the most persistent being whether our ancestor was related to the wife of Daniel

JUDGE SILAS L. BRYAN MARIAH ELIZABETH BRYAN

Father and Mother of William Jennings Bryan.

Boone, whose maiden name was Bryan. William Bryan had three sons, Aquilla, James, and John. Aquilla Bryan, the oldest of the three sons, left Sperryville before or soon after my father's birth, to try his fortune in the Great West which was then inviting adventurers. When he reached the Ohio River the water was so high that instead of descending the river as he had intended, he crossed into Ohio and then waited for the waters to subside. That is the last knowledge we have of him that is authentic. We have met persons who with varying degrees of uncertainty thought they traced their ancestry back to this Aquilla Bryan, but no connection has been established with certainty.

James, the second son, went to Kentucky and located at Glasgow, where some of the family still reside.

John Bryan, my father's father, moved from his birthplace to Point Pleasant in what is now West Virginia. There my father spent part of his boyhood, but his mother died when he was twelve and his father when he was fourteen years old and Silas was entrusted to the care of different members of the family. His oldest brother, William Bryan, to whom I am indebted for the first part of my name, located on a farm near Troy, Missouri, where some of his descendants still live. Russell Bryan, his younger brother, located at Salem, where he raised a numerous family. His children were among my earliest playmates and most beloved companions.

John Bryan, my grandfather, was married to Nancy Lillard, a member of an English family. They lived in Culpeper County. This family was quite large and made up of men and women of character and virtue. My father was named after Silas Lillard, his mother's brother. When I went to Washington as a Member of Congress, I visited Virginia and became acquainted with a number of members of the Lillard family between whom and myself there grew up and has continued a warm friendship.

WILLIAM JENNINGS BRYAN

MY FATHER

As none of the brothers or sisters of my father were rich, he had the advantage of having to work. I do not know that this spur of necessity was absolutely necessary, but it is no disadvantage and it is possibly the best insurance against the influences that sap the energies and industry of young men. He had caught from some one the ambition to learn and though he had to work his way through school, he went further than any of his brothers or sisters in the pursuit of learning. When he was far enough advanced to teach he earned, by teaching, the money necessary to complete his college course, which was taken at McKendree College, Lebanon, Illinois. He had intended to attend a Baptist college, but for some reason changed his plans and entered the Methodist college above named. He took the classical course, graduating in 1849, and was always an enthusiastic believer in classical education for the young. He was a good student and interested also in the literary societies.

As father did not graduate until he was twenty-seven, he was one of the older students, although the age of graduation was probably older then than now. I have had the good fortune to meet several persons who were schoolmates of my father at Lebanon. From these I have learned something of my father as a student.

One incident seems to have made an impression at the time. Father used tobacco—I do not know in just what form at this time, later in life before he quit it entirely he indulged in chewing, smoking, and the use of snuff. He was in the habit of chewing tobacco while he was a student, as I learned from the following incident. Some teacher from another college made a speech to the boys. In the course of the address, the speaker commented upon the use of tobacco, criticizing it quite strongly, paying special attention to chewing. My father thought from what the speaker said he was making personal reference to him—whether true or not I do not know—but at the conclusion of the address father arose and made a speech in defense of the use of the weed. Later in life he became convinced that the use of tobacco was harmful, and just before the date of my birth he quit its use in every form. We thought it responsible for the dyspepsia which manifested itself about 1859 and continued to afflict him sorely until his death twenty-one years later.

Father was a very devout Christian. Just when he joined the Church I do not know, but it was probably at an early age. There came a day, however, when he was a young man, when religion took a very strong hold upon him and held him and became a controlling influence in his life. As a young man he was fond of fun and took delight in the frivolities of his day. One night as he went to a party he took cold and the cold developed into pneumonia. His condition finally became so critical that the attending physician thought it wise to inform him that, while his life was not despaired of, it would be the part of wisdom for him to make such provision for the future as he might think best. When the physician retired, father prayed as he had never prayed before and promised the Heavenly Father that if restored to health he would pray three times a day as long as he lived. He was restored to health and kept the promise.

I knew there was some such incident in his life, but did not learn the details until many years after his death and a few years after my mother's death. The facts were related to me by a caller who lived at one of the county seats which father visited when he was on the Circuit bench. My informant was then a boy and noticing that Judge Bryan bowed his head upon the desk when the noon whistle blew, asked his father why he did so. His father replied, "Judge Bryan is going to eat with us today and you had better ask him for an explanation." When the guest was at the table and the boy hesitated about asking the question, the father came to the boy's rescue and explained to Judge Bryan what the boy had noticed and asked the question the boy had intended to ask. Father moved his chair back from the table and said, "I am glad to answer the question," and then related the incident as it was told to me by the man, then the boy in the story.

This thrice-a-day prayer is the basis upon which numerous elaborations have been built. After my nomination for the Presidency a great many stories were told, differing in detail but all emphasizing the devotional side of my father's life. One story was that he opened court with prayer. Another, that he always prayed for guidance before rendering a decision. The first was not true, but knowing as I do his dependence upon God for guidance, I have no doubt that he invoked aid when entering upon anything important. I may add that my father's attitude on spiritual matters made a very deep impression upon me. There was a family altar in our house and the children were brought up according to the strictest views in religious matters, and my gratitude for such a home environment increased with the years. I shall be happy if my children feel toward me in mature life as I feel toward my father; if they revere my name as I revere my father's name and feel as deeply indebted to me for whatever there is in me of good.

After graduation at the age of twenty-seven, my father moved to Salem, the county seat of Marion County, Illinois, in which two of his sisters lived. At the age of twenty-nine he was admitted to the bar and about the same time or possibly a little earlier was elected superintendent of schools of that county. He began the practice of law in 1851 and in 1852 was elected to the Senate of the State of Illinois, where he served for eight years. He soon became prominent at the bar and prominent also as a public speaker. In 1860, at the age of thirty-eight, he was elected a judge of the Circuit that included about half a dozen counties and was re-elected in 1866, serving until 1872.

IN THE BEGINNING

In 1869 he was elected a member of the Constitutional Convention of Illinois and assisted in the drafting of that constitution. After his death I found in his library two volumes containing a record of the proceedings of the Constitutional Convention. On the fly leaf of the first volume I found a dedication of the books to myself. I immediately examined it, desiring to see what part he took, and was interested to find that at the very beginning of the session he introduced a resolution which reads as follows:

"*Resolved*, By the Convention: First—That all officers to be provided for in the new Constitution in the executive, legislative, and judicial departments, shall be elected by the people. Second—That the compensation to be allowed for official service in the several departments of the government shall be fixed in the Constitution, and shall not be increased or lessened by the legislative department."

It interested me to know that he shared Jefferson's confidence in the capacity of the people for self-government as well as in their right to self-government. He believed in entrusting them with their own affairs, as this resolution indicated. I have credited him with a definite influence in the shaping of my religious views; I am also indebted to him for the trend of my views on some fundamental questions of government, and have seen no reason to depart from the line he marked out.

My father was married at the age of thirty to Mariah Elizabeth Jennings, who had been one of his pupils when he taught school at Walnut Hill, Illinois. Mother was twelve years younger than father and had been his pupil when as a college student he was teaching in the Walnut Hill District, Walnut Hill being in the southeast corner of Marion County, twelve miles from Salem and about four from Centralia. Mother did not have the educational advantages father had secured, but she was as enthusiastic as he in her appreciation of education and in her devotion to it. Her studies after marriage and her companionship with him enabled her to make up somewhat for the shortness of her school days.

My Mother

But before speaking further of my mother, let me add a word here in regard to her lineage. As her maiden name indicated, she was of English ancestry, although, like my father's people, her family had been in the country so long, they were not able to trace any of them to the water's edge. The first of the Jennings of whom we have definite knowledge was Israel, my mother's grandfather. He moved to Illinois from Maysville, Kentucky, early in the eighteenth century and lived to a ripe old age, I think about a hundred years. Family tradition has it that he went from Maryland to Kentucky. His wife, Mary Waters, was a native of Maryland, but we have not been able to locate definitely any of her antecedents and but few of her collateral relatives. Israel Jennings had a large family, most of whom grew up in the neighborhood of Walnut Hill and Centralia.

My mother's mother was a Davidson and this family, too, had been in the United States long enough to lose its old-world connections. The Davidsons were of Scotch descent. Some of the family had been looking up the record recently and they found that there was a certain plaid that was worn by the Davidsons who, though not constituting a clan, were members of a clan. The earliest Davidson of whom we have a record lived in Virginia and went from there to Kentucky. From Kentucky the Davidsons, like the Jennings, moved to southern Illinois, evidently about the same time. I do not know whether it was because of the superiority in the attractiveness of the members of the two families or because of the scarcity of the population, but it is a rather remarkable fact that four Jennings married four Davidsons.

Mother was born on May the 24th, 1834, at Walnut Hill, a rural community near Centralia, Marion County, Illinois. She was reared in the country and attended the public school in the neighborhood. She was married at the age of eighteen (1852) and began housekeeping in the home on Broadway, about halfway between the public square and the railroad. Father helped to hew out the timbers and build their house. The style of it was that which was customary in that day. It had a room on each side of a short central hall, with two rooms upstairs over these lower rooms and a dining room and kitchen in the rear. In this house, the first six children were born. The two older children, Virginia and John, died of whooping cough before the third child was born. Frances, the next child, was born on March 18, 1858. My birthday came on the 19th of March, 1860, two years and one day later. The fifth child, Hiram, called Harry, died in infancy, and the sixth one, Russell, died at the age of seventeen. In 1866, the summer after I reached the age of six, we moved to the farm, about a mile northwest of the center of Salem, where the three younger children, Charles Wayland, Nancy Lillard, and Mary Elizabeth, were born.

Mother was a very competent woman, of rare native ability, of lofty ideals, and as devout as my father. While during the first twenty years of their married life they were members of different churches, there was never the slightest religious discord in the family and I never heard a word said in regard to the differences between denominations. Both of them were firmly wedded to the fundamentals of Christianity, but charitable on all nonessentials. This liberality in the matter of denominations was early impressed upon my mind by the family gatherings. It was in the old days of simple social customs when family dinners emphasized companionship and friendly intercourse rather than elaborate bill of fare. We were in the habit of having all the ministers at our home once a year and I knew all the ministers as "Brother."

While religious subjects occupied a prominent place in the conversation, the meals were not without a sprinkling of humor. I remember on one occasion that the meat for the dinner consisted of a roasted kid. As the plates were being served the conversation turned on the various kinds of meat and the Methodist preacher, Brother Mosser, expressed himself quite strongly as liking all kinds of meat excepting goat meat. Father had spoken of the meat as a roast, without designating the kind of animal that furnished it. After Mr. Mosser's statement he purposely avoided the subject until Brother Mosser was well through with a second helping, when the company enjoyed the joke.

My attitude on the subject of religious tolerance has been inherited, so to speak, from my parents. In memory of these religious social gatherings my good wife has been led to set aside certain days for the bringing together of the representatives of the various denominations in a social way.

I also received from my parents the impressions that have controlled my views on the husband's relation to the mother-in-law. When my father built the commodious brick house in which he lived upon the farm, one room was known as Grandma's room. At that time, my mother's mother was in good health with the prospect of living to a ripe old age. But although my mother's family was one of the largest among the children, it was always understood that Grandma was to have a home in our family if she reached an age when it was not desirable for her to continue to occupy the old homestead at Walnut Hill. The children expected some day to have my mother's mother as a member of the family, and the time came when she was too old to keep house any longer and came to spend her declining years with us. She lived to be more than eighty and

THE BRYAN SISTERS AND BROTHERS

Photo. Kadel & Herbert, N. Y.

Left to right: Ex-Governor Charles W. Bryan, Mrs. T. S. Allen, Mrs. J. W. Baird, and William Jennings Bryan.

it was a pleasure to minister to her during her years of feebleness.

When my wife's parents came to live with us, I recalled this early experience and the respect shown by my father to the mother of his wife. My wife's mother lived with us from 1884 to the spring of 1896 and my wife's father till 1905, and they were welcome members of our family.

My mother had not carried the study of music to the point where she practiced regularly, but she was proficient enough to play many instrumental selections and to play the accompaniment when she sang. Some of the tunes still run through my mind and the words of the songs are still recalled. "When you and I were young, Maggie," was popular at that time, and the war song, "Farewell, Mother, you may never press me to your heart again." The words came back to me when I was for a little while a soldier and I found myself time and again humming the tune that I had heard her sing when I was a boy.

My father being absent at court a considerable portion of the time, the burden of directing the family affairs and taking full control of the children fell upon her. Every duty was faithfully discharged. As I look back upon those early days, I cannot recall a single word that she ever said or a single act of hers that to me seems worthy of criticism. I feel that she was as nearly a perfect wife and mother as one could be. When father died, her oldest child was twenty-two, I was twenty, and the youngest child was ten. She assumed with courage the double responsibility of being to the children both mother and father. She survived my father sixteen years and lived to see her children grown, settled, and successful in life, and was revered by all of them. As a mother, she had one advantage that can hardly be overestimated. Her husband set an example in word and conduct that she could always invoke in the training of the children. Not in a single matter was it necessary to warn the children against following their father's example. Thus the memory of the two is entwined as if of a single character, so much alike were they in all that contributed to character building.

In 1872 my mother took her letter from the Methodist Church to the Baptist Church and from that time until her death became more and more a defender of the creed of that church, though she never carried it to the point of criticizing the doctrines of any other denomination. She had a sense of humor that relieved the conversation in the home. As my father also turned occasionally to the lighter vein and indulged in stories that had a point, I am not sure to which one I am most indebted for my fondness of the stories which I have used in abundance in my speeches. As I proceed with the narrative of my own life, I shall have occasion to refer from time to time to things that my parents said. At this time, I venture to illustrate their sense of humor by two stories for which I am indebted to them.

Some years ago I met an old resident of Salem who had often heard my father speak. Having heard me use in a lecture a story in connection with prohibition, he said it reminded him of a story that my father told back in the sixties. A man who was stricken with lockjaw was taken to the hospital for treatment. The doctor advised, "Give him a little whiskey." In order to administer the liquor, it was necessary to bore a hole through a tooth and inject it through a funnel. It had a stimulating effect; the patient was aroused and making his voice heard through his closed teeth begged them to funnel him again.

I remember one day my mother told a story that was recalled by the charitable attitude of a visitor. It reminded her of another woman so kindly in her treatment of others that she never could bear to have anybody criticized in her presence. One day the children conspired together to see how far the mother could carry her charity. They assembled one by one in her room and began to criticize the devil just to see if their mother would take his part. They had not proceeded far when the mother interrupted them with the admonition, "Well, children, if we were all as industrious as the devil is, we would all accomplish more."

After the children were grown and the three older ones had established homes of their own, mother moved from the farm into Salem. I had then prospered sufficiently to be able to buy her a home near to the home of my oldest sister, and I never spent money that brought me more real pleasure.

In the fall of 1895, she was stricken down with an illness that resulted fatally the following June. I shall never forget her last Christmas with us. We took the children (Ruth was about ten, William six, and Grace four) with us to spend the holidays at Salem. Four of her five children were there and five grandchildren also. Mother sat up in bed and distributed the presents. I never saw her happier; her cheerfulness enlivened our Christmas reunion and is a cherished recollection.

She died ten days before my nomination for the presidency. I went from her funeral to the Chicago convention. Often I have thought of the joy it would have given her if she could have lived to see me nominated. And then I check the thought, for in her weakened condition the excitement might have been too much for her. The fact that she was not spared to share in the proud satisfaction that my nomination brought to the family made me glad that the mother of my successful rival lived to see her son in the White House. A mother's pride is so genuine and so excusable that we forget political differences as we are united in a common humanity.

Such were the parents to whom, and such was the home in which I was born.

My name was drawn from the two families that were united by the marriage of my parents. William was a family name with the Bryans; the name of my father's oldest brother and the name of their grandfather. Jennings was my mother's maiden name. A few years ago I met a man in Missouri who was a little more than a hundred years old. He had lived in Marion County at the time of my birth. In the conversation that I had with him, he claimed credit for having suggested my name. He said that my father wanted to name me William and that my mother desired me to bear the name Jennings. He made the quite natural suggestion that both names be given to me, and so it was. In my youth my name went through all the forms of which it was capable; like the boy of whom James Whitcomb Riley writes,

> "Father calls me William,
> And mother calls me Will;
> Sister calls me Billy,
> But the fellers call me Bill."

Possibly Willy was more frequently used by my mother and brothers and sisters during the early years, while Will became my settled name as I advanced from boyhood into young manhood.

In the spring of 1866 my father decided to move to the country, the reason being that he thought a farm a better place to raise a family. There were three of us at that time, Russell Jones, Frances Mariah, and myself. The site selected was about a mile northwest from the center of Salem—that is, a mile by the road, although not quite so far in a direct line. There were two ways of going out to the place. The Prairie Road way, as we used to call it, took us half a mile west of the square and then a mile north; or the Woods Road that turned to the north about a quarter of a mile from the square and passed through the strip of woods. The house stood in a level piece of land, approached from the east by an avenue a quarter mile long and leading up to what seemed to me quite an elevation. It was not more than twenty or twenty-five feet, and as I have revisited the place in later years I wondered how the hill could have seemed so high. Perhaps it is due to the magnifying power of time, for all the hills in the neighborhood have shrunk, and the streams that seemed deep appear shallow.

The house was of brick and faced to the east and had a porch set in on the front and back side of the main living room. It was of the style quite familiar in Virginia, with a hall running through the center.

A commodious yard about three hundred feet long and two hundred feet wide contained a row of cedars on each side of the walk and several rows of maples. I still measure distances by the distances that I learned to know in this country home. A hundred yards is still the distance between our front door and the gate, a quarter mile is the length of the avenue, and the half mile is the distance from our farm fence to the main street.

My father used to take me out to the farm while the house was being built and the workmen allowed me to help to the limit of my small ability. I would carry a brick on a shingle and in my boyish pride felt that I was having a part in the construction of the building that was to be my home for seventeen years.

A piano was the principal piece of furniture in the parlor and is often recalled. One of the pictures most clearly outlined in my memory is the picture of the family gathered in this room on Sunday afternoon, singing Sunday-school songs and church hymns. Mother played the accompaniment and led in the singing. The Bryan Choir, as father called it, joined with youthful enthusiasm. Father's favorite piece was "Kind Words" and we were wont to close the singing with his favorite song. To these Sunday afternoon exercises, as well as to the Sunday school, I am indebted for these tunes that have run through my mind ever since.

The spare bedroom was set apart for the special entertainment of politicians and divines. The bringing together of these two classes illustrated not only my father's views on the subjects but early taught me to regard the science of government as an entirely honorable one. My father was as much at home with ministers as he was with politicians and statesmen. He saw no necessary conflict—and I have never been able to see any—between the principles of our government and the principles of Christian faith.

One of the pieces of furniture of that day which seems to have disappeared in modern times was the trundle bed. It enabled the younger children to sleep in the same room with their parents and at the same time space in the room to be utilized in the daytime.

Our farm contained five hundred twenty acres in one block, nearly all of it prairie, with a small woods pasture near and an eighty-acre piece of timber about three miles away. We had a park of fourteen acres adjoining the farm where my father indulged his fancy for deer, the number running up at times as high as twenty. We had the usual farm animals, horses, cattle, hogs, sheep, and, of course, the usual supply of poultry which included turkeys, guineas, and ducks as well as chickens. As I look back upon those days, I feel a little disappointed that we did not have geese, fowls that I used to associate with the family visits which we made to our grandparents, who lived near Walnut Hill, Illinois, about twelve miles away. There was a creek in front of the house and the geese that frequented it, always on the lookout, gave their noisy warning at our approach.

My parents were not fanciers of pure-bred stock, although I remember several excellent males that were bought from time to time, as a bull to which we gave the name "White Cloud" which was sent to us from Jacksonville—he was a gift from Dr. Jones, whose name will become familiar to the readers of these memoirs. I remember that we were very proud of him until he became vicious, when we had to dispose of him. My first experience with pigs was with a Chester White boar. I took him to the fair one fall, and have a very distinct recollection of the amount of washing necessary to keep a white pig clean.

IN THE BEGINNING

As we rented the land out and cultivated only a few acres, our place might have better been called a suburban home than a farm, but we had enough farm life to give us experience as children. The boys had the wood to cut and the chores to do. I, being the oldest, used the laboring oar, so to speak, and learned to milk and care for the stock and to do the general chores. If I were required to select the days of my boyhood which were least enjoyed the lot would fall on the winter days of this period. My first business was to make the fire in the Franklin stove and then go to the barn and feed the horses, cows, and hogs. Then came the milking and then breakfast. Sometimes we had a farm hand and I played the part of assistant, but much of the time we did not have enough work to justify the employment of a man in the winter time and the burden fell on me.

More than fifty years have passed since those days and I can see myself engaged in this drudgery, my nose running, my fingers numb, and possessing feelings for which the Sunday-school songs I knew did not furnish fitting expression. And yet, I look back to those days as among the most valuable of my life and I would not for anything have them eliminated. They taught me industry and obedience and they gave me an exercise which no gymnasium can supply. My physical strength has been an invaluable asset and I feel that I am indebted to work upon the farm for the strength that has enabled me to endure fatigue and withstand disease. Our verdicts which we pronounce in youth are often reviewed and set aside in mature life. I am sure that the indictments which I would have framed about the time the chores were done are very unlike the judgments that I now render in retrospect.

Rabbit Hunting

My favorite sport in those early days was hunting rabbits. My father had something of the spirit of the hunter. I presume it came down in his blood from a Virginia ancestry. At any rate, he used to take me out squirrel hunting and I was all interest from the time we began to prepare for the hunt, moulding the bullets the night before for a muzzle-loading rifle, to the time when we came back with one or possibly two squirrels as a reward for an afternoon's tramp. But while I envied my father's skill as a marksman, I never attempted to rival him with the rifle. I began with a shotgun, first with a single barrel and then with a double barrel. These were given to me as soon as my parents thought it was entirely safe for me to use them, possibly a little earlier than it was entirely safe, for I remember three narrow escapes from death by gunshot.

One day I was cleaning the gun in the hallway and it went off, blowing a hole through the baseboard, but I was not in front of it at the time. It scared me and I was careful, but not, I fear, as careful as I should have been. A little later I was putting a double barreled shotgun through a rail fence and foolishly had the barrel pointed toward me. The hammer struck a rail and discharged the cap—but fortunately, the gun did not go off. I could not have escaped death if the fire of the cap had reached the powder. Why it did not, I do not know, for that was its only failure to fire during the hunt.

At another time Henry Webster, my nearest neighbor, went with me out to Tonti, the nearest station on the Illinois Central, to meet my father, who was returning from holding court in one of the courts of his circuit. We got out at a pond near the road to shoot some snipe. I suppose we must have forgotten to let down the hammer. At any rate, the gun that was between us went off and blew a hole through the back curtain. We were singing "O, you must be a lover of the Lord, or you can't go to heaven when you die." Our musical program was suspended by the discharge of the gun and we rode the rest of the way exchanging congratulations upon our escape and wondering how the gun could have discharged.

IN THE BEGINNING

Before I was old enough to use a gun I used to hunt rabbits with a stick, tracking them in the snow and killing them in the little sheltered spots so familiar to hunters of this familiar game.

I had two dogs, Carlo and Dixie, the latter a mixed breed with rat terrier predominating. Carlo was a dog of medium size. If any one pure strain could be multiplied by the many strains mixed in him, he would have been a very costly brute. But as prices are not determined in this way, he would have brought at auction as little as he cost me— nothing. The dogs hunted together, Dixie would go in under the brush piles and scare the rabbits out and Carlo jumped stiff legged around the pile and would take up the chase as soon as the frightened rabbit came out. I followed the dogs, scrambling over fences, helping to pick up the trail when there was snow on the ground, and returning as jubilant in defeat as in victory. Many times when I almost froze during the chores I would warm myself by a chase after a rabbit until all the hardships of work were forgotten. After I began going to school, a part of each Saturday was given over to some kind of sport, usually a rabbit hunt, and one rabbit seemed to be my normal luck, although sometimes I would come back with several.

At times I would get my first game soon after I started and carry it for several hours and sometimes I would trudge along without reward until nearly home and then unexpectedly catch a rabbit. We had a boardwalk which ran diagonally from the front porch to the garden gate and intersected the walk from the kitchen to the barn. As the boards were nailed crosswise on two by fours, the walk furnished a splendid hiding place for rabbits and it trapped many for me.

As I grew older I extended my hunting to quail, prairie chickens, and ducks. The quail, however, was never much endangered by my hunting. It seemed too small for my gun and I was frequently mortified by having a hunting companion give me the first shot and then kill the bird after I had missed it.

With prairie chickens I had better success. Probably they furnished a larger target, but even here I was only a second-rate hunter. One time, I think it was in 1897, I went hunting in Idaho with the father of the famous Chicago lawyer, A. S. Trude. I think he was then about eighty. He had lost one eye, which to a hunter is quite a disadvantage. When we came in from the most successful chicken hunt I ever had we counted up thirty fowls and he was generous enough to insist that I had killed ten of them— half as many as he. I used to wonder what the relative success would have been if he had had two eyes.

Soon after the election of 1896 I became acquainted with William L. Moody, a prominent banker of Galveston. Governor Hogg, his attorney, made me acquainted with him and established him in my affections by telling me that he was the only prominent banker in Galveston who voted for me. When Governor Hogg was describing a hunt he gave a very vivid picture of the hunting at Lake Surprise. Three items of his description are recalled. The first was that you could hunt ducks there in a dress suit, and this I found to be true. We were entertained at a commodious house near the lake, where we had comfortable beds and the best of food. A spring wagon would take us to the lake, where we entered canoes and rowed to the blinds which were hidden in reedy islands in the lake. Here we would sit and shoot until our hunting hour was over. Then boatmen would gather up the ducks, carry us back to the landing place, from which the spring wagon would carry us back to the house. There was nothing to soil one's evening dress had he cared so to clothe himself. On one of my visits I took Mrs. Bryan with me and she sat in the blind and read to me while I waited for the waterfowl to appear. Another item in his description was that the ducks were so numerous that the noise made by their feet in the celery in the lake sounded like the roar of a train and that the noise made by their flying was like the rumbling of distant thunder. These accounts seem quite extravagant, but they were true to the letter. I have never found anywhere such hunting places as Colonel Moody used to furnish at Lake Surprise and never a more genial and hospitable host than Colonel Moody, whose son J. L. or his younger son, Henry, or his son-in-law, Northen, expert with the gun, went with us.

Our trips usually extended from the evening of the first day through the morning and evening of the second day and the morning of the third day. When I first went down there I was inclined to joke about the game law, saying that a law limiting each person to twenty-five ducks a day was never intended for me because I did not expect to come near the limit, and that a law prohibiting more than twenty-five shots at one duck might have been *more* embarrassing to me. But on a later visit, just before a hotel temporarily destroyed the value of the lake as a hunting resort, I had a streak of luck. I killed my quota of twenty-five before sundown on the first afternoon and then killed my quota the morning of the next day so that in the afternoon I had to content myself with pointing out ducks to others. Next morning I again killed my quota before noon, making seventy-five for the three days. This was my record day, surpassing all other hunting experiences.

My father was in the habit of impressing his views upon me by apt illustrations or humor. I recall that during my early boyhood I expressed a desire to take lessons on the piano. He checked my ambitions in this direction with the brief but firm suggestion that the girls in the family could take lessons on the piano but that the boys would learn to make music with the hand saw. I have only inherited half of his views on this subject. When I hear a song that appeals to my heart I envy those who are able to sing. But experience has confirmed in me the views of my father about music in general. One has only so much time. If it is spent on instrumental music sufficient to become proficient it occupies time that must be taken from other things, as for instance, reading, from which I think more practical value is derived. It is a very pleasant thing for a man to be able to furnish music to a company, but it is sometimes done at the expense of other lines of development. If one cannot reach the maximum in both entertainment and service, service is the more important of the two.

My parents believed in the old adage, "Spare the rod and spoil the child," and as they loved me too well to risk my being spoiled, they punished me. As I look back upon these punishments, I find myself more tolerant in passing judgment upon them than I was at the time, although I recall instances where I recognized the punishment as just, and some instances where I felt that I deserved more than I received. They were quite strict with me and I sometimes considered the boys more fortunate who were given more liberty, but on reflection I am not prepared to say that I would have done better under a different system. Other kinds of discipline may be better for other children—that parents must decide for themselves. I am not only satisfied but grateful for the punishment I received.

At the age of ten I was sent to school; before that time my mother taught me at home. Grandma's room—the back sitting room—was my first schoolhouse, and a little walnut table about two feet square, as my memory reproduces it today, was the first stump from which I made a speech. I would learn my lessons until I could repeat questions and answers without the book and then I would stand up on this little table and declaim them to my mother. My first audience, therefore, was a receptive, appreciative, and enthusiastic one.

Webster's spelling book and McGuffey's reader, then a geography, whose author I cannot recall, formed the basis of my education and furnished the themes for my earliest declamations. I would like to own this table, but it has thus far eluded my search.

A difference of opinion may arise as to the inheritance of my ability as a speaker. My father's talent in this line of work may form the basis for argument in support of hereditary ability, but I am inclined to give more weight to environment than to inheritance. It is unusual for the descendants of a prominent public speaker to excel in speaking, and differences among those who inherit equally would seem to raise a doubt as to the value of ancestral abilities. The child of a public speaker has the influence of his father's example and the inspiration that comes from an ambition to be like him. If to this is added the devotion and diligence of a mother who, like my mother, encouraged the tendency, the weight of the argument may be on the side of environment rather than heredity.

I began very young to manifest an interest in speaking and received all the encouragement that a child could from both father and mother. As the profession which I liked leads up to forensic efforts, it must also be taken into consideration no child could have had an environment more favorable to a public career or stronger incentives to follow this particular line of work. As the story proceeds illustrations will be given of the continuity of purpose and the permanence of the ambition.

In School

The first public school I attended was in what we called "The Old College," a building once used for a girls' seminary. When the school was abandoned the building was turned over to the city and my first lessons from a teacher of a public school were given me there.

Mrs. Lamb was the teacher, a woman somewhat advanced in years at that time but an enthusiast on education and a strict disciplinarian.

I next attended a school in a different part of the town

and soon entered the high school, from which I went to Whipple Academy, a preparatory department of Illinois College, Jacksonville.

During these five years in the public school I do not recall much that is worth recording. I walked in to school, a distance of three-quarters of a mile to the first building and about a mile to the second and to the high school. I was regular in attendance and studious, having behind me the coercive power of parents who were determined that I should have an education. I do not recall that I ever failed in an examination, neither do I remember to have been at the head of the class in these earlier days. I might have been called an average—I was not below the average in my studies and well toward the front in deportment. In the high school I began studying Latin and also went a step forward in the art of declamation in the literary society work. We had a debating club in the high school and I recall taking a part in what we called The Senate, and I was a senator from Illinois. It may have been that this experience in a "senate" suggested to me the thought of being some time a Senator of the United States. This ambition received encouragement from my father's race for Congress in 1872 when I was twelve years old.

I early became interested in the political news in the papers and recall very distinctly the eagerness with which I searched the columns of the *Missouri Republican*, the first prominent political newspaper I ever read.

I do not remember the subjects debated, but I recall that in one debate in which the color question came up, I used a sentence which brought forth applause when in the course of a brief speech I described something under consideration as "the darkest picture ever painted upon the canvas of time."

It was during my high-school days that I made my first venture in poetry, but while the jingle was praised by the schoolmates who saw it, the success was not sufficient to turn my head or my mind in that direction.

My father, being a very devout man, lost no opportunity to impress upon me the value of the Bible. To him it was not only the Word of God but the fountain of wisdom. He was especially fond of Proverbs and was in the habit of calling me in from work a little before noon to read a chapter and comment upon it. I cannot say that I shared his enthusiasm at the time—in fact, I was at times a little restless and even wished that I might have been allowed to devote the time to work in the field rather than to the reading and comment. But when he died, soon after I was twenty, the Biblical truths that he sought to impress upon me grew in value and I took up the book of Proverbs and read it through once a month for a year. I have frequently mentioned this experience and advised young men to read Proverbs because of the accumulated wisdom to be found therein—wisdom on all moral questions and expressed with wonderful force and clearness. I have quoted from Proverbs in my political speeches more than from any other part of the Bible or from any other book. Solomon left a rare collection of epigrams and it was the reading of Proverbs that gave me my first appreciation of the value of epigram.

The moulding of public opinion is one of the greatest of the arts, and the essence of moulding public opinion lies in the ability to say much in a few words. No uninspired writer has left so much of wisdom contained in so small a compass. One of the proverbs of Solomon which I early learned and often quoted was "A prudent man forseeth the evil, and hideth himself." This cannot be improved upon so far as the sentiment is concerned or the beauty of expression, but I found that audiences—especially students —did not seem to grasp it. As the object of speaking is to impress truth, I finally took the liberty of presenting this truth in a way most familiar to the student and most easily remembered. The paraphrase ran like this, "The prudent man gets the idea into his head, the foolish man 'gets it in the neck.'" The students instantly caught the idea and I felt that the impressing of the idea did more good than the slang did harm. The consolation of the reformer is that if he is right in uttering the warning and the people do not heed, they will come to him when their necks are sore.

My religious training was not neglected at any period of my life. We had family prayers—one of the sweetest recollections of my boyhood days—and I entered Sunday school early. My father being a Baptist and my mother being a Methodist, I went to both Sunday schools. The only advantage that I know of that can come from the parents belonging to the different churches is that the Sunday-school opportunities are doubled. I would not offer this as sufficient reason for encouraging a difference in church membership on the part of parents, but where there is a difference of this kind, the Sunday school may, to some extent, be an off-setting advantage—at least, in my case it gave to me the double interest in Sunday-school work, an interest which has never waned.

At the age of fourteen I reached one of the turning points in my life. I attended a revival that was being conducted in a Presbyterian church and was converted. Having been brought up in a Christian home, conversion did not mean a change in my habits of life or habits of thought. I do not know of a virtue that came into my life as a result of my joining the Church, because all the virtues had been taught me by my parents. Truthfulness had been so earnestly enjoined that in more than one case I received my parents' commendation for not misrepresenting the situation when truthfulness might bring criticism if not punishment.

I remember that one day we children were playing in the sitting room, and noticing father's pocketbook upon the bureau, it occurred to some one of us—I do not know which—to count the money, so we locked the door and proceeded to inform ourselves upon the amount in the pocketbook. When we were just finishing we heard his footfall in the hall. We hurriedly crowded the money into the pocketbook and opened the door, but not soon enough to avoid suspicion. When he found me alone he asked me what we were doing. I told him we were counting his money, whereupon he took me down town and bought me a saddle, presenting it and telling me, as he presented it, to remember I received it for telling the truth. I do not know of any similar amount of money that ever made so great an impression upon my youthful mind and heart.

As an illustration of the teaching which I received at home I cite two other instances. Before entering school at the age of ten my mother so impressed upon me her opinion of swearing—a matter in which my father also set me a valuable example—that when I entered school I felt a distinct aversion to swearing. I would find myself withdrawing from the crowd when the boys began to swear, and to this day I have not overcome an aversion which I felt in those early days.

The other subject impressed on me was that it was wrong to gamble. My father hated gambling and taught me to hate it. With him it did not matter whether the amount wagered was large or small or whether the person won or lost—gambling was gambling. Some time before I was fifteen I had an experience that almost rivaled the gift of the saddle in the impression it made. My father had bought me a forty-cent knife which I wagered against a ten-cent knife on a proposition where I felt that I could not lose. The boys had given me a number of cards, each containing a series of numbers. These numbers were so arranged that the sum of the first numbers on each card equaled the number asked for. After I had used the cards until I felt confident of their accuracy, I undertook to tell the age of a boy's mother if he would pick out the cards on which the age appeared. The wager was my knife against his and I lost. Upon examination, I found that the number required was the only one which could not be determined by the adding together of the first numbers on the cards containing this number. Knowing my father's views on gambling, I was so terrified at the thought of his learning what I had done that I resolved never to gamble again, no matter how certain I might be to win. The loss of a forty-cent knife has saved me a great deal of money, if I can judge what my experience would have been from the experiences of friends who have bet on elections where I, like they, thought the result was certain.

CHAPTER II

CHURCH AND SCHOOL

IN becoming a member of the Church I entered upon an important epoch—much more important than I thought at the time. I was, of course, too young to know anything about the creeds of the different churches. I knew the names of the churches and had attended all of them at different times and had been connected with the Sunday schools of several of them. The Baptist Church in Salem had a very small congregation at that time. There was preaching there once a month and but very few young people in the Sunday school. The Methodist Church was a larger organization and I went to the Baptist Sunday school in the morning and the Methodist Sunday school in the afternoon. Besides these denominations the Presbyterian and Cumberland Presbyterian and the Catholics had congregations there. The last named ministered to but a few families. After my mother joined the Baptist Church with my father, about 1872, I began to attend the Cumberland Presbyterian Church in the afternoon. It had one of the largest congregations in the city and a great many children in that church were my companions in school. I think no other Sunday school had so large an influence upon my life.

The superintendent was the best Sunday-school superintendent I have ever known—at least, he so seems to me as I look back through the years and recall his devotion to the school, his friendly attitude toward all the children, and our intimate acquaintance with him. He seemed like one of the family; we liked to meet him on the street and enjoyed being sent to his store to make purchases. He was always on hand and the lessons that he drew from the Bible text are yet part of our thoughts and lives. If in the world beyond, he knows, as I believe he does, how affectionately the children remember him, it will be abundant reward for the time he devoted to his work—probably he felt that he received his reward as he went along from a consciousness of service rendered and from the knowledge of the affectionate regard the children had for him.

Then there was Sam Chance, who led the singing. He had one of the sweetest tenor voices I have ever heard; his notes still ring in my ears. He has only one rival among those nonprofessionals to whom I have listened. My wife's father had a tenor voice, not so strong as Mr. Chance's but fully as sweet and as expressive, but I did not hear him until considerably later in life—and then I heard him sing frequently.

There is one fact in connection with my early days that should, I think, be recorded, namely, my parents' willingness to allow me to choose at that early age a church different from their own. It was an evidence of their liberality in denominational matters, notwithstanding the deep and permanent convictions which they had on Christian fundamentals. I noted this liberality first in the attitude of each in the other's church before they became members of the same church. I noticed it also in their treatment of ministers of the various churches who were occasionally assembled at our house at family dinner. I was also impressed by the fact that when we gathered our hay my father was in habit of sending a load away to each minister, including the Catholic priest when a priest resided there.

This liberality was also proof of the deep concern about my religious life. When I asked my father whether he had any objections to my joining the Presbyterian Church—my inclination to join being based upon two facts: first, my conversion at a revival held in that Church; and second being the fact that some seventy young people of the Sunday school, my schoolmates in the day school, joined at that time—he said that he wanted me to join where I felt

I would be most at home and could do the most good. I never knew until after his death that he was disappointed that I did not become a member of his own church.

When, a year later, I entered Whipple Academy at Jacksonville, I took my letter to the Presbyterian Church at Jacksonville and remained a member of it until 1887, when I took my letter to the First Presbyterian Church at Lincoln, Nebraska. Though my connection with the Presbyterian Church at Salem was very brief, the church has had a very warm place in my heart for half a century. Six years ago I presented to the church a pulpit made after a pattern which appealed to me at Dr. Hindman's church, the Northminster Presbyterian Church at Columbus, Ohio. The pulpit was made for him by an elder whose father was an elder in the Presbyterian Church in Scotland.

In front of the pulpit was a cross and in the center was a burning bush—the cross representative of the New Testament and the bush the Old Testament. This so deeply impressed me that I had a replica of the Columbus pulpit made for the church at Salem. I spoke at its dedication in May, 1920, my subject being "Symbols of Service." Dr. Glover, pastor of the Jacksonville Church when I became a member of it, was a man who had ministered to the church for a generation. He became my personal friend as well as my pastor and I feel that he exerted a very beneficial influence on my life at that formative period. His wife, who shared in his devotion to spiritual things, invited me to her home one evening that she might appeal to me to prepare for the ministry. While I had great regard for the ministry, I did not feel that my life work lay along that line and, therefore, while I was willing to hear what she had to say, I was prepared to defend my choice of the law as a life pursuit. I recall that I had fortified myself with the third verse of the twenty-first chapter of Proverbs: "To do justice and judgment is more acceptable to the Lord than sacrifice." When I called at her home I found that sickness of a relative had taken her away from town and, as the invitation was not renewed, I never had occasion to weigh the reasons that she had intended to present.

After Dr. Glover's death, which was before my graduation, Dr. J. R. Southerland was called to the church and the attachment formed between us continued until his death a few years ago. He was succeeded by A. B. Morey. Although his pastorate was brief, it was long enough to become the basis of an attachment between us that lasted till his recent death. His successor had a personality and charm that made a deep impression on me. In one sermon he gave a graphic picture of the right way and the wrong way of doing a thing. He said that to take a tree through a little gate you must take the trunk first, then the limbs would be pressed in against the trunk. If, on the contrary, he attempted to take it through by pulling the limbs through first, the other limbs would catch against the gatepost and prevent progress.

When in 1887 we moved to Nebraska we found Dr. Curtis pastor of the First Presbyterian Church. He was called to a Chicago church and was followed by Dr. Hindman, with whom I became intimately associated, and this friendship I have cherished through years that have followed. Dr. Henry V. Swearingen, who was later Moderator, followed Dr. Hindman. He, too, became one of the inner circle of our friends.

Soon after moving to our country place, Fairview, near Lincoln, Nebraska, in 1902 we took our letters to the Westminster Presbyterian Church. I was elected elder of this church and held the position until we took our letters to the First Presbyterian Church of Miami, Florida, in 1921. But in order that we might know our neighbors better we attended the Methodist Church in Normal. In the Sunday school Mrs. Bryan assisted as teacher, and I was a teacher from time to time as my traveling would permit.

As I look back over the years, I am increasingly grateful

for the religious environment that surrounded me in my youth and the devotion of my parents and for the influence that the Church had upon me in my school days. The period through which one passes in the journey from youth to maturity is quite likely to be accompanied by some religious uncertainty. In the course of nature the child will substitute the spirit of independence for the spirit of dependence. Instead of doing things because he is told to, he must do them upon his own responsibility and from his own convictions. During this transition period the pendulum is apt to swing too far and he sometimes finds himself more self-reliant than he ought to be and less disposed to be influenced by advice of others. It is just at this time when the parental authority is weakening that usually the student begins in the study of the physical sciences. If he is fortunate enough to have teachers who are themselves Christians with a spiritual vision of life, the effect is to strengthen his faith and he advances to a normal religious life. If he is unfortunate enough to fall under the influence of mind worshipers, he may be led step by step away from faith into unbelief. It is a matter of profound gratitude to me that during these days I was associated with Christian instructors so that the doubts aroused by my studies were resolved by putting them beside a powerful and loving God. Knowledge of the experiences of students has made me very sympathetic with students in college and has led me to go from college to college in the hope of helping young men to find solid ground upon which to stand. It was this interest in young men more than anything else which led me to prepare and deliver the address entitled, "The Prince of Peace." (See Chapter XXI.)

WHIPPLE ACADEMY

At the academy I got my first taste of college life. It looked a long road ahead of me when I counted up the two years at the academy and the four years at the college before the day of graduation. And it was the classical course, too. I cannot remember when I decided to go to college—in fact, I do not recall that I ever did decide to go to college. It was decided for me by my parents and when I was too young to fix the day. All I know is that I was going to college from my earliest recollection. I was not only going to college but I was going to take the highest course the college provided, and the plan was later elaborated by the addition of a post-graduate course at Oxford, England. My father was enthused upon the subject of education and my mother fully shared with him this desire for the children. When not long before his death I sat by his bedside and in the presence of my mother took down at his dictation the words of his will, he expressed in a paragraph this ideal which had led him as a poor boy to make a successful struggle for a classical education. He directed that all of the children (I was then twenty and there were four younger than myself) should have the best education that the generation afforded. Not long before he died he bought fifty calves which were to grow until I graduated at Illinois College and then were to be turned into money, the money to be used for a year at Oxford. It so happened that when he died he owed security debts to the amount of about $15,000, the larger part represented by a note given by a man to his sister which father endorsed. In settling up the estate it seemed best to sell the cattle and pay off those security debts, so that my trip to Europe was given up. My mother took enough of the calf money to purchase for me a gold watch which I carried until it was replaced by the precious timepiece given me by the employees in the State Department.

In September after my fifteenth anniversary I was sent to Whipple Academy, Jacksonville, a preparatory school connected with Illinois College. Here again I was the beneficiary of one of the best bits of good fortune that has fallen to my lot. My father, being a Baptist, had intended to send me to William Jewell College in Liberty, Missouri, an institution of his own denomination which he had come to hold in high esteem. If I had been two or three years older I presume he would have carried out this purpose and I would have been brought into contact with other personalities and my life might have been moulded by an entirely different chain of circumstances. My father had a distant relative, a physician of prominence, Dr. Hiram K. Jones, between whom and my father a warm friendship had developed. Dr. Jones was a man of the highest character, of great learning, and lofty ideals. His wife, Cousin Lizzie, as we called her, was one of the sweetest characters which it has ever been my privilege to know. She was a woman of rare intelligence, fond of literature and music, and was possessed of temper that nothing could ruffle. She was so charitable in her attitude toward others that I do not recall having heard her say an unkind word of anyone during the six years that I made my home in the family. Even a criticism made by others would pain her as if it were directed against her and she would protest with a sincerity that was manifested in both tone of voice and in the expression of pain upon her face.

Dr. Jones was the head of the literary circle of the city and for some years a lecturer at the Concord (Massachusetts) School of Philosophy. His specialty was Plato. Possibly no scholar of his day was more thoroughly acquainted with the work of the great Greek philosopher. Dr. Jones' diversion was microscopy and he often called me in to examine the specimens upon which he was working.

Dr. and Mrs. Jones were members of the Congregational Church and he was a trustee of Illinois College, which was founded by a group of Yale graduates who came out to Jacksonville in the early years of the century. As I view in retrospect my own life in the Jones family I find it difficult to calculate the influence which association with them had upon my ideas and ideals. They had no children and

I was only one of a number of schoolboys to whom they had furnished a home, and these, as I came to know them, were as grateful as I became for the splendid environment furnished.

Dr. H. K. Jones had a brother, Dr. George Jones, ten years his junior, who was associated in the practice with him. He was a man of different type but one to whom I became also attached. His wife, an admirable woman, was more or less of an invalid. Their house was in the same yard as that of the elder doctor, so that my acquaintance with them was almost as intimate as with Dr. and Mrs. H. K. Jones. The families furnished a splendid illustration of the strength and tenderness of family ties. Dr. George and his wife had no children and, like the family with whom I made my home, they nearly always had students with them. These were my most intimate friends during these delightful days.

I began Greek in my first preparatory year and Latin in the second year. Like most boys, I was relatively further along in mathematics than in the languages.

When I left home for school father told me that he was able to furnish me with the money that I actually needed but that he could not afford to have me waste money, and then he suggested what I have always believed to be a good rule, that I should keep an account and report to him the use I had already made of the money when I wrote for more. This I proceeded to do and I do not recall that he ever referred to the expenditures except in one case.

I had spent ten cents for blacking, twenty cents for bay rum, and ten cents for candy. I entered the account as "forty cents for blacking, bay rum, etc.," the "etc." covering the candy. It so happened that the next entry was "to the church, five cents." He sent me the money that I asked for, merely adding by way of comment, "I notice that you spent forty cents for blacking and five cents for the church. It seems to me that that is travelling toward the Dead Sea pretty fast." I can imagine that there was a smile upon his face when he wrote this reproof, but it answered the purpose. I never covered any expenditures afterward with "etc." and I never forgot the inference that he drew from the relative size of the amount spent for improvement of my appearance and the amount spent for the church.

I hope that it will not seem to the reader too trivial if I add that this old account book fell into my wife's hands after we were married and she discovered that the first item of my college account was "five cents for a bologna sausage," spelled "ballony." Another entry was, "oysters and needles—15c."

When I first left home I was growing very rapidly. I have reason to remember, because I wrote back home for money to buy a new pair of pants, explaining to my father that my pants had become so short that I was ashamed to attend the church sociables. He wrote back saying that I would soon be home for the holidays and could then replenish my wardrobe and added, "But you might as well learn now that people will measure you by the length of your head and not by the length of your breeches."

College Years

By the fall of 1877 I entered college proper. While I was only a freshman, the two years' experience in the academy had somewhat worn off my freshness and I felt well on the road toward manhood. I had developed so rapidly during the years preceding that I had almost reached my growth. My ambition was to be six feet in height and weigh 180. That was my idea of the proper height and weight; possibly I had obtained my standard of height from my father who was a little more than six feet tall. He did not, however, give me my idea of weight, because he weighed only 154, as I had reason to know.

WILLIAM JENNINGS BRYAN

When I went home from college for a vacation we happened to weigh at the same time. He weighed 154 and I weighed 150. I was rather proud of my weight and said, "I shall soon be as heavy as you are." He replied with a twinkle of the eye, "When you have four pounds more of brains we will weigh the same." The next time we weighed I weighed more than he did and recalling his remark I attributed all the increase as "brain weight."

I did not give much attention to athletics during college. My principal exercise was walking from my boarding place on College Avenue up to my recitations and back and down town and back, as I had frequent occasions to run errands for Dr. or Mrs. Jones. While I played games to some extent, I was not an expert except at jumping. When I played baseball I was usually assigned to the right field, where my inefficiency would least embarrass the club. In my younger days I had been more conspicuous upon the diamond, but my prestige waned when the round bat was substituted for the flat bat and when the ball began to be thrown instead of pitched. The curve was always a mystery to me and I never secured sufficient control of the muscles of my face to restrain the expression of surprise called forth by the curved balls that passed me unimpeded in their flight. But when it came to the broad jump I had to be reckoned with. I was somewhat proficient in the running broad jump, but the only thing in which I excelled was what we used to call the standing jump, known technically, I believe, as the standing broad jump. I began at nine feet when I entered the academy. I gradually increased the distance until I won a prize with a record of twelve feet four inches. I would commence jumping as soon as the frost was out of the ground and jump until I was sore and then I would continue jumping until the soreness disappeared.

I entered many jumping contests, but one competitor after another fell behind. I remember one good-natured

MARY ELIZABETH BAIRD AS A STUDENT, 1880   **WILLIAM JENNINGS BRYAN AS A STUDENT, 1880**
At Jacksonville Academy, Illinois, where she first met William
Jennings Bryan.

rival, Charlie Carter, who, when he discovered that his efforts were hopeless, vented his disappointment in the following good-natured rebuke: "Bryan, my father always told me never to speak of anyone unless I could speak well of him. Whenever I speak of you I always say you are a good jumper." I have thought of this many times since when a stranger introducing himself would say, "Mr. Bryan, I must say that you are a man of wonderful physical endurance." I know by that compliment that he is a Republican, he wants to speak kindly and he can say this much without making any political concessions.

My practice in the jumping forward led me also to practice the jump backwards, in which I left a record of nine feet. I do not recall but one man who surpassed me in the jump backward. There is more of art than strength in this jump, a good deal depending upon so balancing as to use the weight of the body without being thrown off one's feet. Very few can jump any considerable distance backward and the number of those who can jump three jumps backward without falling is still less.

I did not have much chance to hunt while I was in college, although occasionally when there was snow on the ground I went out on Saturday with a college friend. I remember one of these hunts with Oscar Kenneth, one of the members of the class who unfortunately died soon after graduation. We started out early in the morning and hunted until late in the afternoon. The dinner that his mother served to us about four o'clock stands out in my memory as one of the most refreshing meals in my life. It was not that there was great variety of unusual food, but there was plenty and we were hungry—the two necessary elements of a satisfying meal.

I early became acquainted with Glenn Hulett and was frequently his guest. He lives a few miles in the country and we became a terror to the rabbits in the neighborhood. I devote more space to this friend when I speak of my college course. We were rivals and our marks were quite close together at the end of four years' race. But one of the most delightful of rivalries it was. Our friendship was never disturbed by our ambitions. I would have congratulated him as heartily as he did me; if he had been the victor I would have felt that it was an honor to be next to him.

I took the classical course, not as a matter of choice, because I had no choice in the matter. My father and mother decided that question and told me what I was to do, as they had decided for me the question of going to college. I do not know the date of the decision; I only know that from my earliest recollection I was going to college and was going to take the highest course. When I left home, father took from his library two of the largest books, a Greek lexicon and a Latin lexicon, and told me that I was to use the former for six years in the study of Greek and the latter five years in the study of Latin. I did not then know of their importance, but have since been very glad that there were others wiser than myself to decide such questions for me. I have come to place a high estimate upon the study of the dead languages because of the training they give one in the choice of words and because of the acquaintance that they give the student with the derivation of words. I liked Latin better than the Greek—possibly because it is easier. I became so attached to the Latin that I planned to read some Latin every year as a recreation. But I soon became so occupied with work which was necessary that the sentimental was crowded out.

Mathematics was my favorite study until I took up political economy. During the senior year of my preparatory work I took freshman college mathematics and was marked one hundred in geometry. I was a contestant for the freshman prize in mathematics with Sam Montgomery, a boy who was taking the scientific course. I do not know which had the highest marks, because I learned before the prize was awarded that the competition was open only to those who were in the freshman class. This excluded me.

The College Literary Societies

Students of Whipple Academy were permitted to enter the literary societies of the college and I immediately availed myself of this opportunity, joining Sigma Pi (it was not the fraternity which bears this name, but merely the literary society). There was a rival society known as Phi Alpha and I soon caught the college spirit and for six years was prepared to defend my society whenever it was challenged by the "Phis." From the start I took my part in the meetings, beginning with recitations and declamations and later in essays, orations, and debates. My work in the literary societies at Salem had given me some little experience, and yet before this new body of critics I found myself embarrassed by a feeling of timidity. My first appearance called forth more applause from my trembling knees than from the audience.

I may digress for a moment here to commend the work of literary societies. They are an important factor in school life, specially if one contemplates public speaking—an experience into which an increasing number are drawn when they are young though they may have no intention of entering public life.

Of the tasks that fall to the members of literary societies I put the greatest value upon declamations, essays, orations, and debates in the order named. The essay which is often read is, of course, easier to deliver than the declamation. The declamation, on the other hand, employs the words of another and does not require as much thought as the essay. The essay is the preparatory to the oration. It compels an originality of thought which is not necessary in declamation. The oration has all the virtues of the essay and adds to those the virtues of the declamation. It carries the student a step further. The debate is the climax of good speaking.

WILLIAM JENNINGS BRYAN

A debate brings out the ability of the essayist to think and to express himself with clearness and force. It also tests his ability to think upon his feet and to express himself without the aid of manuscript. But still more, it compels him to think quickly and to construct his replies on the moment. He analyzes his opponent's speech as it is made, takes its principal points and frames a reply without time for examination of authorities or for deliberation. The debate is superior also because it is the form of public speaking that wins the largest victories and gives the greatest renown. It gives the most conclusive proof of completeness of preparation, of a thorough understanding of the subject, of earnestness in its preparation, and therefore is most effective in its impression upon an audience.

CHAPTER III

At the Bar

POLITICAL opponents have sometimes referred to me as an unsuccessful lawyer; one president of a great eastern university in a campaign speech delivered in my home city in 1896 argued that I was unfit for the Presidency because I had never enjoyed a large income from my profession. I will not attempt to urge in my behalf the argument that turned Disraeli from the law to politics, that is: "To succeed as an advocate, I must be a great lawyer, and to be a great lawyer, I must give up my chance of being a great man"; but I think I owe it to my friends to give them a glimpse of my career as a lawyer. From this they can form an estimate as to whether I would have succeeded had I continued in the profession.

After graduating from the law school and after admission to the bar I returned to my home at Salem to prepare for a change in residence to Jacksonville, Illinois. During the preceding vacation (1882) I made a trip to Kansas City, which I had considered as a possible location. I was impressed by the reports of the growth of the city and went upon a tour of investigation.

I was deeply impressed with the size and bustle of the city, but was disturbed by the fear that I might not have money enough to support me until I could become self-supporting. If I had known as much about law business then as I learned afterwards I would not have been so timid about starting in a city, but the more I pondered over the problem the more strongly I was inclined to start in Jacksonville, where I thought the beginning would be easier. I reasoned thus: I had spent six years as a student at Jacksonville, was acquainted with many of the literary and business people there. I had graduated as the valedictorian of my class and was also class orator. I do not know whether others were ever guilty of the same error, but I am satisfied that I overestimated the impression that my college successes had made on the general public. But, mistake or no mistake, I decided to hang out my shingle in the charming little city which had come to seem like home to me after six years of student life there. So I planned to take my departure from Salem. I have been rather inclined to observe anniversaries and so I chose the Fourth of July for the date of my entering into Jacksonville—it was an easy day to remember and it gave me an anniversary that was sure to be generally observed.

Here again good fortune attended me. The law firm of Brown, Kirby, and Russell, one of the most, if not the most prominent in the city, was made up of three splendid men. William Brown was one of the ablest lawyers I have ever personally known. He was not only a most delightful companion but his way of addressing a judge or jury came nearer being ideal than that of any other person I have known. I think he had more influence upon my style of speaking than any other person from whom I have taken lessons. The friendship that grew up between us continued until he died, and my admiration for the man grew until he became so heroic a figure that I would have offered him a place in my cabinet had I been elected President.

Judge Edward P. Kirby was an admirable partner for a lawyer like Brown. The latter was a trial lawyer without a superior and with few equals; the former was an office lawyer, a man acquainted with pleadings and precedents and authorities, a man whom everybody trusted. He was especially consulted in any matters of probate and settling of estates.

Robert D. Russell, the third member of the firm, was younger than either of the others and one of the most lovable men it has been my lot to know. He was what is often called "the rising young lawyer," ready, diligent, and the friend of all who needed friends. They were all closely identified with Illinois College and within the circle of Dr. Jones' friends and it was possibly for that reason that I received the welcome they accorded me. Some six months after entering the firm, Mr. Russell, who was a brother of the great actor, Sol Smith Russell, moved to Minneapolis, which led to the turning over of much of the collection business of the office to me.

I remember with what anxious expectations I nailed up my modest sign, "W. J. Bryan, Lawyer," on the doorpost and awaited the rush of clients. I use the word "awaited" advisedly, because waiting was the word. It was then that I experienced my first disappointment. The people whom I knew personally seemed to have very little law business or were supplied with legal representatives. The days passed wearily. There was a continuous tread upon the stairs leading up to the second floor where the firm's offices were, and I would turn to the door each time I heard a hand upon the knob, only to find that the visitor had turned into the office of Mr. Brown, Mr. Kirby, or Mr. Russell. They had clients enough and were busy all the time, but the chair that I had been careful to provide and place at my desk stared at me vacantly.

One of my earliest clients was John Sheehan. He had worked for Dr. Jones when I made my home there. He took care of the doctor's horse, looked after the furnace, mowed the lawn, etc. When I opened my office he was keeping a saloon on East State Street. Soon after I began the practice he called to renew acquaintance and to tell me that, while he had a cousin practicing law, he was going to bring me all the business that he could. The reason he gave was that I was friendly to him when I was a student. This was one of the earliest instances—they have been numerous since—where I saw the return of bread cast upon the waters. It did not cost me anything to be friendly to John when he worked for the doctor. I was amply rewarded by the friendliness that John showed in return, and my impression upon him made him one of my first clients.

He said he knew that I was not in sympathy with his business, but that he thought I might be willing to collect some small bills that men owed him for liquor they had bought. I told him that I did not drink myself nor advise drinking, but that I thought those who bought liquor ought to pay for it. I think the first bill he gave me was for $2.60 and a note from me to the debtor brought a prompt settlement. John was very much pleased when I went to the door of his saloon, called him out, and counted out his $2.60, less twenty per cent commission; but what pleased John still more was that the man from whom I made the collection returned and again became a customer. This gave John an argument that he was quick to employ, as I had reason to know he told his friends that Mr. Bryan could collect a bill without making the man mad.

I was not slow to learn the lesson that this taught. I made it a practice not to make men mad when I was collecting bills. If the man could not pay at the time, I asked him to fix a day when I should call again. If he was not ready at the second call, it never annoyed me; I fixed another time. And so I continued to call until the bill was paid, often a little at a time. This sometimes made clients of the men from whom I collected bills.

I recall that Dr. Jones put some accounts in my hands, one of them against a liveryman. After he had postponed payment until I had called half a dozen times he said, "I could pay this bill if you could collect some bills for me and apply the amount, less your commission, on Dr. Jones' bills." I said, "Certainly," and he turned over a batch of accounts. It was not long before I had collected enough to cover the bill that I held against him and had some others besides. One of the bills brought me one of the first of a series of cases that gave me a good deal of satisfaction. One of the liveryman's bills was against a policeman and he wanted a credit of $25, I think it was, which the liveryman had offered as a reward for the recovery of a stolen horse. It seems that the liveryman had missed a horse one night and, thinking it had been stolen, had offered a reward. The policeman found the horse not long afterward tied not far from the livery stable and claimed the reward. The horse was so near and was found so soon that the liveryman did not think the finding came within the spirit of the offer. I looked the matter up and found that there was a city ordinance making it unlawful for a policeman to receive a reward for work done in the line of duty. I brought suit and having prepared myself on this point I plead the ordinance and defended it on the ground of public policy and won the suit. This success did not come until after the Devlin suit later referred to, but was the outgrowth of early collections.

At the end of each month I counted up my receipts— not a difficult task. I remember that at the end of one month my total receipts amounted to $2.50, and, a little discouraged, I wrote to my sweetheart something of my start in the law. After I had finished the letter and reported the meager returns a man came in and wanted an acknowledgment, for I was a notary as well as a lawyer, and I added a postscript saying that I had taken in twenty-five cents more that month. She wrote back a cheering letter saying that I should not be discouraged and that I was simply passing through the narrows. I replied that that was true if it meant that I was in straitened circumstances.

The outlook was so much less promising than I had anticipated that I entered into correspondence with Henry Trumbull, the son of Judge Lyman Trumbull, the law-school classmate I have referred to, with a view to trying my fortune in Albuquerque, New Mexico, where he had located, his choice being influenced largely by his threatened consumption. Between the Fourth of July and the first of January, nearly six months, my total receipts amounted to a little over $67, or an average of $11 a month.

With the beginning of the new year business picked up. The collections turned over to me by Brown and Kirby gave me a start. Dr. Jones found me a few clients and John Sheehan, whose enthusiasm had been increased by my success in collecting bills for him, brought me a really substantial client, out of whose business I made $200—three times my income for the first six months.

This client was Richard Larkin, an Irishman who had a little grocery store, and who, as I learned afterwards, handled liquors on a small scale. I was made assignee of Mr. Larkin's business, which included the collection of a large number of store accounts. These accounts brought me into acquaintanceship with a large percentage of the Irish who traded in Jacksonville and I made friends of his patrons. I was a persistent collector and a very patient one. It never annoyed me to have to call again and again. I may add here that I formed the practice of keeping my collections separate.

When I would collect a little bill I would take out my commission, put the balance in an envelope and put the envelopes away in a vault so that I could always pay my client the amount due him at any time. This custom of keeping clients' accounts separate was adopted upon the advice of my father. When my father last visited me—the visit which ended by his death—I was treasurer of the college paper and he noticed that I had in my bureau drawer an envelope containing money that I collected from advertisers and subscribers. When he inquired about the money I explained to him that it belonged to the college members and that I kept it by itself. He took occasion to commend and to advise me to follow that rule in regard to all money that I collected from others, saying that if I kept their money separate from my own I would not be tempted to make a temporary use of it and would always have it ready for my clients.

While Sheehan brought me the Larkin business Dr. Jones went on my bond as assignee.

My first lawsuit grew out of Mr. Larkin's business. I had an account against Mr. and Mrs. Matt Devlin. The sum was not large—somewhere between $30 and $40, I think. They objected to some items which he was not willing to omit and I brought suit. Mr. and Mrs. Devlin employed as their counsel Jerry Donahue, one of my classmates at college. When we graduated from Illinois College he studied law at Ann Arbor and I at Chicago. We returned to Jacksonville about the same time and this was his first suit as well as mine. It may seem a trifling thing to report, but a suit for that amount was not trifling to either of us at that time. Mrs. Devlin was an important member of the family and took the leading part in resisting payment. I distinctly recall the expression of disgust upon her face when I concluded my argument in support of my client's claim. She settled back in her chair and said, "Thank God, he's done." When the jury returned the verdict in my favor for the full amount it was with great difficulty that I restrained myself from giving utterance to a similar expression.

As time went on larger matters were brought to me and my clients increased in number and in business importance.

My first calendar year, January, 1884–85, showed receipts of something over seven hundred dollars. The second year something over a thousand, the third about fifteen hundred. As I removed to Nebraska at the end of nine months, the fourth calendar year was not completed. The receipts for nine months were nearly fourteen hundred dollars, making sure that that year would have shown a reasonable increase over the preceding one. I give these facts to show the growth of my practice. The beginning was about as small as it could well be, but the gain was

67

constant and my prospects were equal at least to those of any young lawyer in the city of like age and experience. I had the confidence of the profession and the community, as one instance will illustrate. I had my small bank business with the First National Bank, whose president, Felix Ferrell, had been my Sunday-school teacher when I was in college. One day Mr. Brown came from his office to ask me to become assignee in bankruptcy for one of his clients. I responded in the affirmative. He then asked me whether Mr. Ferrell would go on my bond for $40,000. I told him that I had never asked him to go on my bond and could not answer until I had consulted him. Mr. Brown was connected with another bank and I told him that if Mr. Ferrell went on my bond I would want to give the assignee's account to his bank. This he readily assented to as fair and proper. Then he telephoned Mr. Ferrell, who immediately came to the office. I hope I will be pardoned for saying that what followed was a compliment that I have never ceased to appreciate. Mr. Ferrell was not a man of many words; neither was Mr. Brown; and the conversation was brief and to the point. Mr. Brown: "We want Mr. Bryan to act as assignee in bankruptcy for ——. Will you go on his bond for $40,000?" Mr. Ferrell: "Yes." Mr. Brown: "Thanks." Mr. Bryan: "I am much obliged."

While I was practicing I had the usual experience of young lawyers in being called upon to speak on many different occasions. The lawyer has the advantage over all others in such matters. He is the natural spokesman of those of his school of thought and he is called upon more at banquets than those of other professions, because in the course of business he has to deal with a greater variety of subjects. Every form of question comes before the court and the lawyer is really attending school all his life. Some one has said that every speech represents the sum of the man's knowledge. Consciously or unconsciously, the speaker uses all that he has learned as background for each effort.

AT THE BAR

As I look back over my life I am increasingly impressed with the important part played by little circumstances. They really shaped events. While they seemed trivial at the time, yet in retrospect we can see how the absence of any one of them would have broken the chain of causation. My removal to Nebraska and the events following it furnish numerous illustrations.

To begin with, the one thing that singled Lincoln, Nebraska, out from other Western capitals and gave me a special interest in it was the fact that Adolphus Talbot lived there. We had been in law school together from the fall of 1881 to the spring of 1883. We were members of the class of '83, Union College of Law, Chicago, Illinois. We had been meeting twice a day at recitations for some weeks when the following incident occurred. A lady who was on a visit to the family with which I boarded inquired whether I knew Dolph Talbot. Upon my replying that I knew him as one of the members of the class she proceeded to tell me about a very charming young lady to whom he was engaged. Knowing enough about Talbot to know that he was a jovial good-natured fellow, I thought I would have some fun with him, so I sat down by him when the class was assembling and before the lesson began made up a story about as follows:

"Talbot, when I came up here last fall I felt rather lonesome and advertised for unknown correspondents. A number of young ladies answered me, but after a few exchanges of letters I dropped all but one. She made such a favorable impression upon me that we continued the correspondence until we made known our real names. As she lives at Abington, where you graduated, I thought you might be able to tell me something about her." I then gave him the name of his own sweetheart.

I need not add that he was surprised. My joke was working well. He replied with evident seriousness, "If she is the Miss —— whom I know, she is a very nice girl."

WILLIAM JENNINGS BRYAN

Having obtained the information that I pretended to seek, I tried to change the subject, but he would not change it, and kept returning to the theme, much to my enjoyment. I could see that he was not taking much interest in the lesson that morning and when it was over he followed me downstairs, still returning to the young lady at Abington. I did not have the heart to leave him in suspense all day, so as we separated at the corner of Dearborn and Washington Streets I told him that it was just a joke suggested by the fact that I had that morning met a lady who told me of his engagement to Miss ——. He chased me for a block down the street until I dodged into the Rapier Building, where Judge Trumbull's office was located.

At the afternoon recitation Talbot hunted me up with a broad smile on his face and admitted to me that my joke had him "going," as they say. At the conclusion of the recitation we went out together and during our conversation I learned that we were practically of the same age, had graduated on the same day, had become engaged about the same time. Our fiancées, as we compared notes, seemed to stand out as quite superior to all other young ladies of that age. This was a beginning of a friendship which has for forty years been one of the most delightful that I have known.

I speak elsewhere of the partnership which was an outgrowth of this meeting; I refer to it here as one of numerous factors which combined to take me from Illinois to Nebraska and, in so doing, laid the foundation of my political career.

Some years later, while a member of Congress, I made a speech in Baltimore in which I referred in a humorous way to this incident and after tracing its influence up to the time that I was elected to Congress, concluded: "My election to Congress, therefore, may be regarded as a result of a joke which I played in college."

The man who followed me (I think it was Dr. Gonzales) convulsed the House by referring to my statement and adding, "To come to Congress as a result of a joke is not new; I have known men to go to Congress as a result of a joke they have played upon the whole community."

But to continue the chain of circumstances. In the spring of 1887 I still had desk room in the office of Brown and Kirby. A part of the work turned over to me by Brown and Kirby was the collection of interest on notes held by Illinois College as its endowment fund. Judge Kirby, who was treasurer of the Board of Trustees, suggested that I make a trip to Kansas to call personally on some of the makers of these notes. He explained to me that the college could not afford to do more than pay traveling expenses and a small commission on collections made. As I had never been West, the proposition appealed to me and I made plans for the trip.

When I spoke of the matter at home, my wife's father asked me whether it would be much out of my way to go to Creston, Iowa, and look at a tract of land there which he had held for many years. I examined the map and found that it was not far out of my way and decided to include Creston in the trip. Upon closer examination, I found that I could go from Kansas to Creston either by way of St. Joseph or via Lincoln. The fact that Talbot lived at Lincoln decided me to go by that route.

I reached Lincoln early on Saturday morning in July of 1887, was accorded a hearty welcome and spent that day and the Sunday following with my old law-school classmate. The joke, plus the errand upon which the college sent me, plus the fact that my father-in-law had a piece of land in Creston—the three combined to make me acquainted with Lincoln and the opportunities which it offered to a young lawyer. Here were three little circumstances, each one a necessary factor in my change of residence.

But even these would not have led to my removal to Lincoln had it not been for two other small circumstances. Just before I made the trip to Kansas I had decided to open up an office for myself and I had rented rooms next to Brown and Kirby's office—I had even gone so far as to re-paper the rooms and put them in order for my return from the West. But when I came back from Lincoln I was so deeply impressed with the advantages of the proposed change of location that I arranged for a transfer of lease and began to put my affairs in shape to leave for Nebraska in the autumn.

About the time I had rented the room and began planning for a separate office, I came near entering a partnership at Jacksonville which, if it had been formed, would have prevented my going to Nebraska and by so doing prevented the experiences which followed the change of residence. As I look back upon the little difference which prevented the formation of this partnership I am amazed at the influence that it had upon my life.

Richard Yates, son of Illinois' "war governor," who had graduated from Illinois College two years before my graduation, was the city attorney and a candidate for reëlection. We compared our incomes and found that his, including the city attorney's salary, was about the same as mine without any salary, and that therefore we could divide equally without material loss to either. But his salary constituted a considerable part of his income and he felt that it would not be fair for us to divide equally unless he should be reëlected. As the election was some considerable way off, I did not like to delay action in the matter of partnership until then and I proposed to him that I would take the nomination on the Democratic ticket so as to make sure that the salary would come into our office. To this he objected on the ground that his majority against me (I conceded that the chances were greatly in his favor) would not be as great as the majority he hoped to get against the Democrat who seemed likely to be nominated. Looking to a political life, he counted on the size of his majority to aid him in future candidacies.

72

AT THE BAR

As I recall this incident nearly thirty-five years ago, it seems to me that the two objections to the partnership were both trivial, my unwillingness to risk the small chance of his being defeated and his unwillingness to risk the small loss of majority that he might suffer from my candidacy; and yet these trivial objections prevented the formation of a partnership which would have kept me in Jacksonville.

Another circumstance quite as insignificant might have kept me in Illinois. After the election of President Cleveland in 1884, Mr. James Van Horbeck was appointed United States District Attorney at Springfield. He resided at Carlyle, Illinois, county seat of Clinton County, which was included in my father's judicial circuit when he was on the bench. Mr. Van Horbeck had practiced law under my father and had, I think, been admitted to the bar by him. For that reason he was personally friendly to me.

In the spring of 1887 I went to Springfield and consulted him about appointment as Assistant United States Attorney. He told me that he was not now ready to make the change, but that he would gladly give me the place when there was a vacancy but for the fact that he had promised it to a man endorsed by Congressman Springer. I returned to Jacksonville regretting that circumstances denied me the appointment.

The following September, while I was breaking up housekeeping preparatory for our departure for Nebraska, a carriage drove up to the door and the Assistant United States Attorney called to tell me that he was ready to resign and that the man to whom Mr. Van Horbeck had promised the Assistant's place had moved to Oklahoma and that I could have the position. But it was then too late. My plans had been completed and could not at that time be changed. I was sorry that the information had not come sooner, but if the appointment had been offered me before I went West I would have taken the position at Springfield and would not have gone to Nebraska.

WILLIAM JENNINGS BRYAN

Having laid before the reader the five little circumstances that had a part in my moving to Nebraska, I will only add here that I reached my new home just in time. If I had gone earlier I might have been involved in the divisions in the party and been less available at the particular time which was most favorable for my entrance into politics.

I have described how circumstances combined to take me to Lincoln, Nebraska, where I caught a vision that led to a change in residence. When I returned to Jacksonville I laid the matter before my wife, giving her the reasons for the change as they had impressed me.

First; While I was prospering in Jacksonville, it was only a question of a few years before I would reach the limit of possibilities and Lincoln was a city about four times as large as Jacksonville. Then, too, Lincoln was the capital of a state and I might expect Supreme Court business from outside counties. Illinois had passed through its period of rapid development; Nebraska was growing rapidly. I had found in Lincoln the owner of a weekly newspaper who offered to give me a column of his paper for the answer of legal questions submitted by his readers. This, I thought, would enable me to make acquaintances and become known to the people of the county. And then I had further found there my law-school friend Talbot, who offered me a partnership.

Every argument that impressed me was professional, no thought of politics ever entered my mind. How could it when Nebraska was a Republican state? The Congressional District to which I was moving was Republican; so was the county of Lancaster, the city of Lincoln, and the ward in which I expected to live.

When I had finished my argument my young wife answered in the spirit which she has always shown, "You know Jacksonville; you have seen Lincoln. If you think that the change is for the best, I am willing to go."

We had both attended school in Jacksonville and were

attached to a delightful circle of friends. It was hard to leave these and go to a new country. She was loath to leave the friends who had become so dear to us, and my regret was as deep as hers, but she left the decision to me.

Having obtained my wife's consent, I laid the matter before her father and I cannot forget the generous manner in which he met the situation. I presented to him the same arguments I had laid before my wife and told him of her answer and of my opinion. He replied, "Well, William, it does not make much difference to Lovina (his wife) and me where we live. It does make a difference to you and Mary. You do what you think is best for you and for her, and her mother and I will suit ourselves to your plans."

As a result of an impression more than as a result of clearly defined reasons the die was cast in favor of a change of residence. As I look back to that day I confess that I am somewhat bewildered. Not a single reason that led me to favor the change materialized, but reasons that I never saw and could not therefore take into account justified the change. As I shall show later, my professional success, while as great as we could reasonably expect, covered so brief a period that I could not test the opportunities which appeared to me large enough to justify beginning to practice law in a new state.

And so I arranged to leave for Nebraska on the last day of September and reached Lincoln on the first day of October, 1887, the third anniversary of our marriage. As it was too late in the fall to begin the construction of the home in Lincoln, it was decided that Mrs. Bryan would remain in Jacksonville during the winter with our child and my wife's parents and would join me when the house was completed. When we sold the Jacksonville home I found that Dr. Jones had never put on record the mortgage which I gave him when the house was built, an expression of confidence which I appreciated. The Nebraska home was built by my father-in-law, Mr. Baird, and I rented it until I was in a position to buy it sometime later.

October first, 1887, was a beautiful autumn day. Talbot was at the station to welcome me and he there introduced me to two Democrats who were the beginning of my political friends in that state. One was R. P. Millar, the station agent of the Missouri Pacific Railroad in Lincoln, and W. B. Morrison, a resident of Hickman, about twenty miles south of Lincoln. The partnership of Talbot and Bryan began at once and our offices were in the First National Bank Building. Talbot was the local attorney for the Missouri Pacific Railroad, but it was understood that his salary and fees from the railroad were individual and not covered by the partnership. All other business was the firm's. It was not large at first, because Talbot's connection with the Missouri Pacific had taken him away from the office for a considerable portion of his time and his practice had suffered for lack of a partner.

My first fee came from a man by the name of O'Mara, an Irishman who had heard my Buckhorn School House speech. Although the fee was small, it was a pleasant reminder of the speech into which I had, for professional reasons, tried to inject a reference to my being a lawyer.

When I went to Nebraska I carried with me about $300, a fee which I had just earned in a lawsuit won in the Appelate Court. I also carried with me to Lincoln a letter of introduction to the German National Bank. Joseph Boehmer, the cashier of that bank, had come from Quincy to Lincoln and the letter was from Erwin Wood, who had known him in the former city. I deposited the $300 in the German National Bank and soon became its attorney. The business I received from the bank and through its influence aided me materially in the beginning. Soon after I located in Nebraska we moved our offices to the Burr Block, a building just completed at that time. As I was alone and as I wished to make my $300 go as far as possible, I saved room rent

76

by sleeping on a folding lounge in the office. I economized on food also by buying twenty-one meal tickets for $4.50 at O'Dell's Restaurant and using them two a day instead of three. I ate in the morning and in the evening and contented myself with a lunch at noon, usually an apple and a few gingersnaps. I can remember with great distinctness when the office receipts became sufficient to justify the use of three meal tickets a day.

When I began practice anew in Nebraska my first work was in the matter of collections. I recall one small collection which fell into my hands soon after I joined Talbot. A client who had a little grocery store in the suburbs brought in a small bill which was owed him and told me that he thought the man would pay it if I wrote him a note to stir him up.

I wrote the usual note, framing it in language as polite as I could command, and awaited the call of the debtor. He never came, but the client dropped in the office a few days later to report. As he came into the outer room I noticed a smile upon his face which I interpreted to mean that my note had been successful. When he reached the door I greeted him with,

"Well, I sent him the note. Did it stir him up?"

"Stir him up?" he replied. "I should think it did." Then he took off his hat and showed me a lump nearly as large as an egg on the side of his head, explaining that the debtor had responded to the note, but had called upon him instead of upon his attorney and had hit him on the head with a brick!

I have often thought of this incident when in a campaign I would hear some one boast that he had stirred up the enemy.

I was always interested in the establishment of important legal principles, as two illustrations will show. Not long after I located at Lincoln, Editor Emmons of our local weekly Democratic paper, called on me for advice in regard to a lawsuit. He had been circulating cards advertising his newspaper among the delegates who had come in to attend the county convention. Some of them threw the cards upon the sidewalk and a policeman attempted to arrest Emmons for violating a city ordinance which forbade the throwing of paper upon the street. Emmons resisted arrest and came out second best in the encounter. He went to the office of a justice of the peace and filed complaint against the policeman for assault and battery and the constable refused to serve the papers without fees being advanced. Emmons wanted to know whether it was necessary for him to advance the fees in order to secure redress. I looked for authorities and could find none. One statute specifically gave the constable the right to demand fees before serving papers. After careful consideration of the facts I reached the conclusion in which Judge Cassidy, who was associated with me, concurred: that while the statute made no exception of papers served in criminal cases, such an exception must be presumed, otherwise redress for criminal assault would be impossible to those without means.

Pleading the case upon what I regarded as a fundamental principle, namely, that justice could not be sold and that a remedy in a criminal case could not depend upon the financial ability of the party injured, I drew a petition for a writ of mandamus compelling the constable to serve the warrant without prepayment of his fee. When I took the petition to Judge Chapman and told him the nature of my petition he shook his head and replied:

"You will have to have a very strong case before I will make an officer serve papers without fees being advanced."

"I have a strong case," I answered, "as I think I shall be able to convince you." At the hearing I did convince him and he issued the writ, from which the defendant appealed.

78

When the matter came up in the Supreme Court the hearing was held in a room on the walls of which appeared the seal of the state with the state's motto, "Equality before the law." As that was the basis upon which our fight was being made, I was able to point the judges to the state's motto and it doubtless had its effect in securing a decision, the first, I think, in the United States establishing this important principle. Neither Judge Cassidy nor myself received any fee in this case, but Emmons, who afterwards moved to Oklahoma, had a little post office in his county named after me.

Another case in which I took a deep interest brought me more satisfaction than money. Some beet-sugar factories were established in Nebraska soon after I went there and those in charge of the factories secured a state statute granting a bounty and also sought bounties of counties and precincts. One day a lawyer called with a letter of introduction from J. Sterling Morton to consult me about the legality of a bond issue voted in a precinct in which he lived. My recollection is that his vote was the only vote in the precinct against the bounty. But he wanted to oppose it on the ground that it was unconstitutional. He found me sympathetic. He paid me $25 down and was to pay $25 later. But the account remains open. The fee, however, was immaterial; the case gave me an opportunity to contest the constitutionality of a bounty and I was glad of the opportunity.

We decided to contest the issue of the bonds voted when an attempt was made to issue them. Before they reached this particular precinct a suit was brought to test the validity of similar bonds issued by an adjoining precinct. It was a friendly suit brought by the interested parties against the State Auditor to compel the registering of the bonds, both parties being for an affirmative order. I appeared at the trial and asked for permission to file a brief, stating to the court that I represented a client who was contesting bonds of the same kind in an adjoining precinct. Both sides objected to my request, but the court overruled the objections and allowed the brief to be filed.

When the court decided against the bonds, and in so doing disappointed both plaintiff and defendant, I had satisfaction enough to more than make up for the unpaid portion of my promised fee and was rewarded still further when as a member of Congress this experience enabled me to answer a question which was put to me by an Iowa Republican who knew of the bonds voted but did not know of the court decision nullifying them.

My first case in the Supreme Court came from Greeley County and involved a county-seat election. Those who have ever lived in a county where such elections take place need not be told that the interest in a presidential election is, in comparison, quite negligible. The question to be decided was whether the county seat should be removed from Scotia, a Union Pacific Railroad town on the edge of the county, to Greeley Center, a Burlington Railroad town near the center of the county. The railroads as well as the localities were interested and every voter in the county was at the polls, plus others.

General Barry and John Cavanaugh, two members of the election board, favored Greeley Center, where they lived, but as honest and conscientious officers they were compelled to throw out the vote of one precinct as fraudulent. After the vote was counted it gave the majority to Greeley Center, but Barry and Cavanaugh, true to their oath of office, acted against their personal interests and rejected this precinct.

When the case came up in the Supreme Court Scotia had her attorneys and Greeley Center had hers. The Scotia attorneys wanted the vote in question thrown out. Greeley Center wanted it counted in. Barry and Cavanaugh retained me to represent them as officials, explaining to me that, officially, they wanted me to defend their action, but they personally would like to have their action overruled.

It made my position a delicate one. There was no doubt in my mind about the fraudulent character of the disputed returns. I question whether any records present a case where the fraud was more transparent. The law required that the name of the voter be entered, and those who committed the fraud evidently had to act in a hurry; not having time to manufacture a list of names which would at least look honest, they put down prominent names of presidents, well-known senators, and distinguished men of other states.

In the trial I, of course, was on the side of Scotia and therefore acted with the Scotia attorneys. Before taking up the case on its merits, Scotia's attorneys moved for a delay, and at the request of my clients I joined with the Greeley Center people to oppose delay. This confused the court and one of the judges asked, "Mr. Bryan, for which side do you appear?"

I replied, "I had hoped that my argument would indicate that."

The judge said, "Your argument is clear enough, but I thought you were on the side of Scotia."

"I am," I said, "on the merits of the case, but I am with the attorneys of Greeley Center in opposing the motion." My clients had the pleasure of winning their case and the sorrow of seeing their city fail in its effort to secure the county seat.

Measured by its outcome, my removal to Nebraska was the gift of good fortune. I was most lucky in the selection of a law partner. Adolphus R. Talbot is a rare man—one of God's noblemen. In law school we had come to address each other as Dolph and Will and so when we united our energies in the practice of law, it was a very friendly union. We were about the same height and age, he nearly a year the older—from April around to March—about the same size and not far from the same weight. We were as much alike as two men could be and yet we were quite dissimilar in several respects. He was of English stock, having been born in England; I was very much mixed, with the Irish predominating in my name. He was a Methodist and I a Presbyterian; he was a Republican and I a Democrat. When baldness attacked us, his hair retreated from the front and mine from the rear. In the practice he looked at our side of the case and I inquired as to the arguments that the opposition could advance. But in spite of our points of dissimilarity, no two lawyers ever worked together with less friction. On the first of each month one would take his day book into the room of the other—whichever one happened to think of it first—and we would go over the credits and debits together, each would strike his balance and whichever had the largest net receipts would give the other a check for half and then we wrote "settled" across the two books and never had any other reckoning.

I mentioned the fact that he was a Republican and I a Democrat. At one time he was chairman of the Republican City Committee and I was chairman of the Democratic City Committee.

Our offices consisted of three rooms, the reception room and two private offices. When a man came in and inquired for the chairman of the Committee the clerk would ask him "of which committee?" He was still chairman when I ran for Congress and reported an incident that occurred during the campaign.

One of the members of the city committee called on him to say that he felt that he ought to resign as a member of the committee because he was going to support Bryan for Congress. Talbot assured him that that was not necessary, that the Republican candidate for Congress was only one of many candidates on that ticket and this was only one campaign. The man was finally persuaded not to give up his committeeship and I learned later that the chairman and more than half the committee were supporting me. During my campaign of 1896 Mr. Talbot was a Republican candidate for the Nebraska State Senate and was embarrassed by seeing published in the Lincoln papers glowing eulogies of me which he had written to papers in other states in answer to inquiries.

Talbot's personal friendship was always greater than his Republicanism, despite his prominence in the party. For more than thirty years he has been one of my nearest and dearest friends. Whenever I am relieved for a moment from the pressure under which I have lived, a pressure so great as to prevent any leisurely review of the past or unhurried contemplation of the future, and I allow myself to think of the latter days, I dream of a brief period before the close of life when, my work done, I can commune with lifelong friends and recall the joint struggles of early days. I always think of Dolph as one of those with whom companionship will be most satisfying.

When I was elected to Congress, I felt that I should give my entire time to my work and therefore I turned over to Mr. Talbot the unfinished business and only appeared where it was necessary to please some particular friends among our clients. The only conflict of opinion we ever had over fees was when I went to Congress. He insisted on giving me a larger percentage of the fees which came from the left-over business than I thought I deserved and it was not without a good deal of argument that we reached a compromise of our differences.

The firm name was continued while I was in Congress and I expected to resume the practice when I returned to Lincoln in 1895, but by that time the fight over bimetallism was just beginning and I received about the same time three invitations from widely different points, one to answer John Sherman at Salem, Oregon, another to answer him at Cincinnati, Ohio, and a third to answer John G. Carlisle at Memphis, Tennessee. It soon became apparent that I must either refuse political invitations or suspend practice again. I was too much interested in the fight for which I had helped to lay the plans to disappoint those whom I had helped to enlist, and so I decided to postpone for another year my return to law.

Then came the Presidential campaign of 1896 which so completely identified me with national politics that I felt that I must keep up the fight for at least another four years. So I retired from the firm.

My last appearance as a member of the Nebraska bar was in the United States Supreme Court in a maximum rate case which arose over a law passed in Nebraska and contested by the railroads. The Attorney-General of Nebraska, Hon. C. J. Smythe, one of my closet political friends, represented the state. I was so deeply interested in the result of the trial that I volunteered to appear without pay in order to present the one point in which I was concerned.

The proposition upon which I based my argument was taken from a book written by Governor Larrabee of Iowa, who became a leader of the agriculturists of that state in their effort to secure reasonable railroad rates. I read the book soon after I entered Congress and attempted to secure the incorporation of the principle in a pooling bill that passed the House while I was a member. My amendment to that bill was defeated, but it attracted enough attention to call forth one of the earliest epithets applied to me. A Richmond, Virginia, paper quite conspicuous for its sympathetic support of the corporation side of public questions, had an editorial denunciation of my amendment which appeared under the title of "Nihilist Bryan."

INTERCOLLEGIATE DEBATING TEAM

Representing six middle western colleges.   The lady is Miss Jane Addams;   the tallest figure standing is that of Mr. Bryan.

CHAPTER IV

THE LURE OF THE COLLEGE PRIZE

I FELT the lure of prizes from the start and took part in every contest for which I was eligible. A prize always stirred me to activity, and a recollection of its influence upon my studies has led me in later days to stimulate students to similar activity by the establishing of prizes in a number of institutions of learning.

The principal prizes I established were in the public school at Normal, the precinct in which our country home near Lincoln was located, and in some nineteen institutions —seventeen of them state universities—in which I established a prize for the best essay on the science of government. When, some years later, Mr. Philo S. Bennett consulted me in regard to the best use of some money which he desired to leave by will, I recommended similar prizes and upon his death distributed for him funds for the establishment of such prizes in twenty state universities.

In my first year in the academy—"Junior Prep" as it was called—I entered the declamation contest, using as my theme Patrick Henry's famous speech, "Give me liberty or give me death." The judges did not seem to regard me as especially promising. At any rate, I was not near enough to even second place to give me any intense interest in the returns. The next year I entered the declamation contest again, this time taking as my subject by the advice of Mrs. Jones, "The Palmetto and the Pine." The sentiment was most excellent, but my delivery seemed to lack something— enough to enable two of the contestants to pass me. I came third in the estimate of the judges and Dr. Jones thought that my failure may have been due to indistinctness of articulation. I do not know whether that was true or not, but it spurred me up on that particular subject and distinctness of articulation became a controlling passion with me.

In the freshman year I entered the declamation contest for the third time, after having divided the second prize in Latin prose composition with a fellow student. I was gaining ground. In my first contest I came down toward the last, in my second contest I ranked third, in my third contest I won half of the second prize, in my fourth contest—freshman declamation—I rose a point higher and had the second prize all to myself. I did not like dramatic pieces, but at the earnest solicitation of my instructor in rhetoric I took Bernardo del Carpio for my freshman declamation. Of course, the matter was very much on my mind during the days immediately preceding the contest, so much so that a night or two before the declaimers were to appear in public on the stage of Strawn's Opera House I had a dream that made an indelible impression upon me because it came true. In my dream, we seemed to have finished our declamations and were awaiting the announcement of the award of the prizes—a moment of great suspense, as all will admit who have passed through the experience. Then the chairman of the committee of judges appeared and wrote upon the blackboard the names of the victors. I could see my name very distinctly occupying the second place, but I could not make out the name of the man who was awarded the first prize.

My dream not only assured me of my success in securing second prize but it even disclosed to me the books which I selected (the prizes were given in books to be selected by the students themselves. The second prize in this case was $10.00). I selected an Oxford Bible with a concordance and a volume of Shakespeare. As I am writing these words I turn to this treasure and find on the first page of the Bible the following: at the top the Greek letters Sigma Pi and my class '81 and following that these words: "Presented to W. J. Bryan, Salem, Illinois, by the faculty of Illinois

College, May 28, 1878. Second prize in declamation."
The copy of Shakespeare bound in calf is still in my library
and on the first page is a duplicate of the first page of the
Bible above referred to.

I digress here to say that I received the usual training in
public speaking. Professor Hamilton was our instructor;
he was a large man with a strong face and a piercing eye.
He rather leaned to the dramatic and recommended dramatic pieces to us. I rather preferred the oratorical style.
He complimented me by saying that I declaimed the oratorical pieces so well that he could not be of much assistance to
me along that line. He trained us in modulation of the
voice, gesticulation, etc., and I presume that his instructions
were beneficial to me, although I have been so much more
interested in the subject matter than in the form of presentation that my use of his advice has been unconscious
rather than intentional.

As our absorption of ideals is gradual and constant, I
do not know to what extent I am indebted to him for the
settled opinions which I have formed on public speaking. I
think that instruction in gesticulation becomes valuable as
one forgets the instructions and moves his arms and body
without thought of the instructions. It is hard to be
graceful in gesticulation when one is thinking about the
movements to be made, just as it is difficult for one to speak
naturally while he is engaged in artificial effort. But the
training that one receives, both in the modulation of the
voice and in action, finally becomes a part of him—a second
nature, so to speak—and he obeys the suggestions that he
has received without a thought.

In my sophomore year I entered the contest in essay and
won the first prize—my first first prize—with an essay on
the by no means novel subject of "Labor." This pleased
my father more than the previous prizes won. He said that
he would rather have me gain prominence for my own thought
than by repeating the words of others.

WILLIAM JENNINGS BRYAN

In my junior year I entered the oratorical contest influenced by a double ambition, because the successful orator in this contest would, as a matter of custom, represent the college in the intercollegiate contest the following fall. My subject on this occasion was "Individual Power" and I left nothing undone that would contribute towards success. I had had in mind for nearly five years the honor of representing the college in the oratorical contest. It so happened that soon after my arrival in Jacksonville I had the privilege of attending a contest in which Fred Turner, the orator of Illinois College, represented our institution. From that night this vision was before me and my work as a declaimer, as an essayist, and in the delivering of orations was to this end. I was successful—securing the first honor here as in the contest in essay the year before.

Possibly another digression here may be excusable. My good wife often refers to it when someone has in later years commented as to what they have described as the ease with which I speak. She says that they do not know how hard and for how many years I worked as a college boy and as a young man when I was in training. The incident which she often related is as follows. The contest came in May, 1880, some seven months after we became acquainted. Mrs. Jones, who was very fond of Miss Baird, conceived the idea of having a May Day party out in a woods pasture belonging to Dr. Jones. It so happened that this woods pasture adjoined the grounds of an insane asylum and it also happened that a man who had formerly worked for Dr. Jones was cultivating a farm close by this spot selected for the party. I went out to the grove an hour or so ahead of the rest of the party and spent the time delivering my oration with the trees as an audience. When Miss Baird and the other members of the May Day party approached the woods pasture the former employee left his plow and ran out to the road waving his hand in warning, calling out: "Don't go in there. There is a man over there shouting and waving his hands. I think he must have escaped from the asylum." Mrs. Jones and my wife-to-be guessed at once the cause of his alarm and entered the pasture in a mood to enjoy the day.

In the following October (1880) I went to Galesburg, Illinois, to represent my college in the contest to which I had looked forward for many years. My subject was "Justice." After the prize had been awarded, General John C. Black of Chicago, with whom I afterwards served in Congress, one of the judges in this contest, took me to his room in the hotel and gave me encouragement and advice. He told me that he had marked me one hundred on delivery and high enough on thought and composition to make me his first choice (the marks of the other two brought me down to second place). He then gave me his advice on various styles of oratory, contrasting the style of Edmund Burke, whose sentences were long and involved, and the style of Victor Hugo, whose sentences were short and pithy. He said that I leaned rather to the style of the latter and advised me to cultivate longer sentences. I have not forgotten his advice, but have found it difficult to follow it, possibly because I have always labored under the coercion that made me so anxious to present a subject clearly that I could not give much attention to ornamentation and figures of speech.

In my oration on "Justice" my introduction was, I think, as appropriate as any that I have ever employed. I learned quite early the wisdom of a beginning that immediately catches the attention. I noticed this in speeches, of which I early became an eager reader, and observed in Wendell Phillips when he delivered his famous lecture, "The Lost Arts," at Jacksonville during my student days. The great orator was in the habit of commencing with some reference to some local object of interest, which he linked to his address. Dr. Conwell employs the same art in his remarkable lecture on "Acres of Diamonds."

As it is my purpose to make my memoirs as useful as possible to the young people who read them, I am led to add that Paul has given to the public speakers of the world probably the most perfect illustration of easy and felicitous entrance on the presentation of a theme. His speech at Athens was before the most critical of his audiences and he was especially happy in selecting an opening phrase which at once enlisted the attention of his hearers:

"Ye men of Athens, I perceive that in all things ye are too superstitious.

"For as I passed by, and beheld your devotions, I found an altar with this inscription, TO THE UNKNOWN GOD. Whom therefore ye ignorantly worship, him declare I unto you.

"God that made the world and all things therein, seeing that he is Lord of heaven and earth, dwelleth not in temples made with hands;

"Neither is worshipped with men's hands, as though he needed any thing, seeing he giveth to all life, and breath, and all things;

"And hath made of one blood all nations of men for to dwell on all the face of the earth, and hath determined the times before appointed, and the bounds of their habitation;

"That they should seek the Lord, if haply they might feel after him, and find him, though he be not far from every one of us:

"For in him we live, and move, and have our being; as certain also of your poets have said, For we are also his offspring.

"Forasmuch then as we are the offspring of God, we ought not to think that the Godhead is like unto gold, or silver, or stone, graven by art and man's device.

"And the times of this ignorance God winked at; but now commandeth all men every where to repent:

THE LURE OF THE COLLEGE PRIZE

"Because he hath appointed a day, in the which he will judge the world in righteousness by that man whom he hath ordained; whereof he hath given assurance unto all men, in that he hath raised him from the dead." (Acts 17:22–31.)

My speech on Justice began: "Plutarch tells us that men entertain three sentiments concerning the gods; they fear them for their power, respect them for their intelligence, and love them for their justice." The local paper had a complimentary account of my speech—they generally praised where they could performance of students—and these early bits of eulogy are very satisfying to participants in contests—especially those who fail to win prizes. I came second, my college backer insisting, as college boys are wont to do, that I ought to have had first place.

The fifty dollars handed me by the treasurer of the oratorical association was the largest sum that I had earned up to that time. The first draft upon me was made for the purchase of an engagement ring for my intended wife. I had waited from June until October in order to purchase the ring with money that I had myself earned. It was a modest ring—a garnet set in gold—but it was sufficient to satisfy our simple tastes, and adorn Mrs. Bryan's hand until it was lost during the campaign of 1896. It was my custom to earn the money to pay for any gifts to Miss Baird, and during a large part of my college days I added to my spending money by clerking in a hat store on Saturdays.

This contest was quite an event in college life and, as was customary, a delegation of the students went along to boost for their representatives. I had gone upon a similar expedition when Richard Yates represented our college and won the first prize at Champaign, Illinois, two years before. The successful competitors in a number of these intercollegiate contests contested for the interstate prize at a later meeting which was at the time held in Jacksonville. By winning second prize I became the alternate and would have represented the state at the interstate contest had the winner of first prize failed to appear. Although this was a very remote contingency, I prepared myself for it, but Mr. Erskine, orator of the state at Galesburg, was there and I not only had no opportunity to enter the larger contest but was the victim of a good deal of ridicule when the man who defeated me came near the close of the list in the interstate contest. For several days I was greeted by college friends with substantially the same question: "If Erskine came last, where would you have been?"

At the Galesburg meeting, I was, because of my residence at Jacksonville, the place of the next contest, made vice-president of the interstate association. The work of arrangement fell to President Montgomery of Indiana and Secretary Howard of Iowa. In the correspondence that took place prior to the date of the contest at Jacksonville I was in correspondence with Montgomery and Howard. We had never met, but in the intimacy between us developed by the correspondence we had exchanged guesses as to each other. Howard and I discussed Montgomery, Montgomery and I discussed Howard, and Howard and Montgomery discussed me. When the time came for the meeting Montgomery and Howard arrived at Jacksonville at the same time and our acquaintance ripened into a permanent friendship. Judge Montgomery has since held a high judicial position in his state and I have frequently enjoyed the hospitality of his delightful home when I visited Seymour, Indiana. Howard afterward moved to Indianapolis and then to New York and was a Republican in his early days. He became a supporter of mine in 1896 and until his death in New York some years ago was a colaborer in the political vineyard.

I was a contestant for one prize in my senior year and there I came second, but I was even more pleased to have

WILLIAM JENNINGS BRYAN IN HIS EARLY DAYS
Portraits taken before his first nomination.

the prize go to Sam Eveland than to have won it myself. Sam was one of the lovable members of the class and one of the most interesting men I ever knew. He was brought up in Michigan. His education was neglected and he went early into the logging camps. As a young man he tramped from section to section in search of work. He went by chance one evening into a church where a protracted meeting was in session. He was converted and decided to be a minister. With Sam it was really a new birth. His life was as completely changed as was the life of Paul. I have never known a man more completely consecrated to the service of God and to the life patterned after the example of Christ.

He went to school in spite of the embarrassment that a grown person finds in studying with children. He was fourteen years older than myself, and I graduated at about twenty-one. I was about the average age for the class. He was not a brilliant man, but no one could surpass him in industry and in patient plodding. He was as truthful as a child; everybody loved him. When the professor of political economy announced "Pauperism, Its Causes and Remedies," as the subject of the thesis and that each member was expected to write, I remarked that we might each give our experience and let the prize go to the one who knew most about the subject, and that is the way it went. Sam Eveland won the prize. Evidence, if evidence was needed, of the value of personal knowledge in the presentation of any subject.

Still another digression here. When I went home to spend the Christmas holidays I went out to the county poorhouse, thinking that I might get some information for my thesis. I acquainted the superintendent with the object of my visit and he gave me access to the inmates. The first man I met was, to my surprise, a brother of one of the most prominent citizens of the county, a man of wealth, family, and influence. I found that this inmate was an unmarried man. My questions did not bring out much information beyond the fact that he had not saved anything and found himself a pauper during his later days. The second man whom I met was also unmarried and I jotted down "celibacy" as a cause of pauperism.

I began in my mind to sketch the path of the unmarried man without responsibility, he gives free rein to his desires and pleasures, wasting his life in enjoyment, and finally comes down to old age with no provision made for the days of failing strength. I thought I had made some progress in preparing my case. Then I met the third inmate.

"Are you married?" I enquired.

"Yes, my fourth wife left me when I came here."

"Have you any children?"

"Twenty-six." And my first theory was exploded.

After time for reflection I thought that possibly there might be a golden mean—that was before the word "golden" had been made odious by bad association—between the irresponsibility of the unmarried man and the burdened spouse and father. I have not yet been able to understand how a man could raise twenty-six children without having at least one among them who could care for him in his old age!

Returning to Eveland again: I cannot resist the temptation to record facts that come to my memory when the name of this dear friend is recalled. First was one of his experiences in courtship. I was rather a patriarch among the boys during my last year in college. I reached my twenty-first anniversary less than three months before graduation and I was engaged, as they say, during my entire senior year. This was known among the boys and some of them came to me for advice—among them Sam.

He took me aside one day and with evident emotion told me that he had at last found the girl for whom he was looking. He described her to me and according to his description she would make a model wife for a pastor. He said that he had laid his claims before her the night before and that she had accepted him.

I was rather surprised at the suddenness with which he had proposed and suggested to him that it might have been better to have gone about it more gradually, but he was a very practical sort of a fellow and, having found the kind of wife for whom he was looking, he did not see why any period of romance should be injected between the discovery and the filing of his claim. I congratulated him, though I confess it was with some misgivings as to whether the agreement reached was really conclusive.

A few days afterward the poor fellow came to me distressed beyond description to tell me that he had called upon the young lady again and found that she did not understand that they were engaged. In fact, it was not long before he brought back that familiar report that while she could not marry him she would always be his friend. Later he was more successful and found an exemplary lady about his own age who was deeply religious and who became his wife.

The day before his marriage, he called on me. "Bryan," he said, "I want you to do me a favor. As I am a minister, I am afraid that the preacher who will officiate will not be willing to accept a fee from me. So I will give you the money and you can hand it to him."

Of course I responded favorably, and took the coin away with me in my pocket. Between that hour and the hour when he and his chosen one were to be united in the holy bonds of wedlock I framed a little speech to be made to the minister when it came time to act as Sam's paymaster. Everything went well. The invited guests were as happy as the bride and groom, the pastor was on hand and the ceremony was duly performed. After the congratulations I took the minister off to one side and began to deliver Sam's message. When I reached the proper point I put my hand into my pocket and to my amazement discovered that I had changed my trousers. The minister had to take my word for the fee until I could go home and get the money and hunt him up. Whenever I saw Sam afterward and we became reminiscent, this embarrassing episode was sure to be recalled. But my, what a smoke a little fire kindleth! All these recollections were unloosed when I thought of being defeated in a thesis contest by a classmate who had once been a tramp.

CHAPTER V

EARLY NATIONAL CONVENTIONS

I FORMED early the habit of attending national conventions. It so happened that the Democratic National Convention of 1876 was held in St. Louis, only seventy miles from my birthplace. My father and mother were attending the Philadelphia Exposition at the time, but my enthusiasm reached a point where I decided to go to the convention with some of the other boys—I do not recall that any of them were as young as myself. I sold enough corn to secure the small amount necessary, the railroad fare being only a few dollars and my other expenses being small. I recall that I stayed all night at East St. Louis, sleeping in a room with more than thirty others on cots.

Next day I appeared at the convention hall, but not knowing anyone from whom I could secure a ticket, I had to content myself with standing around watching the distinguished Democrats, to me unknown, go in and out of the convention. But here again my lucky star helped me out. A policeman, taking pity on me, put me in through a window and I had the pleasure of hearing John Kelly make his famous speech against Tilden. That was my initiation into national politics. Since that time I have attended every Democratic National Convention but three, and I was in close touch by wire with two of the three, those of 1900 and 1908. The Cincinnati Convention of 1880, therefore, is the only one that I have actually missed since I was sixteen years old. I was still a college boy in 1880 and Cincinnati was so far from Salem that I was able to withstand the temptation which overpowered me four years before.

When the convention of 1884 was held at Chicago I was living at Jacksonville, but my income was so meager that I decided that I could not afford a trip to Chicago, but here again fortune favored me. I was invited to deliver a Fourth of July address at Greenwood, not many miles from Jacksonville. In accepting the invitation I answered the inquiry about compensation by saying that I expected nothing more than my traveling expenses. When I was through speaking, the chairman of the committee asked me about my expenses. When I stated the amount, something less than three dollars, he handed me a twenty-dollar bill with the remark,

"That will cover your expenses."

I was so surprised that I almost forgot to thank him. I decided that I would construe my good luck as a providential provision for convention expenses and arranged to go to Chicago. On the train I fell in with Carl Epler, son of Judge Epler, one of the circuit judges presiding in the Jacksonville circuit, and we made the trip together.

At Chicago we went from one headquarters to another and listened to the arguments in favor of the various candidates. My personal preference was Senator Bayard of Delaware. In one of the senates of which I was a member when a schoolboy I represented Delaware and took the name of Senator Bayard. I was open to conviction, however, and ready to hoorah for the candidate who won the nomination.

As it is in all national conventions, it was difficult to get a ticket of admission. Finding Hon. Telas W. Merritt, of Salem, a prominent politician at the Illinois headquarters, I asked him if he could secure tickets for Epler and myself. He said he could not secure any tickets, but that he knew one of the doorkeepers, whereupon he took us to Joseph Chesterfield Mackin, a Chicago politician, and said in his stammering way—he stuttered—"Joe, pa-pa-pass these b-b-boys in." Joe passed us in and we returned to his door regularly during the sessions of the convention. I am sorry to have to remark in passing that Joe was soon after sent to the penitentiary for "ballot-box stuffing"—this was through no fault of Mr. Merritt's or of ours and I only mention it because I never think of the incident without also thinking of what befell Joseph Chesterfield after we had thus become acquainted with him.

When the 1888 convention was held in St. Louis I was a resident of Nebraska. Having helped elect Hon. J. Sterling Morton a delegate, I had no difficulty in getting a ticket to this convention. I remember being very much impressed by a nominating speech made by Senator Daniel of Virginia.

The Democratic National Convention of 1892 was held at Chicago. I was a member of Congress then and was renominated a few days before the convention, in fact, went from the Congressional Convention to the Chicago Convention. By this time I had become acquainted with a good many public men and also with a good many politicians. I spoke at Creston in the Boies Campaign the fall of 1891. Here I met a prominent Democratic politician of that section by the name of Duggan. I happened to meet him at Chicago and learned from him that he was doorkeeper. He offered to let any of my friends in and I soon found out how easily one could add to his list of friends when he could reward them with admission to the national convention. Before the sessions were over I had put a liberal number of western Democrats under obligation to me by bringing them into acquaintance with Mr. Duggan.

At the Chicago Convention I heard Bourke Cockran make his celebrated speech against the third nomination of Mr. Cleveland, but took no part in the convention's deliberations.

In 1896 I began attending Republican Conventions as well as those of my own party. The first was the McKinley Convention, which was held at St. Louis about two weeks before the Chicago Convention at which I was nominated. I was at that time editor of the *World-Herald* and attended the convention ostensibly in the character of a newspaper man. As a matter of fact, however, I was there to encourage the Silver Republicans in the fight they were making. Beginning in 1893, I had been more and more intimately acquainted with the Silver Republicans like Senators Teller, DuBois, Pettigrew, and Cannon, and Congressmen Shafroth, Towne, Hartmann, and others. I was in conference with them during the course of the fight over the platform and sent back editorial correspondence to my paper.

The convention turned out as I expected and the looked-for bolt took place. I felt sure that the action of this convention would have a large influence at Chicago.

CHAPTER VI

A Brief History of the Chicago Convention

FOR some months prior to the Chicago Convention of 1896, I had received letters from different parties in different states suggesting my candidacy. John W. Tomlinson, a delegate from Alabama, wrote me; Mr. Cassady, a delegate from Mississippi; Mr. Felix Regnier, a delegate from Monmouth, Ill.; Hon. M. A. Miller, a delegate from Oregon; Gov. J. E. Osborn, of Wyoming; Ex-Gov. Baxter, of Wyoming, and a number of others. They all presented the same arguments, and the arguments presented were the ones that led me to believe that there was a possibility of my nomination.

During the year 1895 I visited Springfield at the invitation of bimetallists and spoke at a convention which was the beginning of the organizing of the silver forces of that state. I met Governor Altgeld there and have letters which I received from him afterward suggesting the possibility of my receiving the nomination for Vice-President, he being favorable to Congressman Bland for President.

When I delivered my Tariff Speech in Congress in March, 1892, I received a telegram from a friend in Jacksonville which ran about as follows: "How old are you? Am for you for the Democratic Presidential Nomination if you are old enough."

This was one of the earliest outbursts of enthusiasm. From time to time newspapers mentioned my name in connection with the nomination. This occurred with increasing frequency after my Silver Speech in August, 1893. I had prepared the address on Bimetallism signed by some thirty-three members of Congress and had given it to the public about the fifth of March, 1895. I prepared it after consulting with Mr. Bland, whom we all recognized as the

101

leader of the silver forces in Congress. I had him sign it first, and I signed it second. No senators, as I recall it, signed it, and only about one fifth of the Democratic members. Others to whom it was presented objected on the ground that it might divide the party. A short time after that appeal was published, President Cleveland wrote a letter to a Chicago Club, in which he indicated that the fight was to be on the money question, and this aroused the silver Democrats to the realization of the fact that they would have to control the organization or be read out of the party. A conference was called for June at Memphis, Tenn. There the Democratic Bimetallic League was organized with Democratic senators as its officers. I attended this conference at Memphis—in fact, I had spoken in Memphis a month before in answer to Mr. Carlisle. He went to Memphis to deliver an address intended to line up the South in favor of the gold standard.

For the next year I traveled throughout the country, lecturing in some places and making public speeches in other places—everywhere helping, as best I could, in the organization of the silver forces. At Wilmington, Delaware, I paid the hall rent and introduced myself, and spoke to a handful of people in a small room. At one other place I helped to pay the expense of the meeting. It was through these speeches that I became acquainted with a number of the delegates who were present at Chicago. I perhaps was personally acquainted with more delegates than any other man who was mentioned as a candidate. My own state would have instructed for me if I had permitted it, but I objected on the ground that I did not want to be presented as a candidate for two reasons. First, there was no likelihood of my being instructed for in any other state, and, second because I wanted to help other men who were candidates to secure their own states.

I went to Chicago a few days before the Convention to

confer with the leaders who were making their plans for the control of the convention and was present when Senator Daniel was selected for temporary chairman. We already had a majority of the delegates instructed for bimetallism. At that time the sentiment seemed to be divided between Bland and Boies and Matthews, and as I looked over the situation, I did not think that the outlook for my candidacy was encouraging. In fact, I told Mr. Tomlinson that I did not want him to feel bound by his pledge to me if he found it to his advantage to support some one else. He gave me an insight into his political purpose when he told me that he had no interests of his own to advance, and that, as he still believed I was the most available candidate, he preferred to advocate my nomination whether there was any chance of my success or not.

I had an engagement to speak at the Chautauqua in Crete, Nebraska, between the preliminary conference at Chicago and the convening of the Convention. I was advertised for a debate there with John Irish of Iowa, one of the prominent advocates of the gold standard. I went to Nebraska to fill this engagement and then returned to Chicago with the Nebraska delegation. In the debate with Irish I used the sentence with which I closed my Chicago Speech—the sentence which refers to "the cross of gold and the crown of thorns." I had used it a few times before that time, recognizing its fitness for the conclusion of a climax, and had laid it away for a proper occasion.

Some of my friends spoke of me for temporary chairman of the Convention, but this position, as I have said, went to Senator Daniel, and a very wise selection it was. Then there was some talk of me for permanent chairman and this seemed a possibility when I made the brief trip to Nebraska. On the train I made some preparations in anticipation of an opportunity to speak at the Convention, although there was no certainty that this opportunity would come to me.

WILLIAM JENNINGS BRYAN

While I spent all my spare time in arranging the arguments for any speech that I might deliver at the Convention, I prepared only one new argument and that I have always regarded as the most important argument presented, although it has never received a great deal of attention from those who have commented upon the speech. I do not recall that it has ever received prominent attention until recently, when it was selected in England as the passage to be quoted in a description of that speech published in London. The passage reads as follows and was intended for a double purpose: first, to awaken small business men to an appreciation of their importance; and, second, to rebuke the gold advocates who were continually talking about business men but who regarded those engaged in big business as the only business men to be considered:

"We say to you that you have made the definition of a business man too limited in its application. The man who is employed for wages is as much a business man as his employer, the attorney in a country town is as much a business man as the corporation counsel in a great metropolis; the merchant at the crossroads store is as much a business man as the merchant of New York; the farmer who goes forth in the morning and toils all day—who begins in the spring and toils all summer—and who by the application of brain and muscle to the natural resources of the country creates wealth, is as much a business man as the man who goes upon the board of trade and bets upon the price of grain; the miners who go down a thousand feet into the earth, or climb two thousand feet upon the cliffs, and bring forth from their hiding places the precious metals to be poured into the channels of trade are as much business men as the few financial magnates who, in a back room, corner the money of the world. We come to speak for this broader class of business men."

When I got back to Chicago the situation, so far as my prospects were concerned, had not perceptibly improved and I found that my first fight would be to get my delegation seated, it having been shut out of the temporary organization by action of the National Committee in which the Gold Men had a considerable majority.

I might add here that the night before I made my speech in the Chicago Convention, the North Carolina delegation held a meeting, and as the majority of the delegation voted in favor of my nomination, the entire delegation was given to me by the unit rule, and I was so notified by one of the delegates, I think it was Mr. Josephus Daniels, who was national committeeman that year, and has so continued up to this day. Before the delivery of my speech I had assurances from several other states. I think that a majority of the Kansas delegation had indicated a preference for me in case Bland was not nominated. Senator Patterson has since told me of an incident that impressed him.

Senator Towne and Congressman Hartman were with Senator Patterson, and they came over to ask me to support Senator Teller. As Senator Patterson relates it, I listened to their arguments and when they were through, said to them that I did not regard Senator Teller's nomination as a possibility, that I was perfectly willing to vote for him myself because I regarded the money question as the paramount issue, but that we had won our fight in the Democratic party while the Republicans had lost their fight in the Republican party, and that it was easier to bring the disappointed Republicans over to the Democratic party than to carry the victorious Democrats over to the Republican party. Knowing that the gold Democrats would vote, I thought they could make a much stronger fight against one who, up to that time, had been identified with the Republican party, than against one who had been all his life a Democrat.

I still believe the reasoning sound, and I say this after reflection upon the ability, character, and patriotism of

Senator Teller, whom I then admired and for whom my admiration has grown with more intimate acquaintance. When I stated that I did not believe Senator Teller could be nominated, Senator Patterson asked me who could be nominated, and I told him that I thought I had as good a chance to be nominated as anyone, for by that time I thought I saw a considerable improvement in my chances. He asked me what strength I had in the Convention. I told him that Nebraska would be for me whenever I wanted its vote, that half of the Indian Territory would be for me on the second ballot, and I was intending to give the rest of my strength as far as I had learned it (I am not sure whether North Carolina had acted then or later in the evening); but before I could go any further, some one came up and interrupted the conversation, and Senator Patterson and his associates, not considering the matter of sufficient importance to wait longer, took their leave.

The Senator has told me with some amusement of the conversation that followed when he, Mr. Towne, and Mr. Hartman reached the street. They looked at each other and smiled at the presumption of a man who calculated on the presidential nomination with only his own state back of him and the Indian Territory on the second ballot. Had they waited longer I would have given them better evidence that my hope had a substantial foundation, but I am afraid that I could not have given them enough evidence to make them share my expectations.

The possibility of my nomination led me to urge Mrs. Bryan to attend the Convention, a precaution of which I was afterwards glad when the Convention resulted as it did. We took rooms at the Clifton House, where my delegation had headquarters.

As some comment has been made upon the fact that our delegation had rooms at the Clifton, I might explain that we tried to get rooms at the Palmer House, but all the other delegation from Nebraska had secured headquarters there, and we went to the Clifton, not so much because it was less expensive there as because it was nearer to the Palmer House than any other hotel. Our delegates were prepared to meet whatever expense was necessary, but they wanted to be near the center of political activity, and the Clifton House suited their purpose. I may add, however, that as the rates were lower at the Clifton House, I can point to a less pretentious hotel bill than I would have had at the Palmer House. I took $100 with me and after paying the hotel bill of Mrs. Bryan and myself during the Convention week I had about $40 left, a sum probably as small as anyone has spent in securing a presidential nomination. It did not, of course, include my share of the expenses of the delegates or the expenses of the preliminary contest in which the delegates were selected, but even this sum was inconsiderable, as no money whatever was spent in entertaining delegations or delegates.

My ambition had been to be chairman of the Committee on Resolutions, but I found that Senator Jones aspired to that place, and as he was a much older man, and the president of the bimetallic organization formed at Memphis, I did not care to be a candidate against him, and gave up the thought of that place. As our delegation was shut out of the temporary organization by the National Committee, it would have been impossible for me to be chairman of the Committee on Resolutions, but the committee did not act until after I had given up the idea. Then there was some talk of my being voted for as permanent chairman, but by this time the papers had begun to discuss the possibility of my being a candidate, and I was objected to by the friends of other candidates. As my time was occupied in the contest before the Credentials Committee, I did not get a chance to attend the convention during the earlier sessions, and although I was called for when others were called for, I did not have a chance to speak to the Convention.

The exclusion of my delegates was a good illustration of

machine politics. As has been shown elsewhere, there was not the slightest ground for the opposing delegates. There was irregularity in our Conventions and it represented more than nineteen-twentieths of the party vote in Nebraska. But the Gold and corporation faction had control of the old National Committee and the other delegation was seated, making us the contesting delegation before the Credentials Committee of the delegates. The delegates desired me to lead the fight before the committee and this kept me from attending the sessions of the Committee on Resolutions for which I was selected by our delegates.

The contest before the Credentials Committee of the Convention was one-sided, the opposition bringing in no minority report. I was more exultant over the seating of our delegation than I was over my nomination. In the former case I could rejoice with the boys, in the latter case my rejoicing was sobered by a sense of responsibility.

As soon as our delegation was seated, I went at once to the Committee on Resolutions, of which I was a member by selection of my delegation, and found the platform practically completed. I looked at a draft of it and found that the money plank was there as I had written it two weeks before. While in St. Louis, attending the Republican Convention, I had called upon Mr. Charles H. Jones, then editor of the *Post-Dispatch*. He was a very able man, entirely in sympathy with the progressive ideas of the party. I found him engaged in writing a draft of the platform to be presented at Chicago. I prepared a plank covering the money question and he inserted it in the platform which he was drawing.

I hasten to explain that the language which I employed was language which had been incorporated in many state planks beginning more than a year before. I explain elsewhere the origin of the most prominent plank in the platform. There was no part of the plank which had not been thoroughly discussed and quite unanimously approved by the advocates of bimetallism.

When that plank was adopted by the Committee on Resolutions, it is probable that the members did not know that I had written it—at least, I have no reason to believe that they did know—and they approved of it in my absence. There were two planks which, according to my recollection, I added after I joined the committee. Some one suggested that we had no plank on arbitration and, if my memory serves me well, I wrote that plank and it was accepted. And then some suggested that there was no plank on the Venezuela question, and I wrote that plank. It will be seen, therefore, that I had very little to do with the writing of the Chicago platform, although since the Convention I have been given credit for writing it.

And now came an unexpected stroke of luck. Soon after we went into the Convention to report the platform, a page came to me and said that Senator Jones wanted to see me. I went to his seat and he asked me if I would take charge of the debate. I asked him if he did not want to conduct the debate himself and he replied in the negative. The request came as a surprise, for he had never intimated to me that he wanted me to do this, and I had never suggested it to him or anyone else.

I digress for a moment to remind the readers that this was a position to which I aspired in the beginning but for which I was not willing to be a candidate after I heard of Senator Jones' aspirations. I had seen my chance of temporary chairmanship disappear and then the chance for the permanent chairmanship—which afterward had become impossible because the possibility of my nomination made the other candidates hostile to the suggestion. And now, having passed through the circle of disappointment, I found myself in the very position for which I had at first longed.

Before continuing the narrative the reader may be interested, as I was, to know why this good fortune befell me.

After the Convention was over and Senator Jones had been made chairman of the National Committee at my request, I asked him how he happened to turn the defense of the platform over to me. I know that it was not with any thought of favoring me as a candidate, because he was a supporter of Mr. Bland and too loyal to him to have knowingly given an opportunity to any possible candidate if there was any likelihood of the opportunity being used to the disadvantage of his choice. And I myself had no thought of the effect produced by the speech. While I had, before the Convention met, regarded my nomination as a possibility I had relied upon what I called the logic of the situation rather than upon the influence of a speech.

The speech that I expected to make was not different from the speeches that I had been making except in the setting, to which I had not given special consideration. My interest was in the subject and I felt that I was master of the subject and could give expression to the sentiment of the Convention as represented by a little more than two-thirds of its members. Senator Jones answered my question by saying that I was the only one of the prominent speakers who had not had an opportunity to address the Convention. He referred to the speeches made by the temporary and permanent chairman and by others who were called out by the Convention while I was attending the meeting of the Committee on Credentials. He knew of the part I had taken in the organizing of the fight and how I had traveled over the country for a year helping in many states and said that his invitation to me was due entirely to a sense of fairness, and hence I honored him more for it than I could have done had it been due to partiality for me.

But to return to his request. I asked him what members of the committee wanted to speak on the platform and he said that no one had asked for time except Senator Tillman. I then went to Senator Hill, of New York, he was the leader of the minority, and arranged with him about the time to be allotted to the discussion. We agreed to an hour and a quarter on a side. I believe that was the time named. I then went to Senator Tillman and asked him whether he wanted to open or close the debate. He said he would like to close and that he wanted fifty minutes. I told him that that was too long for a closing speech and that I hardly thought the other side would agree to our using so much of the time in closing. I went back to Senator Hill and presented Senator Tillman's request and he objected to it, as I supposed he would, and said that if Senator Tillman wanted to use as much time as that he ought to use it in opening. I then returned to Senator Tillman and stated the case, and as he, Senator Tillman, felt that he needed more time than Senator Hill was willing to use in closing, he decided to open the debate and left me to close it. This again was an advantage, but it was an advantage that came by circumstance, for I would not have felt justified in refusing to allow Senator Tillman to close the debate if he had been willing to accept a shorter time.

I had spoken long enough to know that, comparing myself with myself, I was more effective in a brief speech in conclusion than a longer speech that simply laid down propositions for another to answer.

Fortune favored me again. For some reason—I do not now recall what the reason was—the debate on the platform was put over until the next day and I had time to think over my speech during the night and to arrange my arguments in so far as one can arrange arguments for a closing speech. I fitted my definition of the business man at the place that I thought best and kept my "cross of gold and crown of thorns" for the conclusion. When it became known that I was to have charge of the debate my delegation was quite buoyant. They had known of debates in Nebraska and they were confident that my closing speech would make an impression on the Convention.

When the Convention convened I felt as I always do

just before a speech of unusual importance. I usually have a feeling of weakness at the pit of my stomach—a suggestion of faintness. I want to lie down. But this being impossible in the Convention, I got a sandwich and a cup of coffee and devoted myself to these as I waited for the debate to begin. During these moments of suspense Clarke Howell, with whom I became acquainted in 1893 and whose father was one of the leaders in the silver movement, sent me a note scribbled on an envelope. It read, "This is a great opportunity." I wrote under the words, "You will not be disappointed," and sent the envelope back to him.

Senator Tillman's speech did not present our side to the satisfaction of the friends of bimetallism. It was a strong speech—he could not make any other kind—but it presented the question as a sectional issue between the south and west with northeast states on the other side. While that division was very clearly presented in the Convention, we did not regard it as a necessary division; we believed that the restoration of bimetallism would be beneficial to the nations everywhere, not only to this country but all over the world. When Senator Tillman was through, Senator Jones took the platform and announced to the Convention that the Committee did not endorse the sectional argument by Senator Tillman. This increased my responsibility because it threw the whole burden on my closing speech.

Senator Hill followed Senator Tillman and made a very strong speech. He was at his best and presented the arguments on his side with consummate skill and adroitness. The effect upon the audience was apparent and the nervousness of our delegation increased as he proceeded.

He was followed by Senator Vilas, a man of high standing in the party, large experience in politics, and great ability as a lawyer. He pounded the advocates of free coinage without mercy.

Near the close of his speech Governor Russell of Massachusetts, who was the third and last man on the gold side, came back to Senator Hill's seat with evident excitement and protested that Senator Vilas was not going to leave him any time. My seat was so near Senator Hill's that I could hear the conversation. I immediately stepped across the aisle to Senator Hill and suggested that I was willing to have the time extended to give Governor Russell the time he wanted, the same period to be added to my time. Governor Russell was very appreciative of the suggestion and Senator Hill at once agreed to it. I cannot say that it was entirely unselfish on my side, and I think I would have made the suggestion if the extension of time had fallen to some one else, but as it was, it added about ten minutes to my time and I needed it for the speech I was to make. This was another unexpected bit of good fortune. I had never had such an opportunity before in my life and never expect to have again.

There never was such a setting for a political speech in my own experience, and so far as I know there never was such a setting for any other political speech ever made in this country, and it must be remembered that the setting has a great deal to do with a speech. Webster says that the essentials for a successful speech are eloquence, the subject, and the occasion. I felt that I had at least two-thirds of the requirements. I had a subject of transcendent importance. The demonetization of silver in 1873 had so decreased the world's supply of standard money as to bring about a shrinkage in values that covered a period of more than twenty years. This shrinkage in prices caused by the increase in the purchasing power of the dollar had led to three international conferences in which the leading nations had sought in vain for a remedy. Many prominent Republicans were on record as in favor of remonetization as the only means of fighting for the restoration of the parity between money and property. The Republican Convention had declared for the maintenance of the gold only until it was possible to restore international bimetallism by agreement and the platform pledged the party to an effort to secure international bimetallism. The cause was great enough to bring about a revolt in the Democratic Party—a fight won by the rank and file against all the power of the administration, and of the power of the big corporations and the metropolitan press. I was to make the final speech to a Convention in sympathy with our fight.

After an unsatisfactory opening of the debate and after our side had been pounded unmercifully by the giants of the other side, all that was necessary to success was to put into words the sentiments of a majority of the delegates to the Convention—to be the voice of a triumphant majority. The occasion was there and complete in every detail. I had no doubt that I could meet the expectations that had been aroused by this extraordinary combination of circumstances, because I had spent three years studying the question from every angle and I had time and again answered all the arguments that the other side had advanced. All that I had to do was to analyze the speeches of Hill, Vilas, and Russell as they were made and then present the answer as effectively as I could.

The delegates had been hammered by the very able speech of Senator Hill; they had been provoked by the language of General Vilas, and still further irritated by the speech of Governor Russell, and they were in a mood to applaud. Fortunately my voice filled the hall, and as I was perfectly familiar with the subject, I was prepared to answer in an extemporaneous speech the arguments which had been presented—that is, extemporaneous in so far as its arrangement was concerned. No new arguments had been advanced and therefore no new answers were required.

The excitement of the moment was so intense that I hurried to the platform and began at once. My nervousness left me instantly and I felt as composed as if I had been speaking to a small audience on an unimportant occasion.

From the first sentence the audience was with me. My voice reached to the uttermost parts of the hall, which is a great advantage in speaking to an assembly like that.

I shall never forget the scene upon which I looked. I believe it unrivaled in any convention ever held in our country. The audience seemed to rise and sit down as one man. At the close of a sentence it would rise and shout, and when I began upon another sentence, the room was as still as a church. There was inspiration in the faces of the delegates. My own delegation I can never forget. No man ever had a more loyal sixteen friends than I had on that day. Their faces glowed with enthusiasm.

Two faces stand out as in memory I look over the hall. Ex-Governor Hogg, of Texas, was a large man, probably six feet two or three inches in height, and heavy. He wore no beard and his face was beaming with delight. He stood by the aisle to my left, and about in the same relative position on my right stood Ollie James, a member from Kentucky, also a large man with a smooth face. As I turned from one side of the hall to the other, these two faces impressed me, for like the rest of the audience, they were in full sympathy with the sentiments to which I gave expression. They could not have responded to the expressions of my own face more perfectly if I had been speaking a speech that they had prepared.

The audience acted like a trained choir—in fact, I thought of a choir as I noted how instantaneously and in unison they responded to each point made.

The situation was so unique and the experience so unprecedented that I have never expected to witness its counterpart.

At the conclusion of my speech the demonstration spread over nearly the entire convention. As is customary at such times, the standards of the various states were carried through the aisles followed by the delegates, the Nebraska standard at the front. During the demonstration many persons came to me to tell me of the votes in their delegations; in some cases whole states were pledged. Others came to ask questions.

I remember that one man came to report that I was accused of drinking to excess. It was easy to answer him with the assurance that I was and always had been a tee-totaler. Another man came to tell me that some one in his delegation accused me of saying that I would not support a gold candidate if one were nominated by our convention. I replied that I had stated that I would no more support a gold standard or a gold platform than I would an army marching on my home. The delegate said that he would not either and went back to carry my answer.

After the nomination Hon. Arthur Sewall, my running mate, came to tell me of an experience which in the confusion had made no impression upon me. He said that he came up and told me that they would nominate me that night if my friends would prevent adjournment. He quoted me as answering, "Should I want to be nominated tonight if they would be sorry for it tomorrow?"

To another, as he reported to me afterwards, I said, "If the desire to nominate me will not last until tomorrow, would it last during the campaign?"

The nomination came on the following day on the fifth ballot. I had been so busy all the forenoon that I had not had time to shave. When the bulletin was brought in announcing my nomination I knew that the crowd would soon turn from the Convention to my headquarters, and I hurried down to the barber for a shave. I mention this as evidence that I was not excited, but the barber was—so much so that he could hardly handle his razor.

Mr. Sewall, who became my running mate, was one of the first to call to congratulate me. When they met for the selection of Vice-President I sent for some of the leaders and told them that I had no choice for that position and did not care to advise further than to say that I had no

WINNING THE NOMINATION

William Jennings Bryan and the Chicago Convention in 1896, when he delivered his famous "Cross of Gold" Speech.

objection to the nomination of a Southern man if the Convention thought proper to do so. I did not mean to advise such a nomination, but I wanted them to know that I did not share the objection so often raised to a Southern man. I felt then, as I have felt since, that a man otherwise eligible should not be barred because he lived in the South, even though he were an ex-Confederate, as most of the men old enough to be candidates were. I had become convinced, even then, that the voters were not so much interested in the locality of the candidate or in his position during the Civil War as they were in his attitude on public questions.

Honorable Arthur Sewall was nominated, the chief argument being that I lived so far West that they should have an Eastern man to balance the ticket. Mr. Sewall had gained distinction as the only silver man on the National Committee representing eastern states. He had voted to seat the Nebraska delegation when the question was before the committee. I did not know Mr. Sewall until he was nominated, but I learned to love him as I became acquainted with him. I soon learned that he was a thorough Democrat. I sounded him along the various lines and never in a single instance did I find him holding views inconsistent with the most fundamental Democracy. He was a well-to-do man but a believer in the Income Tax; he was a national banker but preferred the Government note to the bank note. His sympathies were with the common people and he was true to their interests on every subject. Because of Mr. Watson's nomination by the Populist Convention, Mr. Sewall did not take an active part in the campaign. Had he made speeches I am sure that he would have become more popular in the West than in the East, because his views were entirely in harmony with the sentiment in those sections that dominated the Convention.

This word in behalf of Mr. Sewall is due to him. I can never forget the last time that I met him. I was speaking in the South when he happened to be near where I was to speak. He wired me inquiring the time of my train, and learning that I would pass over a certain road, he met me. He appeared with me on the platform at several points where crowds were gathered, and just as he was leaving me at a place where quite an enthusiastic crowd was gathered, he said with tears in his eyes, as he bade me good-by, "Mr. Bryan, how these people love you," and I am sure that they loved me no better than Mr. Sewall did, and his affection was reciprocated by me.

The Convention closed on Saturday and Mrs. Bryan and I spent Sunday with the family of Judge Lyman Trumbull, who had died a short time before the Convention. Then came the trip to Lincoln by way of Salem, my birthplace, where we had left the children while we went to attend the Convention.

This is the story of my connection with the Convention that has had such an important influence upon my public life. I put it in writing at this time so that the story will not be lost in case my life should be ended before I have time to prepare a more detailed sketch.

In speaking of the Convention it has been my purpose to record only the incidents that were personal and of which others would have less knowledge than I. I prefer to let disinterested parties describe the impression made by the speech and the demonstration.

CHAPTER VII

LEADING UP TO MY SECOND NOMINATION

THE number of letters which I received after the election of 1896 made it certain that unless some change in conditions occurred, I would be renominated in 1900, for although defeated, the six and a half millions of voters came out of the campaign of 1896 a compact and undismayed army. The elections of 1897 indicated a growth in our party's strength and things went well until the Spanish War broke out, then attention was turned from economic matters to questions affecting the war.

I telegraphed to President McKinley on the day that the war was declared offering my services, but never received a reply. I know that the telegram was received, because the President asked Senator Allen, of Nebraska, what position I could fill, and Senator Allen communicated the question to me. I wrote the Senator that I was willing to do any work to which I might be assigned, but suggested that as I was personally acquainted with General Wheeler, it would be agreeable to be assigned to his staff if the rules permitted. Senator Allen did not receive my letter until after General Wheeler had gone South, and I afterwards learned that the rules of the army would have prevented my being assigned to his staff, as I was not a commissioned officer and had had no experience. Shortly afterwards Governor Holcomb, of Nebraska, authorized me to raise a regiment—I had already enlisted as a private in a company organized at Lincoln. I raised the regiment and served something more than five months, resigned the day that the treaty with Spain was signed, so that my military career began constructively with the offer of my services on the day that war was declared, and with the termination of my services on the day that the war was formally closed by treaty.

During my army life I refused all social invitations and attended strictly to the duties of the office. I also avoided any discussion of political questions, giving as an excuse that I had military lockjaw. After I began to recruit a regiment, but before I was sworn in, I had occasion to make a speech at a dinner in Omaha, where the subject of imperialism was approached, and I then announced my opposition to colonialism, and so far as I know, I was the first public man to express myself on this subject. Ex-President Cleveland and Senator Hoar, according to my recollection, made speeches, or gave interviews, a few days afterwards along the same line.

My reason for leaving the army was that I saw that the sentiment in favor of imperialism was widespread and that many Democrats had been led to join in the cry for expansion, as it was then termed. I believed imperialism to be dangerous to the country, and so believing, I resigned my position in the army in order to oppose it. It required more courage to resign than it did to enlist, for I knew that the unfriendly papers would criticise me for leaving the army just as they had criticised me for entering it. They stated that, having no military experience, I was not fit to take charge of a regiment and that it was unfair to the soldiers in my regiment to be under my command. When I resigned they stated that I had deserted my soldiers and that it was unfair to the soldiers for me to leave them while they were still in service.

When I left the army the question before the country was the ratification of the treaty, and I announced the next day after I put on citizen's clothes that I favored the ratification of the treaty and the declaration of the nation's purpose to give independence to the Filipinos. As my reason for taking this position has been explained and defended in my speech on imperialism made when I accepted the nomination in 1900 (see Chapter XXI), I need not set forth this reason here. I have never regretted the position taken; on the contrary, I never showed more statesmanship than I did when I insisted upon the termination of the war and the making of the promise embodied in the Bacon resolution.

The Democratic party was in the minority in the Senate and in the House, and a Republican President was in the White House. Our party, therefore, could not pass a resolution through either body, and it had no voice in the selection of the treaty commissioners. It required two thirds of the Senate to confirm the treaty, and a few Republicans were willing to act with the Democrats to reject it.

But the Republicans and Democrats stood in different positions. The Democrats had to furnish the bulk of the votes to reject the treaty, and had no influence with the administration. The Republicans who opposed the treaty were few in number but hoped that, through their influence with the administration, they might be able to modify the terms of the treaty. But the Democrats would have had to have borne the responsibility for the continuation of war expenditures and for any dangers that arose during the continuation of the state of war. Hostilities were feared and parents were clamoring for the return of their sons, and it was difficult for Democrats to defend an act that would continue the state of war and postpone the making of the treaty.

Then, too, several of the great nations of Europe, such as England, Germany, and Russia, were interested in the Orient and might resent the setting up of a republic there. England was not interested in the spread of the ideas of popular government in India, neither was Germany interested in having colonies take up the ideas of self-government, and Russia was at that time the most despotic of the European empires. If we had insisted upon the recognition of the independence of the Philippine republic, it might have brought us into conflict with the interests of several

European powers, and it was not necessary for us to take this risk because we could give independence to the Filipinos more easily than we could force Spain to give independence. By ratifying the treaty, we settled the question with Spain and gave to ourselves the entire control of the Philippine situation.

It then became an easy matter for us to make to the Filipinos the same promise that the treaty made to the Cubans. The ratification of the treaty did not bind us to hold the Philippine Islands; it simply severed the Philippine Islands from Spain. I felt confident that it was easier to persuade the American people to promise independence to the Filipinos in connection with the ratification of the treaty than to continue war and force Spain to recognize a republic in the Philippines. I still believe that we followed the line of least responsibility and that we are better off today for having settled the war and made the Philippine question purely an American question than we would have been had we, a minority in Congress, attempted to compel a majority to carry out a plan by which the majority would in turn be compelled to force Spain to recognize the independence of the Philippine republic.

The Bacon resolution, which was a part of my plan, came so near being adopted that it required the vote of the Vice-President to defeat it. It will be seen, therefore, that although I was a private citizen, the Senate came within one vote of carrying out a plan which I had outlined and for which I had been severely criticised. Had the plan been carried out, we would have been saved the tremendous expense which has followed our attempt at colonialism and we would have been spared the menace to which our meddling in Oriental politics has subjected us.

For a while the excitement regarding expansion, as the Republicans termed it, and imperialism, as we termed it, aroused suggestions as to other candidates. Admiral Dewey was spoken of and even went so far as to indicate his willingness to accept the nomination, although he did not indicate with which party he expected to connect himself. Admiral Schley was also spoken of as a candidate, but refused to consider the matter.

As the convention of 1900 approached, however, it became evident that no other candidate would be presented to the convention, and when the convention was held, the delegates from all of the states and territories but one, if my memory is correct, were instructed to favor my nomination. It is possible that two or three of the states instead of instructing, passed resolutions expressing a preference for me. When the convention met at Kansas City, I was not present. Mr. R. L. Metcalfe, editor of the *World-Herald*, and a delegate at large, was the Nebraska member of the Committee on Resolutions.

Mr. C. H. Jones, who prepared the draft of the Chicago platform, had prepared the draft of the Kansas City platform, using very largely the phraseology that I had employed in the discussion of the questions. About the only plank that aroused discussion was the plank restating the Chicago platform for the restoration of bimetallism and the opening of the mints to the free coinage of silver at the ratio of sixteen to one. The Eastern delegates were opposed to the restatement of this proposition, although they were willing to reaffirm the platform as a whole without any special reference to this plank. As it was intended, however, to restate nearly all the other planks of the Chicago platform, it was evident that the failure to restate this plank was equivalent to a repudiation of it, notwithstanding the general endorsement of the Chicago platform as a whole. I insisted upon the restatement of the plank because I thought that a refusal to restate it would, under the circumstances, be considered a repudiation of that plank, and while I recognized the force of the arguments made by some of our friends, namely, that the increased production of gold since 1896 had reduced the importance of the question, I was not willing to run upon a platform which either ignored the question or put me in the attitude of pretending to endorse it when the endorsement was not genuine.

I considered the matter very fully, and nothing ever distressed me more than being compelled to differ from so many of my trusted friends. A number of those who had been loyal to me in the former campaign were persuaded by the arguments of the Eastern delegates who favored the reaffirmation of the platform without a specific restatement of this plank, and but for my objection, the resolutions committee would have so acted. Even with my objection known, the vote in the committee was quite close. Several friends sent a representative to Lincoln to ask me to leave the question of the platform to the convention, and I replied that I would gladly do so, but when asked if I would be a candidate in case the convention decided to leave out that plank, I replied that I would not consent to be a candidate under those circumstances. I had fought for four years for the reaffirmation of that platform and I was not willing to go before the country on a deceptive promise, as I felt it would be a deceptive promise if the convention merely reaffirmed but refused to reiterate.

I told the friends there that I could afford to lose the nomination, that it was not necessary to my happiness, but that I could not afford to lose the confidence that the voters had in my honesty and that I would decline to be a candidate if the convention in its wisdom saw fit to write the platform as was then proposed. So unwilling was I to put my judgment against the judgment of the committee that I was on the point of sending a communication to the convention declining to be a candidate under any circumstance, for I felt that the support of the convention would not be a hearty support if it approved of a platform against its own judgment, and yet I was not willing to be a candidate under conditions that required me to apologize for the platform.

Yours truly
W. J. Bryan

Sincerely yours,
Mary Baird Bryan

Photo. Pacific & Atlantic Photos, Inc.

PORTRAITS OF MR. AND MRS. BRYAN, TAKEN IN 1900

MY SECOND NOMINATION

I was prevented from sending this communication by the fact that the delegates were instructed for me and that it was not the fault of those who gave the instructions that the delegates were considering the propriety of yielding to the demand that came from the East. Some have thought that my refusal to consent to this change in the platform resulted in my defeat, but I have never entertained this view of the subject. I believe that the acceptance of the modified platform would have resulted in a more disastrous defeat than the one which I suffered. In fact I believe that had I consented to run on such a platform, I would have so disappointed the rank and file who made the fight for me in 1896 that I would have had something of the experience that Mr. Parker had four years later.

I did agree to the plank making imperialism the paramount issue, because I believed that with changed conditions the question of imperialism was at that time more important than the money question. The trust plank was given the second place in importance, and the money question was not discussed to any extent during the campaign. The fact that the platform reiterated the demand for independent bimetallism made it less necessary for me to discuss the question than it would have been had the platform attempted to avoid the subject. As it was, the substitution of imperialism as the paramount issue discouraged a great many of our active workers, and while I gained in the New England states and in what used to be called the middle states, those in the neighborhood of New York, I lost in the South, in the Mississippi Valley states and in the West.

A word more in regard to the contest in the committee at Kansas City. I was in telephonic communication with friends at Kansas City, and the Kansas City *Times* was being edited by a close political friend who sent a representative to Lincoln, with whom I was to confer, and it was willing to carry out editorially any suggestions that I should make. The resolutions committee harangued over the platform far into the night and as the time approached for the paper to go to press, the editor sent his representative to me to get an indication of the outcome in case the committee rejected what was known as my plank. I told him that the paper could safely have an editorial written upon the assumption that I would not be a candidate in case the convention rejected that plank. I did not tell him so, but I had no thought of letting the fight drop with a mere resolution of the committee. I would have gone to Kansas City if necessary and made a fight in the convention for an adoption of the plank; if the convention had then rejected the plank, I then would not have been a candidate.

The committee, however, by a very small majority, declared in favor of the plank, and no minority report was filed. It has sometimes been stated that the vote of the delegate from Hawaii decided the result in the committee. If so, it might be interesting to know that a Democrat passed through Lincoln years before on his way to Hawaii and asked me for a letter of introduction to President Dole. The man brought with him a letter from a friend which contained a sufficient endorsement to justify me in giving the letter desired. I saw nothing more of the man until after the Kansas City convention. When I learned that he was present at Kansas City and that he made it his business to advise the Hawaii member of the Committee on Resolutions and to fortify him against the persuasion that came from the opposition, I did not know, of course, to what extent his loyalty may have influenced the vote of the Hawaiian member, but if it did have influence, it is another evidence that bread cast upon the waters may return after many days, for it was a favorable return that this man made for the slight service that I rendered him in giving him a letter of introduction.

It ought also to be known that Mr. Richard Croker, the leader of Tammany, played an important part in this matter. Mr. Croker met with an accident a little while before the

MY SECOND NOMINATION

Kansas City Convention, and while he was laid up by the accident, he read my book entitled "The First Battle." The arguments in favor of silver convinced him of the correctness of our position, or at least removed the prejudice he had against our position. When he came back from his trip abroad he announced that he was in favor of my nomination and he sent me word that he would support the platform that I wanted. When New York's member of the resolution committee was to be selected, Mr. Croker favored Judge Van Wyck in place of Senator Hill, and he did so because he was afraid to trust Senator Hill on that question. Mr. Van Wyck voted against my plank on the committee. I have always believed that he would have voted with me had his vote been necessary—but he refused to join in any minority report. As soon as it became known that the committee had included the plank for which I asked, Senator Hill began an agitation in favor of a minority report, and I was informed at the time that Mr. Croker, upon learning of it, notified Mr. Hill that New York's votes would be cast in favor of the majority report. This ended the fight and the platform was unanimously adopted. Mr. Croker was an enthusiastic supporter during the campaign, and after the election wrote me a letter expressing his regret at my defeat and saying that he still expected me to be elected to the presidency. He was one of the few Eastern Democrats who wrote me after the election. I have appreciated Mr. Croker's support of me because I believed it entirely disinterested. He never asked a promise of me; never said anything to indicate that he had any personal reason for favoring me, and I have every reason to believe that he stated his real reason for supporting me when he gave as his reason that he believed that I was in public life because of my interest in the public and not because I had any pecuniary advantage in view.

Hon. A. E. Stephenson was nominated for Vice-President at Kansas City and his nomination was entirely satisfactory.

He is a man of splendid character and was faithful to the core in 1896 when the President and nearly all of his prominent appointees deserted the party. I explained to General Stephenson that if elected I would ask congress to enact a law to make the Vice-President ex-officio member of the cabinet in order that he might be present at all consultations and be fully informed as to all administration plans. Such a law I think would add dignity to the office of Vice-President and at the same time prepare the Vice-President for the better discharge of the duties of the office in case of the President's death. I had resolved on this recommendation as far back as 1896 and may have spoken to Mr. Sewall of it, but am not sure about it. The matter had so impressed me that the first issue of the *Commoner* contained an editorial on the subject.

CHAPTER VIII

THE BENNETT WILL CASE

THE friendship between Philo S. Bennett and myself, which began in 1896 and continued until his death, was one of my closest and dearest friendships outside of my family, and yet it brought upon me an experience which gave rise to more malicious misrepresentation than any other incident of my life. It was the only time in which I have been called upon to serve a friend at great expense to myself both in feelings and in money. I am glad to put upon permanent record the facts in connection with it. It is now possible to discuss the case with more freedom than was possible during the lifetime of Mrs. Bennett.

Philo S. Bennett was a citizen of New Haven, Connecticut, but was engaged in business in the city of New York. His firm, Bennett, Sloan & Company, were wholesale grocers, specializing in tea.

I never met Mr. Bennett until the campaign of 1896, when he was on the reception committee on the occasion of my campaign visit to New Haven.

Speaking some six hundred times during the campaign, it was of course impossible for me to recall the members of all the reception committees which took part in meetings. It so happened that at New Haven, Connecticut, Mr. Bennett rode in the carriage with me along with John B. Sargent, a prominent hardware manufacturer of that city. I had known of Mr. Sargent for some years, because he was one of the few Eastern manufacturers opposed to a protective tariff. He had made a trip around the world and on his return gained a considerable prominence by interviews in which he declared that American manufacturers could compete with the world without a tariff; basing his arguments on observations he made as a traveler. The proposition that I remember best was that American labor was so much more efficient than foreign labor that our power to compete in the markets of the world increased as the percentage of skilled labor in the manufactured articles increased.   Mr. Sargent's name had therefore become known to me and I remembered the personal meeting with him and the support which he gave to our cause, but would not have been able to remember Mr. Bennett but for our correspondence which brought him to my attention just before the election.   The following letter is the first which I received from him:

BENNETT, SLOAN & Co.
New York, October 30, 1896.

Hon. William J. Bryan
Lincoln, Neb.
DEAR SIR:

The betting is three to one against you in this state at the present time; but notwithstanding that, I am impressed with a feeling that you will win, and if you are *defeated*, I wish to make you a gift of $3,000; and if you will accept the same it will be a genuine pleasure to me to hand it to you any time after the 10th of next March.

You have made one of the most gallant fights on record for a principle, against the combined money power of the whole country, and if you are not successful now, you will be, in my opinion, four years later.

The solid press of the East, and all the wealth of the country have, ever since the canvass opened, concealed the truth and deceived the people regarding the whole question.   They have succeeded in making 25 per cent of them believe that if you are elected the country will be governed by a lawless, disorganized mob.   If you are elected I trust that you will, as soon as you can, issue a letter or make a speech, assuring them that the great body of the people are honest and can be trusted.

This letter is intended only for yourself and wife to ever see. A feeling of gratitude for what you have done in this canvass for humanity, for right and justice, prompts me to write and make this offer.

I am one of the electors at large on the silver ticket in the state of Connecticut, and accompanied you from New York to New Haven, and rode in the carriage with you and Mr. Sargent from the station to the hotel.

Hoping for your victory, and with kind regards, I am,
Sincerely yours,
P. S. BENNETT.

Mr. Bennett's first letter indicated such a sympathetic interest in our party's position on public questions that our acquaintance grew. It became more intimate as I met him from time to time on my trips to the East, and our friendship continued unbroken until his accidental death in 1903. I seldom passed through New York without seeing him. He invited Mrs. Bryan and me to spend a summer vacation with him and Mrs. Bennett at their summer home in Maine, but it was never possible to accept his invitation except as we met him for a day or two in New York or New Haven. He was so much older than I that the relationship between us was more like the relation between parent and child, he giving me the benefit of his greater experience and larger business acquaintance.

It will be noticed that this letter was written just before the election and the offer contained in it was contingent upon my defeat. The letter did not come to my attention until after the election, by which time I discovered that the campaign had brought upon me a continuing expense in the way of correspondence. The number of letters received amounted to twenty-five hundred or sometimes three thousand a day. It soon became apparent that my correspondence would cost me more than it ever cost me to live before I was nominated. Mr. Bennett's offer, coming at such a time, was quite welcome, but before accepting it I took the precaution to inquire by letter addressed directly to him whether he was pecuniarily interested in silver mining. Believing that the silver question would continue to be an issue, I was not willing to put myself under financial obligation to anyone who was in a business way interested in silver as a metal. My interest in silver was solely as a matter of the public interests; the demonetization of silver seemed at that time the only way of increasing the volume of money.

I quote from his reply dated November 20, 1896:

New York, Nov. 20, 1896.
Hon. William J. Bryan,
    Lincoln, Neb.
DEAR SIR:

I have yours dated the 13th inst. I do not now, and never have owned a dollar's interest in a silver, gold or any other mine, and do not expect to in this century.

If just as agreeable to you, I will make the gift in three different payments, sending you check for $1,000 the 15th of each March for the next three years.

I would like to have you use it all for yourself and family, and not give a penny for the cause of silver or any other political purpose.

The newspapers report that you are to enter the lecture field. If this is true, when you go to New Haven it would afford me pleasure to entertain you while there. I am confident you will have a full house and be received enthusiastically.

I am anxious to have you seen and heard on the platform in the East by the gold advocates, for I think it will help to remove from their minds some of the prejudice that now exists. To me it seems one of the best methods you have open for that purpose; it will also help hold your old friends.

You of course fully understand the *power of money and brains coupled together*. You may rest assured that both will be used lavishly to prevent you from securing the nomination for President in 1900. From now on if you mingle and keep in touch with the people, I believe they will remain true, and you can secure the nomination against the all-powerful forces named.

I hope that before 1900 you will in some manner gain the support and goodwill of part of the business element. Here in the East and middle states they were almost solid against you in November. It is important that you should have it next time in order to carry any electoral votes in this part of the country, for the money power, as it is generally understood, will be a unit against you.

I have just received the Boston *Herald*, containing a speech by Mr. F. A. Walker on bimetallism, delivered on the 7th inst.

I suppose you know that Mr. Walker has his eye on the presidency, and hopes to secure the nomination some time from the friends of bimetallism. Keep close watch on him. After reading his speech I will forward it to you.

I send you a few clippings which you will probably feel interested in reading.

With kind regards, I am,

Sincerely yours,

P. S. BENNETT.

Perhaps I ought to qualify what I have said about Gen. Walker, for I have no *positive* knowledge that he expects the nomination.

In April or May of 1900 I received a letter from Mr. Bennett asking whether I would be home at a certain time in the near future, without giving me any intimation of the object of his proposed visit. Upon receiving my answer in the affirmative, he appeared one morning at our home in Nebraska. He laid before me a will which he had made some years before, stating that he desired to make some changes in it.

He said that he felt as much interested in the reforms which I was advocating as I did myself, but that he was unable to present them to the public as I was in the habit of doing. It had occurred to him that if he made provision in his will for a sum that would be given to me at his death I would be able to make, without compensation, speeches that I delivered in the form of lectures, and he desired to set apart fifty thousand dollars for that purpose, saying that he would leave ten thousand dollars in care of Mrs. Bryan, five thousand dollars to each of my children and twenty-five thousand to myself. He felt that in this way he could share in the work and would feel that he was making a contribution that was within his means.

I inquired whether he would have that sum to spare after making provision for his wife and relatives. He told me that he was worth about three hundred thousand dollars, and that he was giving one hundred thousand to his wife, a sum which he said would furnish her a larger income than she could use during the remainder of her life. They had no children, their only child, a daughter, having died some years before. They lived comfortably but without ostentation and they had estimated the amount necessary to provide for all the wants of his wife should she be left a widow. He went further and explained that the money which he left her would at her death go to her relatives and the amount he was allotting to her was all he cared to leave them. The amount he left to his own relatives, a sister and a half brother, had been decided by him without any consultation with me.

In fact, he did not consult with me about any item of

the will except that fifty thousand dollars which he wanted to give to me and thirty thousand dollars which he desired to devote to altruistic purposes. I ventured to call his attention to the fact that after giving to his wife and his relatives the amounts he desired left them and after giving fifty thousand to me, there still remained thirty thousand dollars of his estate. We talked over the various uses which could be made of this. In the course of the conversation I told him that I had established prizes in nineteen colleges, nearly all of them state universities. These prizes were given each year for the best essay on the science of government; my plan being to give two hundred fifty dollars to the institution, the interest from which would be used to furnish annual prize money. The plan pleased him and he decided to leave ten thousand to me in trust for this purpose. I was to select twenty state universities which I had not myself endowed, giving to each five hundred dollars for the purpose outlined above. That left twenty thousand dollars and Mr. Bennett expressed a desire to use it to aid poor boys and girls to secure an education, explaining that he himself had lacked educational opportunities when he was young and that it would give him satisfaction to aid those similarly situated. I discussed with him how this might be done and he asked whether I would be willing to distribute ten thousand for the aid of boys and Mrs. Bryan a similar amount for the aid of girls. He remarked that her wide acquaintance would enable her to distribute the money over the United States to the best possible advantage. These provisions were written into the will. He had a small sum left and I told him of a plan that I had in mind to buy the ground upon which I was born and upon it build a city library.

He had so impressed me by his devotion to the political ideals and principles with which I had been identified that I told him it would be very pleasant to me to have his name linked with mine in this library. The plan appealed to him and the provision was made. The library has been built and is known as "The Bryan-Bennett Library." We contributed equally to the cost of the building, but I had previously bought the land and subsequently contributed five hundred dollars for the purchase of books.

When we came to consider the fifty thousand dollars to be left to myself, I told him that I was not an old man and was likely to live for many years and that I would not promise to accept the money at the time of his death because I might not need it at the time. There was so little opposition to my second nomination that it seemed quite certain that I would run again and I told him that if I was elected I would be in a position where I would not need any financial assistance. He thought I would need the money more in case of my election than my defeat. I had no desire to accumulate means beyond a provision against old age and I preferred to have him give the money to his wife, with instructions to give it to me if at the time of his death I desired it. He preferred to give it to me directly and asked me whether I would be willing to distribute it in case I did not desire to accept it, reminding me again that he had made what he regarded as ample provision for the members of his family and wanted this sum devoted to the public. He said it gave him pleasure to contemplate the benefit which his bequest would bring to other young people, situated as he himself had been in his youth.

He insisted that I should distribute the fifty thousand dollars among charities and educational institutions if for any reason I refused to accept it. Having no thought of the possibility of a contest, I promised to do this, and it was this promise that compelled me to oppose the breaking of the will.

The money was left to his wife in trust, the terms of which would be made known to her in a letter deposited with the will.

I have gone into this in detail because the alternative

obligation which he imposed upon me was the matter that embarrassed me at the time of his death. He explained to me that he had given to his wife all that she could use and his estimate was borne out by subsequent facts. He left his wife about one hundred thousand dollars. When she died in 1919 she left an estate of one hundred thirty-six thousand dollars. It shows an increase rather than a diminution of the amount left her.

Mrs. Bryan, who at that time used the typewriter and helped me with a considerable part of my correspondence, copied the will at Mr. Bennett's request.

When the new will was drafted, being, as I have said, a copy of the old will except as to the five bequests above mentioned, he took it back to New York with him unsigned; then, fifteen hundred miles away from Nebraska and several days after the drawing of it, he executed the will and put it in a safety deposit vault of his own selection and of which he only had the key, notifying me of what he had done. There the will lay until his death more than three years later. The will was never mentioned in any conversation between us and never referred to in any letters. And I did not know at the time of his death whether the will was in existence.

In one of his letters written upon a wedding anniversary he remarked that he was almost old enough to be my father, adding that I could not be nearer to him if I were indeed his son. I mention this because while it made no reference to the will when he thus expressed himself, he may have had in mind the provision of his will.

Between the making of the will and his death I saw him frequently and heard from him from time to time. In the fall of 1903 he made a trip to Idaho, and arranged to stop at Lincoln on his way west. It so happened that I was away from home, so that I missed an opportunity to have what would have been a farewell visit with him. He expressed himself as greatly pleased with Fairview, our

country home. It was on this trip that he met his death
by accident at a point near Boise, Idaho. He was riding
in the open stage coach commonly used on the mountain
roads when the brake broke on a hill and the team became
unmanageable. He was thrown from the coach, striking
against a tree, and died instantly. His widow wired me and
I went to New Haven to attend the funeral. She greeted
me affectionately, put the flowers which I brought on the
coffin with her own flowers and invited me to speak at the
grave, which I did. Below will be found my remarks.

"At another time I shall take occasion to speak of
the life of Philo Sherman Bennett and to draw some
lessons from his career; today I must content myself
with offering a word of comfort to those who knew him
as husband, brother, relative, or friend—and as a friend
I need a share of this comfort for myself. It is sad
enough to consign to the dust the body of one we love—
how infinitely more sad if we were compelled to part
with the spirit that animated this tenement of clay.
But the best of man does not perish. We bury the brain
that planned for others as well as for its master, the
tongue that spoke words of love and encouragement,
the hands that were extended to those who needed help
and the feet that ran where duty directed, but the spirit
that dominated and controlled all rises triumphant over
the grave. We lay away the implements with which he
wrought, but the gentle, modest, patient, sympathetic,
loyal, brave and manly man whom we knew is not dead,
and cannot die. It would be unfair to count the loss of
his departure without counting the gain of his existence.
The gift of his life we have and of this the tomb cannot
deprive us. Separation, sudden and distressing as it is,
cannot take from the companion of his life the recollection of forty years of affection, tenderness and confidence, nor from others the memory of helpful associa-

tion with him. If the sunshine which a baby brings into a home, even if its sojourn is brief, cannot be dimmed by its death; if a child growing to manhood or womanhood brings to the parents a development of heart and head that outweighs any grief that its demise can cause, how much more does a long life full of kindly deeds leave us indebted to the Father who both gives and takes away. The night of death makes us remember with gratitude the light of the day that has gone while we look forward to the morning.

"The impress made by the life is lasting. We think it wonderful that we can by means of the telephone or the telegraph talk to those who are many miles away, but the achievements of the heart are even more wonderful, for the heart that gives inspiration to another heart influences all the generations yet to come. What finite mind, then, can measure the influence of a life that touched so many lives as did our friend's?

"To the young, death is an appalling thing, but it ought not to be to those whose advancing years warn them of its certain approach. As we journey along life's road we must pause again and again to bid farewell to some fellow traveler. In the course of nature the father and the mother die, then brothers and sisters follow, and finally the children and the children's children cross to the unknown world beyond—one by one 'from love's shining circle the gems drop away' until the 'king of terrors' loses his power to affright us and the increasing company on the farther shore make us first willing and then anxious to join them. It is God's way. It is God's way."

After the funeral I talked with her at her home and told her about the will drawn at my house about three and a half years previously. I told her I did not know where the will was and had no knowledge of what had occurred since and therefore did not know whether it was still in existence, but I told her of the bequests as I recalled them. She made no objection whatever to the bequest to me, but did express surprise and dissatisfaction with two other items in the will. The will as drawn made his partner, Mr. Sloan, and myself executors. I had an imperative engagement which took me away from New Haven for a few days and when I returned to present the will for probate I found that she and the other residuary legatees had employed a lawyer and decided to contest the fifty thousand dollars willed to myself.

I explained to her and to her attorneys that I would not receive any of the money for myself without her approval, but that having promised Mr. Bennett to distribute the sum if I did not receive it, I could not refuse to carry out his directions unless relieved by the court. The will was not contested on the ground that any improper influence had been brought to bear upon him, but merely on the technical ground that the provision to Mrs. Bennett did not sufficiently define the trust according to the Connecticut statute regulating wills. If the money had been given to me directly there would have been no contest and if I had not promised to distribute the sum in case I refused to accept it, I would have immediately relinquished all claims. However, having been taken into Mr. Bennett's confidence and having learned the disposition he wanted made of it, I did not feel at liberty to consult my own pleasure or my own interest.

My position was made plain to the probate judge, the circuit court and to the supreme court, so that it was known to all that I had no personal interest in the result of the suit but was simply carrying out the wishes of a dead friend. I received the most courteous treatment from all the officials who took part in the case. I employed Judge Henry G. Newton, a prominent member of the bar, to represent the estate in the defense of the will. At one time in the trial he interposed objections to an improper question and I asked him to make no objections to any questions that Mrs. Bennett's counsel might desire to ask, whether proper or not. I was not willing that any limit whatever should be placed upon interrogations, feeling that any objections might be open to misconstruction. At the conclusion of the hearing Judge Cleveland expressed himself very strongly as to the impression made by my testimony.

In the course of his written opinion, the judge said: "This court finds that neither the twelfth clause of the will (which was the clause in question) nor the letter therein referred to, was procured by undue influence." And the judge, in his written comment on the testimony, said:

> "The testimony of Mr. Dewell, who had known him for a quarter of a century, shows that the testator was a sharp, able business man, a man of decided opinions from which he was not easily turned aside. But whatever presumption, if any, might be raised by reason of Mr. Bryan's drafting the will, has been, in the opinion of the court, abundantly overcome by the evidence. Mr. Bryan testifies that the idea of a bequest in his favor, so far from being suggested by him or Mrs. Bryan, was a complete surprise to both; a statement in which the court has entire confidence in view of Mr. Bryan's frankness on the witness stand and his evident desire to fully disclose all his relations with the testator and all the circumstances surrounding the drafting of the will.

The three $10,000 funds left in trust to me were distributed as follows:

BENNETT PRIZE FUND

Delaware College, Newark, Del.................... $400
Bowdoin College, Brunswick, Me.................... 400
A. and M. College of Kentucky, Lexington, Ky...... 400

Harvard University, Cambridge, Mass..............	$400
Dartmouth College, Hanover, N. H.................	400
University of Tennessee, Knoxville, Tenn...........	400
St. John's College, Annapolis, Md.................	400
University of Idaho, Moscow, Idaho...............	400
University of Montana, Missoula, Mont.............	400
University of Utah, Salt Lake City, Utah...........	400
University of Washington, Seattle, Wash...........	400
University of South Dakota, Vermilion, S. D........	400
University of California, Berkeley, Calif............	400
Nevada State University, Reno, Nev..............	400
University of Colorado, Boulder, Colo..............	400
South Carolina College, Columbia, S. C............	400
Cornell University, Ithaca, N. Y...................	400
University of Wyoming, Laramie, Wyo.............	400
University of Vermont, Burlington, Vt.............	400
University of Oregon, Eugene, Ore.................	400
Yale University, New Haven, Conn.................	400
Brown University, Providence, R. I................	400
University of North Dakota, Grand Forks, N. D.....	400
University of Pennsylvania, Philadelphia, Pa........	400
Princeton University, Princeton, N. J..............	400

Each college is to invest the amount received and use the annual income for a prize for the best essay discussing the principles of free government. I had already established similar prizes in nineteen states and the twenty-five colleges selected for the Bennett prize were selected from other states so that every state but one now contains a college giving such a prize.

Educational Fund for Boys

The fund for the aid of poor boys desiring a college education was distributed as follows:

Illinois College, Jacksonville, Ill..................	$1,000
Park College, Parkville, Mo......................	750

College of William and Mary, Williamsburg, Va..... $750
Doane College, Crete, Neb...................... 500
Howard College, East Lake (near Birmingham, Alabama)................................ 500
Hendrix College, Conway, Ark................... 500
Tuskegee Normal and Industrial Institute, Tuskegee, Ala....................................... 500
Kenyon College, Gambier, Ohio................. 500
Muskingum College, New Concord, Ohio........... 500
St. Olaf College, Northfield, Minn................ 500
Hillsdale College, Conway, Ark.................. 500
University of the South, Sewanee, Tenn............ 500
Trinity University, Waxahachie, Tex.............. 500
Ripon College, Ripon, Wis...................... 500
Nazareth College, Muskogee, I. T................ 500
Hope College, Holland, Mich.................... 500
Butler College, Indianapolis, Ind................ 500
Sutherland College, Sutherland, Fla.............. 500

EDUCATIONAL FUND FOR GIRLS

The fund for the aid of poor girls desiring to obtain a college education was distributed by Mrs. Bryan as follows:

Georgia Normal and Industrial College, Milledgeville, Ga.. $500
Eureka College, Eureka, Ill..................... 500
Hastings College, Hastings, Neb................. 500
Wesleyan University, Buchannon, W. Va........... 500
Henry Kendall College, Muskogee, I. T........... 500
Williamsburg Institute, Williamsburg, Ky.......... 500
Wesleyan University, University Place, Neb........ 500
Baylor University, Waco, Tex.................... 500
Iowa College, Grinnell, Ia...................... 500
Tulane University of Louisiana, New Orleans, La.... 500
State Normal and Industrial College, Greensboro, N. C.. 500

Hiram College, Hiram, Ohio...................... $500
Kingfisher College, Kingfisher, O. T................ 500
Academy of the Visitation, Dubuque, Ia............ 500
Williams Industrial College, Little Rock, Ark........ 500
Ewing College, Ewing, Ill......................... 500
Bethany College, Lindsborg, Kan................... 500
University of Arizona, Tucson, Ariz................ 500
University of New Mexico, Albuquerque, N. M...... 500
The Mississippi Industrial Institute and College,
    Columbus, Miss............................... 500

CHAPTER IX

The St. Louis Convention

IMMEDIATELY after the election of 1900 I announced that I would not be a candidate in 1904. Having been defeated twice, the second time by a larger majority of the popular vote and of the electoral college than the first time, I thought that it was not wise to be a candidate again until the things I had fought for were so clearly vindicated as to lead the voters of the party to demand my nomination. And having reached the conclusion that I should not be a candidate, I thought it only fair to others who might be candidates to let them know that I would not be in the field.

The result was a contest for supremacy between the radical element of the party and the conservative element. The conservative element had the advantage in that it was able to point to two defeats under my leadership. This advantage was at once seized upon and the conservative leaders promised victory if they were put in control.

Mr. Hearst announced himself as a candidate and received the support of the more radical of the radicals, but did not command the support of all who had supported me. He was especially weak in the South and when the Convention met, the conservatives had a two thirds majority.

Judge Parker, of New York, was the man on whom they had centered, but his delegates were not for the most part instructed. I recognized the difficult position which I occupied and I recognized, too, that those who had fought for me were very much discouraged by the second defeat. I was in a position to know this. After the 1896 election I received as many as 2500 letters a day, all containing promises of support and assurances of victory in 1900.

After 1900 I received very few letters that expressed hope for the future of the Democratic Party. Most of my correspondents were disappointed; they did not see how we could win after the defeats we had suffered.

As the campaign of 1904 approached, I tried through my paper and in my speeches to awaken an interest in the coming campaign and to organize the radical element of the party to resist the encroachments of the conservatives. But it was useless. I did not think it wise to support any particular man for the nomination, and this was probably a mistake, for it is difficult to attack a candidate and have no candidate to suggest in his place. A number of Democrats said to me that if I would only pick out a man, they would support him, but if I would not do so, they must select for themselves. I mentioned a number of candidates as available, Mr. Hearst among others. But no other candidate appeared with any considerable strength except Mr. Hearst. Mr. Wall had Wisconsin, and Mr. Gray had Delaware, and Mr. Cockrell had Missouri, but Mr. Hearst had the only considerable following.

I decided to go to the convention as a delegate, at least I announced my willingness to do so, but even in Nebraska a club had been organized to support Mr. Parker and an effort was made to carry the Convention for him. This effort, however, failed and we carried every county, I think, but one, in the state, and the state convention elected a set of delegates who, to a man, supported my position.

I went to the St. Louis convention from a sense of duty and not because I expected to win any victory there, or even to avoid a humiliating defeat. Remembering that the gold Democrats had left the party and by leaving had lost their influence in the party, I was afraid that if the platform was written by the conservative element it would drive a large part of the radical Democrats out of the party. My purpose, therefore, in going to the convention was to get a platform that would not sacrifice what the party had been fighting for, and would, if possible, secure a candidate who could be voted for by those who had been enthusiastic in my support. I was more successful in the matter of the platform than I had hoped to be.

The first fight in the convention was over the Illinois delegation. Mr. Hearst had a considerable majority in the Illinois state convention, but the organization was against him, and the temporary chairman proceeded to run the convention with the gavel without regard to the wishes of the delegates. A crowd had been brought down from Chicago and stationed near the platform to prevent any interference with the program that had been laid down by those in charge.

While they could not prevent a resolution endorsing Mr. Hearst, they selected a delegation, a majority of which was opposed to him, and the selection was made by the most high-handed methods. The delegates from the several congressional districts made a selection of national delegates, but these were ignored and new names substituted to meet the purpose of those in charge.

When I read in the paper an account of the convention, I telegraphed M. F. Dunlap to meet me at St. Louis and I questioned him in regard to the convention. Believing that an outrage had been perpetrated upon the Democrats of Illinois, and believing that the action of the convention might have a decided influence upon the national convention, I proposed that a contest be made. I went to Chicago and laid the matter before Mr. Hearst, but he felt that it might be a reflection upon the instructions for him to attack the convention that gave the instructions. Mr. Dunlap and I then decided to make the fight ourselves, and each bearing half the expense, we proceeded to secure a petition from a majority of the delegates of the convention asking for the seating of certain men as delegates at large and of the men who had been chosen in the several districts by a majority vote.

WILLIAM JENNINGS BRYAN

Before the convention met we had a signed request of more than a majority of those who actually took part in the convention asking for the action which we suggested. Of course, this was resisted and the Parker men being in control of the convention, the contestants were overruled and the opposing delegates seated. I got a proxy from the Nebraska member of the Committee on Credentials and went into the committee and presented a minority report. I opened and closed the debate on this question and it was the first victory won in the convention, for, although I was voted down by the convention, even without the delegates, I had such an overwhelming majority of the audience with me, that their expression of opinion very much strengthened me in the contest that followed.

The *Post-Dispatch*, one of the Parker papers, had a two-column editorial entitled "The Passing of Bryan," in which the editor discussed at some length the insignificant part that I was taking in the convention. I had entered the convention the day before while some one was speaking and I took my seat unnoticed. This was commented upon as an indication that I no longer had influence in the party.

The delegates had just about had time to read that editorial when I entered the convention to make the minority report; and possibly because of the vindictive spirit that ran through the editorial, my entrance was made the occasion for a demonstration that lasted some twenty minutes. This was the first notice served upon the delegates that they were not to have things all their own way. The reception accorded my speech in behalf of the Illinois contestants increased the impression, and by the time I took up the fight in the full committee, the conservative element was aware that I had with me a large majority of the audience and a respectable minority in the convention.

I was of course a member of the Resolutions Committee, being selected for the place by my own delegation. Senator Daniel was made the chairman of the committee and he appointed a sub-committee to draft the platform. As a matter of courtesy I was put on this sub-committee, but I was the only one in the beginning who represented our side of the fight. Senator Newlands was afterwards added and he was of great assistance in the struggle which followed.

We spent one session, lasting from eight o'clock until midnight, on the tariff plank, and I was finally voted down. During the next session I was occupied in the convention in the fight over the Illinois delegation, and while I was absent the sub-committee went over the rest of the platform and was ready to report to the full committee at the evening session. At the time the committee was appointed the papers published a platform which was described as the platform agreed upon by the leaders of the party. It was not strange that I had not seen the platform, for I was not counted among the leaders by those in control of the convention, and it was not supposed that I would have any influence in the writing of the platform. I had gone over this platform and marked the planks to which I objected and had this copy with me when the full committee met to consider the work of the sub-committee. I took my place at the table not far from Senator Daniel, and we began the most memorable contest through which I have ever passed.

From eight o'clock in the evening until noon the next day—sixteen hours—the battle raged over the wording of that platform. As we took up plank after plank, I moved to strike out and to substitute, and as fortune would have it, I succeeded in securing a majority for each proposition, so that when the platform was completed, I had written a great deal more of it than I had written of the Chicago platform upon which I myself ran. I did not get into the platform all that I wanted, but with the help of a majority of the committee, I kept out of the platform everything to which I objected.

The fight over the gold plank attracted most attention, although the majority against the gold plank was larger than the majority against any other plank stricken out. The vote, as I recall it, was thirty or thirty-five to fifteen. Nearly all of the Southern members voted against this plank. While I voted against it, I did not take much part in the argument, because there were plenty of Parker men to talk against it.

At one time Senator Daniel, who was urging the plank, asked if any Democrat thought that the adoption of the plank would weaken the party in his state. More than half of the committee arose, among them some of Mr. Parker's stanchest supporters.

During the course of the discussion, I asked Senator Hill when he had decided that the gold plank should be inserted in the platform. He replied that he had reached that decision only a few days before the convention. In asking the question I thought that he might answer that he had believed so for months, and I then intended to ask him why it had not been inserted in the New York platform —that platform having been silent upon the subject. His answer, however, showed that it was a newly conceived purpose. I also asked him Judge Parker's views on the subject and he said that he did not know. I asked him if he had ever talked with Judge Parker on the subject and he said that he had not. This seemed remarkable to me and it struck the convention in the same way when the conversation was reported to the convention.

I saw that it was impossible to secure the insertion of any money plank, and I did not, therefore, spend much time in urging it. I consented to a plank suggested by Senator Carmack which stated that the quantitative theory of money had been established and that the increase in the volume of money had removed the money question from the arena of politics. But that plank was objected to by Senator Hill, and seeing that the best we could do was to prevent any expression on the subject, we contented ourselves with leaving out the money question entirely.

I urged a plank in favor of the income tax, but while nearly every member of the committee, excepting Senator Hill, expressed himself as favoring the income tax, a considerable majority opposed the insertion of the plank, some of them on the ground that it would interfere with the collection of a campaign fund. I finally agreed to withdraw the income-tax plank if the committee would agree to a stronger anti-trust plank, and when this was consented to, Senator Hill and I drew up an anti-trust plank, it being made as strong as the committee would permit. The labor planks were also inserted during the debate. There were two questions upon which there was no dispute, the election of senators by the people and the party's position on the subject of imperialism. The committee was unanimous on these questions.

The fight over the tariff question was probably the closest and most spirited fight that we had. The original proposition was strongly suggestive of protection, at least it gave very little encouragement to the tariff reformer. Several of the Parker men joined with us in strengthening this plank, among them Mr. Cable, of Illinois, who had been instructed for Mr. Hearst and was in sympathy with the Western element of the party, and Mr. Hamlin, of Massachusetts. Senator Bailey did efficient work on this plank, going so far as to threaten to bring in a minority report if they attempted to report the plank that was suggested in the original draft of the platform. During the course of the discussion I had somewhat spirited debates with several members of the committee, but while the feeling was quite intense on both sides, the debates were conducted with courtesy and no ill feeling was left when the committee adjourned.

I am not sure that I ever rendered my party more service than I did during this fight over the platform, for the platform which we adopted did not surrender the party's position on the questions which had been an issue before, it merely left out some things about which we could not agree. The convention breathed a sigh of relief when the announcement was made that the committee had agreed upon a platform, and the platform was adopted by the unanimous vote of the convention.

As soon as the platform was adopted, the presentation of candidates began, and Judge Parker, Mr. Hearst, and Senator Cockrell were presented. Then came the seconding speeches. As the time rolled on these speeches were limited to four minutes. When Nebraska was called, I arose and yielded to Wisconsin, that Wisconsin might present Mr. Wall. When Wisconsin was called the state yielded to Nebraska and I seconded the nomination of Senator Cockrell.

I was somewhat in a quandary as to what to do. My main object was to prevent the nomination of Judge Parker, who was so closely identified with the men who had defeated the party in two campaigns that I felt sure he would be so handicapped by this support as to make his election impossible.

I had no particular choice in selecting Senator Cockrell, but was governed by two considerations. First, he stood for everything that I had been fighting for and I could therefore urge his nomination without surrendering or abandoning anything. In the second place, he was an ex-Confederate soldier and I thought that there was a possibility that with him we might break the Southern support of Judge Parker, and I believed that Senator Cockrell would poll a very much larger vote than Judge Parker could possibly poll.

I had more to say than I could say in four minutes, and therefore I asked for a suspension of that rule. I announced to Congressman Clark, the presiding officer, that if allowed unlimited time, I would second the nomination of Senator Cockrell, but if the request was denied I would present the name of someone else for nomination, because in making a nominating speech there was no limit upon time.

Mr. Clark asked the convention for unanimous consent to suspend the rule, and although it was four o'clock in the morning, and the delegates were weary, no objection was made. I have always regarded this as a compliment as well as a great courtesy. Two thirds of the delegates were for Parker and they knew that I was against him; I had fought him and the platform which his leaders had urged, and yet there was no objection when I asked unanimous consent for a suspension as to the time limit, that I might address the convention against Mr. Parker's nomination.

The speech made on that occasion is a matter of record and is generally known as the "I Have Kept the Faith" speech, for what was considered the most striking passage in it was the one in which I stated, in returning the standard which had been placed in my hands, that they could dispute whether I had fought a good fight; [they could dispute whether I had finished my course, but they could not deny that I had kept the faith. (See Chapter XXI.)

My effort, however, was futile. The delegates had gone so far in their determination to nominate Judge Parker that no effort of mine could prevent it, and when the roll was called, he had the necessary two thirds. If I had been asked my opinion as to the availability of candidates, I would have decided in favor of Governor Pattison of Pennsylvania. He was the one man suggested who would have been acceptable as a compromise candidate.

Judge Parker was acceptable to the Eastern element, but not to the radical element of the party. Mr. Hearst was acceptable to the radicals, but not to the conservatives. Mr. Gray would have been more acceptable to the conservatives than to the radicals. Mr. Wall, while not for silver in 1896, supported the ticket and would have been acceptable to the radicals, but he lived too far west for the conservatives. Governor Pattison was a candidate before the Chicago convention and was a gold Democrat, but he supported the ticket that year. He lived in the East, but he had a record that commended him to the radicals, and I believed then, and still believe, that he came nearer meeting the requirements of the occasion than any other man we had, but his own delegation sided in with New York and left him no chance.

He died soon after the convention and as his death would have demoralized our campaign, it is fortunate he was not nominated. Notwithstanding the fact that I was looked upon as a disturber of harmony, I had been anxious that we should find some one upon whom the party could unite and for whom we could make a strong fight.

After being up all night for two nights—one night on the Committee on Resolutions and another at the convention (and I had only slept for a few hours for several preceding nights)—I was utterly exhausted and as soon as I concluded my speech, I returned to the hotel and retired. In fact, it was more than fatigue. I went to the convention with a severe cold and it developed so far as to threaten pneumonia. It was against the advice of my physician that I attended the convention, and the first night I attended the meeting of the Committee on Resolutions wearing a mustard plaster over my chest. As soon as I reached the hotel the doctor put a plaster of antiphlogistine on my chest and I remained in bed until night. During the day Judge Parker sent his famous telegram which threw the convention into an uproar. The delegates brought me news from time to time and no one could foresee the result. Several delegates came over and expressed themselves in very emphatic language to the effect that they "had been bunkoed." I tried to soothe them by telling them that it was no more than they might have expected and that they ought to have known from the tactics pursued that it was not a compromise which had been demanded but a surrender.

Finally the situation became so tense that I decided to

go over to the convention. Taking advantage of the absence of the physician, I dressed and hurried over, pale and worn. I went to the platform and made my last stand against the Parker element. His telegram had announced that he regarded the gold standard as irrevocably established and the Resolutions Committee brought in a resolution declaring that as the question was no longer an issue, his personal opinion was not material. I introduced an amendment calling upon him to give his opinion upon certain other phases of the money question, as he had seen fit to give it upon the gold question. But after reflection I withdrew this, not only because there was little chance of its adoption, but because I was afraid that his answers to my questions, if he answered them, would simply commit him to the wrong side of the question.

When the vote was taken the committee's resolution was adopted by about the same vote which was cast in favor of his nomination, and the resolution was not a very important one after all, because it only stated the fact which we all recognized, namely, that the money question was not an issue any longer. It would have been better, however, if the resolution had stated that it was no longer an issue because the principle contended for by the Democrats had been vindicated and because an unexpected increase of money from another source had rendered the restoration of bimetallism unnecessary.

His telegram, however, put an end to whatever hope there was of Mr. Parker's election. He had remained silent and by so doing he had alienated the rank and file of the party. If the election had occurred a week after the convention, he would scarcely have received half the votes of the party, but as time went on, the Democrats became more reconciled to the situation and recognized that he had simply expressed his own opinion and in no wise committed the party.

I took part in the campaign, justifying myself by the

fact that the Democratic platform was good as far as it went and that our candidate stood for a number of reforms, while President Roosevelt was pledged to no reforms. I offered my services to the national committee and spoke in several of the states, neglecting my own state to do so. And while I have reason to believe that I was instrumental in increasing his vote, I found it difficult to arouse enthusiasm.

I heard many amusing stories of the campaign illustrating the lack of enthusiasm. One man told me that at a ratification meeting three cheers were proposed. The chairman gave two of them and the man who told me gave one, which made the three—the remainder of the audience refused to join. At a meeting in Indiana where the Democratic candidate for governor was present, the chairman proposed three cheers for the ticket and got no response whatever, but the audience, after giving three cheers for the Republican candidate, adjourned.

I look back to the St. Louis convention as one of the best illustrations I have had of the fact that one cannot see very far ahead. I went to the convention expecting to be disregarded by a hostile majority. I never knew one hour what was coming next, but continued on my way meeting the questions as they arose and doing what seemed to me to be right at the time.

In the convention in which I expected humiliation I found victory, for I think the victory at St. Louis was really a greater personal triumph than the victory at Chicago, and did more to strengthen me in the party. My support of the ticket convinced many who had doubted my democracy that I was in fact democratic in my principles and loyal to the Democratic party as an organization.

When I went to St. Louis I could not, of course, see the outcome, and I would not promise in advance to support the nominee, but I was convinced during the course of the convention that the Democratic party was sound at heart

ACCEPTING THE NOMINATION FOR THE PRESIDENCY, 1908

and that its surrender to the conservative element was but temporary.

This encouraged me to continue the fight within the Democratic party, and the platform was such that I had something to stand on and to fight for. The platform committed our candidate to certain important reforms, while the Republican platform committed the President to no specific reforms, and I felt that if we could but get rid of imperialism and the spirit of war which the President seemed to embody, we might be better prepared to enter upon the fight for economic reforms.

Looking back upon the campaign of 1904, I think that it was probably best that Mr. Parker was nominated, because his nomination gave the conservatives a chance to test their ability to win victory, and their failure made it possible for the party to reorganize itself and become a positive and progressive force. Had we nominated a radical at that time, he would, in all probability, have been defeated, because the conservative element would not have supported him; had we nominated a compromise candidate he would also, in all probability, have been defeated, but the nomination of a man clearly identified with the Wall Street element removed, for the present at least, the fear of another conservative triumph in the party.

At the Democratic National Convention at Denver in 1908 Mr. Bryan was nominated for President for the third time. His position on the Trust question at that time is set forth in a statement and telegrams which will be found in the Appendix.

CHAPTER X

THE BALTIMORE CONVENTION

AFTER my third defeat in 1908 I felt that nothing but a revolutionary change in the political situation would justify a fourth nomination. Not seeing evidence of such a change and not being willing to obstruct the plans of other aspirants, I announced that I would not be a candidate in 1912. As a result of the Congressional election in 1910 the Democrats gained control of the House of Representatives and Champ Clark was elected Speaker.

Clark entered Congress in 1892, from which time my acquaintance with him began. As is the custom, he came to Washington after his election and before his term began in March of 1893. I recall our first meeting at that time. He said that he had used my record as an argument in his race for the nomination. The Democratic member of Congress from his district was serving his first term when Clark announced his candidacy. His argument against the sitting member was that he had not accomplished anything during his first term. The member replied that it was not customary for a new member to do much during his first term; that it took time for a man to secure prominence and influence in Congress. I had been made a member of the Ways and Means Committee during my first term when I was only a little past thirty.

From that time on I met Clark in the 53d Congress and afterwards at Democratic national gatherings. While I was not more intimate with him than I was with a thousand other Democrats scattered throughout the Union, I followed his record with interest and rejoiced at his growing influence.

After his election to the Speakership in 1911 I regarded him as the logical candidate and invited him to speak at my

birthday banquet on March 19, 1911. My purpose in inviting him was to let those who were friendly to me know that
I regarded him as an available man for the nomination.
Governor Wilson was being talked of more and more, but
I felt that Clark was more in sympathy with the policies
of the party and, therefore, better suited to lead our forces
in the coming presidential campaign. Clark came, but I
learned from him afterwards that it was with some reluc-
tance. This surprised me and I was surprised still more
when, as the campaign proceeded, I found that his friends
were tying up with the Harmon forces wherever a combination was necessary to defeat the Wilson forces.

Wilson, on the other hand, was becoming more radical
in his utterances and was gathering about him an increasing
number of the progressive element of the party. He was
also exciting the opposition of the reactionary element. As
the campaign proceeded I received many letters from different parts of the country warning me that Harmon men were
getting on Clark delegations.

Having learned from a friend who was present at the
meeting that Wall Street had picked out Governor Harmon
as its Democratic candidate, I at once brought the matter
to the attention of the Democrats of the country and insisted
that he could not expect to be the candidate of a progressive
Democratic Party. I was fond of Harmon personally, but
I was satisfied that his business connections and his bias
made it impossible for him to be the exponent of the masses
in their struggle for reforms. I had confidence in Clark
personally, and, knowing that a man cannot refuse the
support of those who for different reasons may favor him,
continued to count Clark and Wilson as equally acceptable
to the progressive element of the party.

In the Nebraska primary I announced myself as a candidate for delegate-at-large, saying that I would willingly
support either Clark or Wilson according to instructions,
but that I would resign as delegate in case the state

instructed for Harmon, giving as a reason that I was not willing to aid in turning the party over to Wall Street. I ran about five thousand ahead of the ticket and considered my election as an endorsement of my opposition to Wall Street domination.

Some of my prominent political friends came into Nebraska and made an active canvass of the state in favor of Clark and against Wilson. George Fred Williams and Ex-Senator Pettigrew were among the number. They were both strongly against Wilson. They quoted Adrian Joline's letter and also extracts from Mr. Wilson's utterances on the money question. They urged the support of Clark on the ground that he always supported the things that I advocated and was, therefore, nearer to me in his political ideas and ideals. I favored a division of the delegation so as to avoid a fight between two progressive candidates, but Mr. Wilson's manager insisted on having two thirds of the delegation and thus prevented a joint ticket.

I was so anxious to preserve an attitude of perfect neutrality between the two that I tried to make the vote in my precinct as nearly equal as possible. There were two voters at my home and I advised them to vote one for Clark and one for Wilson. Had they done so there would have been only one vote difference between the votes of the candidates, but when the time approached they thought that one of the candidates was going to have quite a lead and so, following the spirit instead of the letter of my advice, voted together for the one they thought was weakest, but were mistaken in their calculations and their two votes thus gave the successful candidate a lead of three majority over the other.

When the returns from the state came in it was found that Clark had the instructions but that Wilson had a majority of the delegates (bound by instructions, of course, but friendly to Wilson).

Some time in the spring, Norman E. Mack, the committeeman from New York, wrote me and asked if I would like to be temporary chairman. I answered that I did not think it would be wise for me to be temporary chairman. My reason for not wanting to enter the race was that some of the metropolitan papers were construing my neutrality between the two leading candidates as evidence of a desire to be a candidate myself. I was afraid that I would be accused of trying to stampede the convention, that being the possibility upon which the unfriendly papers dwelt at greatest length.

As the convention approached it became apparent that the progressives would be in control of the convention and that Clark would have more votes, although neither would have a majority.

I wrote to Governor Wilson and suggested to him that we should have a progressive chairman and that as neither had a majority the choice would naturally fall to the candidate having the largest number of votes. I called his attention to the fact that Ollie James, the candidate of the Clark delegates, was a progressive and a fair-minded man and suggested that he accept James in case it should prove impossible to elect the man of his own choice. He answered, saying that he preferred O'Gorman. I mention this fact to combat the unfair criticism of Mr. Clark's friends directed against me after I changed my vote.

At Chicago I watched the Republican Convention select a candidate under the pressure of influence from Wall Street. What I saw there made me sensitive to the influence of Wall Street in our own convention. While I was at Chicago the Democratic National Committee met and selected Judge Parker as temporary chairman. In the contest before the committee the Clark men had supported Ollie James and the Wilson men Judge O'Gorman. Neither having a majority, Parker finally received the support of the Clark men and became the choice of the committee. Josephus Daniels, then the member of the committee for North

Part of Mr. Bryan's copy of his letter to Champ Clark

THE BALTIMORE CONVENTION

Ft. Wayne, Ind.

May 30

MY DEAR CLARK:—

I venture to make a suggestion for your consideration. I believe the fight over wool will prove a crisis in your life as well as in the party's prospects. A leader must *lead;* it is not always pleasant to oppose friends, and one who leads takes the chances of defeat, but these are the necessary attendants upon leadership. Wilson is making friends because he *fights.* His fight against Smith was heroic. He fought for the income tax and for a primary law. The people like a fighter. You won your position by fighting and you must continue to fight to hold it. Enter into the wool fight. Don't be content to take polls and sit in the background. Take one side or the other and take it *strong.* If a tax on wool is right, lead the protectionists to victory. You can do it and it will make you strong with that wing of the party. If free wool is right, as I believe it is, lead the fight for it and get the credit for the victory if victory comes. Don't inquire about how the fight is going to go—make it go the right way if you can. If you fail you lay the foundation for a future victory. The right wins in the end—don't be afraid to wait. My opinion is that you will not have to wait long, but whether long or not, one can better afford to be defeated fighting for the right than to win on the wrong side. I hope you will pardon this intrusion upon your thoughts, but the party needs your assistance—a blast from your bugle may save the day, and it will, in my judgment, strengthen you personally.

Regards to the family.

Yours

BRYAN

Carolina, called me up by telephone and asked me what I thought of the selection. I told him that I not only would criticise the selection but the committee that made the selection. I then prepared a telegram to each progressive candidate reading as follows:

"In the interest of harmony I suggested to the sub-committee of the Democratic National Committee the advisability of recommending as temporary chairman some progressive acceptable to the leading progressive candidates for the presidential nomination. I took it for granted that no committeeman interested in Democratic success would desire to offend the members of a convention overwhelmingly progressive by naming a reactionary to sound the keynote of the campaign. Eight members of the sub-committee, however, have, over the protest of the remaining eight, agreed upon not only a reactionary, but upon the one Democrat, who, among those not candidates for the presidential nomination is, in the eyes of the public, most conspicuously identified with the reactionary element of the party. I shall be pleased to join you and your friends in opposing this selection by the full committee or by the convention. Kindly answer here."

Governor Foss of Massachusetts, Governor Marshall of Indiana, and Governor Baldwin of Connecticut, all declined to join me in my fight against Parker. Governor Wilson of New Jersey and Governor Burke of North Dakota went to my support.

Woodrow Wilson sent the following reply:

"You are right. Before hearing of your message I clearly stated my position in answer to a question from the Baltimore *Evening Sun*. The Baltimore convention is to be the convention of progressives—the men who are progressive in principle and by conviction. It must, if it is not to be put in a wrong light before the country, express its convictions in its organization and its choice of the men who are to speak for it. You are to be a member of the convention and are entirely within your rights in doing everything within your power to bring that result about. No one will doubt where my sympathies lie, and you will, I am sure, find my friends in the convention acting upon a clear conviction and always in the interest of the people's cause. I am happy in the confidence that they need no suggestion from me."

Champ Clark replied as follows:

"Have consulted with committee having my interests in charge and agree with them that the supreme consideration should be to prevent any discord in the convention. Friends of mine on the sub-committee of arrangements have already presented the name of Ollie James to the sub-committee. I believe that if all join in the interest of harmony in an appeal to the entire national committee to avoid controversies in matters of organization that the committee will so arrange as to leave the platform and nomination of candidates as the only real issues on which delegates need divide."

Governor Marshall's reply was:

"You may be right, but as Judge Parker, as a member of the committee on resolutions from the state of New York at the national convention at Denver, helped to report our platform of 1908 and as he came to Indiana that year to advocate your election and mine, and as he returned in 1910 to advocate the election of Senator Kern, I do not see how his selection as temporary chairman will result in a reactionary platform in 1912."

Governor Burke of North Dakota sent the only explicit acceptance of the challenge offered by the Wall Street crowd. Governor Marshall was willing to support Parker, while Clark's answer was a straddle. Governor Wilson's telegram, while not as direct as I would have liked, began with a sentence that led the delegates to accept it as a promise to oppose the Parker candidacy, which his delegates did. The account of this incident is given by Governor Wilson's secretary, J. P. Tumulty, in his book on "Wilson as I Knew Him," page 105.

I soon afterwards left the Chicago Convention and proceeded to Baltimore, hoping all the way that the Clark delegates would oppose Parker and thus give us a progressive temporary chairman to sound the keynote of the convention. When I reached Baltimore I found the situation unchanged. A Clark delegate called on me soon after my arrival and intimated that I might have the permanent chairmanship if I did not oppose Parker. Of course, I did not entertain any such proposition, but proceeded to hunt for a candidate to put up against Parker, after having made a personal appeal to Parker himself. I had a frank talk with him on the afternoon before the convention met in which I told him that he had no part in the reforms for which the party now stood and could not possibly give expression to the thoughts and purposes of the delegates who constituted a majority of a progressive convention. I made no impression on him further than to arouse his ire, as such a protest naturally would.

I first called in Ollie James, the candidate of the Clark men when the matter was before the committee. I felt sure that he could defeat Parker. He laid the matter before Mr. Clark's managers and returned to tell me that they objected to it and that therefore he could not allow his name to be used as a candidate. I then sent for Judge O'Gorman, Mr. Wilson's candidate in the contest, but he, being a member of the New York delegation, had pledged his support to Judge Parker, although he advised Judge Parker not to be a candidate.

Failing to secure a candidate from the delegates supporting Clark and Wilson, I made an appeal to Senator Kern, but found that he, too, was embarrassed by the fact that he was there as delegate supporting Governor Marshall. The Indiana delegates, following the wishes of Governor Marshall, were nearly all supporting Judge Parker. The matter was made more delicate for Senator Kern by the fact that he was already being discussed as a candidate and naturally hesitated to do anything that would divert attention from his state's candidate to himself. Senator Kern urged me to be a candidate for the place as others had, but I explained to him that my first desire was to present an argument against Judge Parker's candidacy, which I could not do if I was myself a candidate for the place.

When Senator Kern left my room the night before the opening of the Convention he did not answer positively whether he would allow me to present his name, but said he hoped I would not. I heard next morning, not from him directly but indirectly, that he had a plan, but I did not learn the details of it. Not having received from Senator Kern a positive refusal to allow his name to be presented, I placed him in nomination after the committee had offered the name of Judge Parker. My speech will be found in the Appendix.

I have regarded my use of the "pillar and cloud" of fire of the children of Israel as one of the most appropriate references that I have ever made to the Bible in a political argument, but there was so much confusion in the convention that it seemed to make but little impression and I think I saw but one reference to it in the papers. It illustrates an experience that one frequently has; a phrase upon which one sets great store is often ignored, while a sentence which is spoken on the spur of the moment and without thought of its being considered important, will attract widespread attention.

In the course of my speech against Parker I used a quotation from Tennyson, "He never sold the truth to serve the hour," which was printed in large letters over Jefferson's picture which hung at the right of the platform. When I used this quotation Mrs. Bryan, who was just back of the platform, heard a man near her say to another, "I told them that he would use that quotation if they put it up there."

As I look back upon the convention I have a growing appreciation of the part played by Senator Kern; it was the best piece of acting that I ever saw off the stage. In fact, I have not seen it surpassed on the stage. As soon as I had finished my speech he arose and made an appeal to Judge Parker to join him in withdrawing from the contest, that the convention might agree upon some one who could receive the united support of the convention. He made an eloquent plea for harmony and then paused for Judge Parker to answer. There was deathlike silence for a moment. Then Senator Kern appealed to Mr. Murphy, chairman of the New York delegation, to use his influence with Judge Parker to secure his withdrawal in the interest of harmony. Again a silence that was deathlike. Then Senator Kern turned to the presiding officer and in a spirit of defiance announced that if there must be a contest Mr. Bryan was the only man to lead the people's side and placed my name in nomination.

As the roll call proceeded it became apparent that Judge Parker had the support of Governor Harmon's delegates, Congressman Underwood's delegates and a considerable percentage, though not all, of Speaker Clark's delegates. (The vote stood Parker 579, Bryan 508.) Parker was elected, but the victory did not arouse the enthusiasm which might have been expected. The shadow of the vote darkened the convention, because the friends of Mr. Clark began to suspect what its effect would be on the country.

Judge Parker was conducted to the platform to deliver

his address as temporary chairman, but the hall was in confusion and the aisles were full of people going out. So large a percentage of the audience retired that those in charge of the convention hastily conferred and announced that Judge Parker would deliver his address at the evening session and then adjourned the convention. I have not consulted the precedents, but do not know of any similar experience. As soon as it was evident that I was defeated I went with my wife and children to the hotel. They were naturally disappointed and sympathetic, but I explained to them why I had made the fight and assured them that my purpose had been accomplished. I was satisfied that the country would be aroused when it knew that a supposedly progressive convention had selected as temporary chairman the man most conspicuously identified with the Wall Street side.

I was not disappointed. I had scarcely reached the hotel before telegrams of congratulation began to pour in. Then followed such a demonstration of the power of public opinion as has never been witnessed in a convention before or since. The effect of the contest upon the Democrats of the country was electrical. The party, sound at heart, felt that it was being betrayed by its political leaders and "the folks at home" communicated with the delegates. Many joined in one telegram, the language varying from courteous appeal to vehement denunciation.

The Montana delegation was cast for me with the exception of one vote. The result was immediately carried by bulletins throughout the country and shortly the Montana delegation received a brief telegram signed by a number of angry citizens saying, in substance, "Send us the name of the —— who voted for Parker. We want to meet him when he comes home."

These telegrams continued to pour in during the convention as each new incident gave new excuse for expression. The total number of telegrams received, according to the local agents of the two telegraph companies, was estimated at one hundred and ten thousand, or an average of about one hundred to a delegate. I received 1182 telegrams and they averaged three names to a telegram. One of them, from Virginia, was signed by one hundred and forty names. I learned later as I traveled through the West that the Democrats in the agricultural section would congregate at the railroad stations, read the bulletins as they were taken from the wire, and then join in sending a telegram to the delegates whom they knew, the signers "chipping in," as they say, to pay the expense of the telegrams.

When I was given credit for having exerted an influence on the convention, I replied that I had simply turned the faucet and allowed public sentiment to flow in upon the convention, deserving no personal credit except for knowing where the faucet was and the height of the stand-pipe from which the public opinion flowed.

But to return to my narrative; early in the evening a committee from Mr. Clark's headquarters called to offer me the permanent chairmanship of the convention. This encouraged my family and the friends about headquarters, because it was proof conclusive that Mr. Clark's managers were feeling the reaction from the victory of the afternoon. I declined the invitation, telling the messengers that those who owned a ship should furnish the crew; that when my friends controlled a convention, we never asked the minority to supply the officers. We were all kept up late that night listening to the messages that came from the various headquarters, all indicating confusion and consternation.

The next morning I was delayed in getting to the Committee on Resolutions and found when I reached the convention hall that a committee had been sent to the hotel in my absence to ask me to accept the chairmanship of the Committee on Resolutions. They soon returned and made me the offer. I expressed my appreciation of the honor done me, but suggested that the majority should furnish the chairman, as it might become necessary for me to present a minority report and it would not look well for such a report to be presented by the chairman. Mr. Kern was then chosen chairman and I was asked if I would serve on the sub-committee. This I gladly consented to do, as I desired to contribute as much as possible to the making of a progressive platform.

Before the sub-committee withdrew to begin its work I offered a resolution to the effect that the committee after agreeing upon a platform should hold it until after the nomination of a candidate for President, so that he might be consulted about the platform before it was adopted. One of the Eastern delegates arose and asked in a tone of surprise whether I thought it possible that a nominee of the convention would object to any platform that the convention had adopted. I replied, "Our candidate did in 1904." The questioner subsided amid the laughter of the committee, and the resolution was adopted.

We then had an illustration of the sensational character of reports that are sent out from conventions. The morning papers under big headlines told about my being defeated for chairman, the unfriendly papers in varying tones of gleefulness described my demise. The afternoon papers with headlines as large announced that Mr. Bryan had risen from the grave and taken charge of the Committee on Resolutions—basing the statement on the fact that the innocent resolution that I had introduced had been adopted.

My association with the other members of the sub-committee was pleasant and harmonious. I never worked with a more congenial crowd. The completeness of the harmony may be gathered from an incident. Just before the opening of the second day's session I met Judge O'Gorman, who told me that Senator Martin had stated to him that instead of being a firebrand as some of the committee feared I would be, I was the most conservative man on the committee. When the committee assembled I went up to

171

Senator Martin and addressing him in serious tones said, "Senator, I am sorry to hear you have been making unkind remarks about me."

The Senator assured me, with a look of honest surprise upon his face, that I had been misinformed, that he had spoken of me only in the most kind and complimentary language.

"But," I explained to him, "you told Judge O'Gorman that I was the most conservative man on this committee. What will my friends think when they hear this and know that you are on the committee?"

He enjoyed the humor of it and we went on working together as if we had always agreed on the policies of the party.

I assured the committee that I had no desire to write into the platform of another candidate any view that I had that had not already been endorsed by the party. I opposed any retreat on public questions and found the committee quite ready to endorse all that the Democrats in Congress had done since they believed, as I did, that our fight must be made upon the party's record. I was successful in reiterating in our platform many of the planks contained in previous platforms which I had helped to write, but I did not ask for the incorporation of anything new. The platform incorporated a phrase which had appeared in three previous platforms, namely, "A private monopoly is indefensible and intolerable." I first used the phrase in a speech at an Anti-Trust Conference at Chicago in 1899. The sentence used was almost identical with the sentence above quoted, and incorporated in the platform of 1900 and 1904 and 1908 and finally in 1912. I digress far enough from the narrative to say that this sentence was incorporated in President Wilson's speech of acceptance and in his message to Congress on the trust question.

I think I should mention a fact that one plank in the platform which has often been attributed to me, namely the plank reading: "We favor a single Presidential term and to that end urge the adoption of an amendment to the Constitution making the President ineligible for reëlection, and we pledge the candidate of this convention to this principle," was proposed by Governor Beckham of Kentucky. I very gladly supported the plank, but for obvious reasons would like to have it known that I did not offer it at this time. I have always believed in the single term for the President. When in Congress I introduced a resolution, proposing the necessary amendment to the Constitution. In each of my Presidential campaigns I made the statement that if elected I would not be a candidate for a second term, giving my reasons.

I will add that in every speech that I made during the campaign following I pointed out that this pledge against a second term enabled the President to serve the people with singleness of purpose unembarrassed by any selfish interest.

The platform also laid the foundation for the currency legislation secured in President Wilson's first term. The language employed in the discussion of banks was a distinct departure from the language usually employed, just as the language employed in the discussion of labor marked a new departure. The plank on independence to the Philippines was substantially the same as that contained in the three previous platforms of our party. An amendment providing for election of United States Senators by the people advocated in three preceding platforms was urged upon the states.

While I was occupied with the work of the Resolutions Committee most of the time Wednesday and Thursday I was from time to time in conference with the progressive element of the convention and learned of the activity of the same element that had controlled the Republican Convention at Chicago. I found that the representatives of Morgan, Belmont, and Ryan were at work. Belmont and Ryan were themselves delegates, the former from Chicago and the latter from Virginia. Being convinced of the intimate relationship between these financiers and Mr. Murphy, I became increasingly alarmed lest they should be able by the control of the New York delegation to make the nomination. The ninety delegates from New York were bound by the unit rule and Charles P. Murphy, the Tammany leader, had enough delegates to enable him to vote the entire delegation at his will.

When I returned to headquarters Wednesday night my brother, Charles W. Bryan, who had been closely associated with me in Nebraska, laid before me the information he had secured and suggested the resolution which I introduced the next night.

I took Wednesday night to think over the subject, and Thursday morning, before going to the committee room, dictated a resolution along the line he had suggested and left instructions that he call in as many of our friends as possible and get their opinion on it. The resolution, as I had prepared it, contained two paragraphs; the first was substantially the resolution as adopted by the convention; the second embodied the plan that was the outgrowth of my own experience in my three campaigns.

> "*Resolved*, That in this crisis in our party's career and in our country's history this convention sends greetings to the people of the United States, and assures them that the party of Jefferson and of Jackson is still the champion of popular government and equality before the law. As proof of our fidelity to the people, we hereby declare ourselves opposed to the nomination of any candidate for President who is the representative of or under obligation to J. Pierpont Morgan, Thomas F. Ryan, August Belmont, or any other member of the privilege-hunting and favor-seeking class.
>
> "*Be It Further Resolved*, That we demand the with-

174

drawal from this convention of any delegate or delegates constituting or representing the above-named interests."

I had never had a national committee entirely loyal. In the first campaign some of my committee did not attend the meetings. They were opposed to my election and yet retained their membership on the committee. The situation was so bad in 1900 that I thought that the committeemen who represented predatory wealth had little sense of political honor and should not remain on the committee when they were not in sympathy with the aims of the party. In the second paragraph, therefore, I included authority for the removal of unfriendly members of the committee.

When I returned to the hotel Thursday evening I found my brother very much discouraged, as he said that none of the men whom he consulted thought it wise to introduce the resolution, the criticism being directed mainly to the second paragraph which they thought might arouse opposition on the ground that it interfered with the rights of the states to select committeemen.

All my political friends appeared to be at the hall at the time and I suggested that I might strike out the second paragraph, whereupon he expressed a fear that the first paragraph alone might not draw the line with sufficient clearness.

He suggested a second sentence that dealt with Belmont and Ryan, who were delegates, in order to put teeth in it as he said. I framed the sentence, embodying his suggestion, and started for the convention not quite certain whether to chance the resolution or not. On the way to the convention I decided to introduce it. I felt some timidity about taking the responsibility without any encouragement from those who were nearest to me and most in sympathy with what I was trying to do, and reached the decision more from conviction that it was my duty to act than from reasons with which I could justify the act.

As I went to the platform some one pulled me aside to introduce me to Mrs. Taft. This little incident led me to change a sentence in the first paragraph referring to Mr. Taft's nomination in Chicago. I had included a few words not necessary to the resolution but comparing the attempt that was being made in our convention with the successful effort of Wall Street to control the Chicago nomination. When I found that Mrs. Taft was there I felt that it would be ungenerous to give her pain by such a reference to her husband and I therefore struck out the offensive words. President Taft afterwards learned of it, and in his characteristic way thanked me for the consideration shown his wife.

I do not recall just who took part in the debate on the Morgan-Belmont-Ryan resolution. Flood of Virginia led off with a denunciation of the resolution. He stood at one side of me a few feet away. I next met him after I became Secretary of State. He was chairman of the Foreign Relations Committee of the House and called at the Department on some matter in connection with his committee. I did not recognize him until he gave me his name and then I made him feel at home by remarking, "The last time I saw you I saw only your profile."

Honorable Cone Johnson of Texas made a speech in which he condensed a great deal in a few words. I became better acquainted with him afterwards when he came into the State Department as solicitor.

I went to Permanent Chairman Ollie James and asked for his recognition. It was necessary to suspend the rules and that required a two-thirds vote. I have many reasons to cherish the friendship of Ollie James, but he never did me a greater favor than when he recognized me on this occasion.

The resolution came as a surprise to my friends as well as to our opponents. "Dropping a bombshell into the crowd" is a phrase often used to describe the sudden precipitation of an issue. The phrase never more accurately described a situation. The explosion was immediate and vehement. The convention was in an uproar. Many were on their feet shouting denunciation. Old politicians accustomed to surprises in conventions were dazed. One member of the Congress rushed to the platform and, gesticulating violently, denounced me until he frothed at the mouth, and almost hysterical he was carried away by friends. I sat upon the platform where I could see the seething crowd. Urey Woodson, near me, was one of the Parker crowd. He was my friend in the earlier campaigns, but went off with Wall Street element in 1904 and had become prominent among the reactionaries. His apostasy had not led to any rupture in our relationship, although we understood that we were no longer co-workers. He had a box near me and was watching the proceedings as much mystified as his associates on the floor of the convention. I was near enough to him to remark, calling him by his first name, "When your machine ran over me it moved so slowly that I was able to inspect the works from the underside and I am now telling the convention what I saw."

My aim was to get a roll call, because I felt that whichever way the convention voted it would be difficult to nominate a man who had the support of the New York delegation. If they passed the resolution it excluded anyone who was the representative of Morgan, Belmont, or Ryan or under their influence; if they voted it down, the rebuke from the country would make it impossible for New York to select a candidate.

Just before the roll was called I announced that I would strike out the second paragraph of the resolution. I do not know how many in the convention understood what I had done; they were too excited to distinguish between the two paragraphs. When the roll was called the tumult reached its height. A state would be called; its chairman would announce its full vote, "aye." Then half the delegation would jump to their feet and demand a poll, shaking their fists and shouting in violent language. I do not think there were ever before so many people in one hall, wildly excited and swearing at one another without someone being hurt. I heard afterwards of delegates who were loudly expressing the hope that somebody would take me out and hang me. One delegate, whom I afterward aided to a high position, stated that he would give twenty-five thousand dollars to anybody who would kill me. I have no thought that these men who poured out their threats would have carried them out. I only mention them to show the state of super-excitement.

Polls were taken in nearly all the delegations and some of them changed from a solid vote against the resolution to a solid vote in favor of it. As the roll call proceeded the opposition became frantic and delegates piled over each other to vote for the resolution, with the result that it finally carried by a vote of about 4½ to 1. Even New York voted for the resolution.

Some one reported to me afterwards that Murphy turned to Belmont and said, "August, listen and hear yourself vote yourself out of the convention." Virginia voted 23½ votes for the resolution. It was a great victory for progressive Democracy. Nearly all the Wilson delegates voted for the resolution and nearly all of the Clark delegates also, although many of the Clark leaders voted "no" and in so doing greatly lessened the political chances of their candidate. Clark's leaders are more responsible for his defeat than Clark himself, or would have been if it were possible for a candidate for President to excuse himself for allowing his managers to do what he would not do himself.

The effect of the Morgan-Belmont-Ryan resolution can hardly be overestimated. One of the London papers compared it with St. George slaying the dragon. One of the Baltimore papers pictured it in a cartoon as burning the word "progressive" into the hide of the Democratic donkey. The passage of the resolution stirred the enthusiasm of the progressive Democrats and gave a new impetus to the shower of telegrams from the rank and file of the party. Having, as I thought, insured the convention against the nomination of anyone by Wall Street influence, I retired from the convention, while the delegates proceeded to place candidates in nomination.

Balloting began on Friday. Up to this time I had not taken my seat with my delegation, although I had appeared twice on the platform—Tuesday, when I made my speech against Parker, and Thursday night, when I introduced the Morgan-Belmont-Ryan resolution. My reason for absenting myself was that I did not want to risk attracting attention, having in mind the oft-repeated charge of unfriendly papers that I wanted to stampede the convention in my own favor. My intention was to keep out of the hall until the nomination was made and then appear at a time when I could make a speech in support of the candidate, whoever he might be.

On Friday night I was in the room of the Resolutions Committee when a great demonstration broke out in the convention hall. After waiting a while for it to subside, I went to the hall to inquire the cause. I found the convention in an uproar—the New York delegation had gone over to Clark on the fifth ballot. New York had started out voting for Harmon, thus verifying my predictions in regard to Wall Street's choice. I knew that New York's second choice was Underwood, but the throwing of the vote to Clark was by many believed to be evidence of an understanding between the Clark leaders and the New York delegation. I never heard anything other than circumstantial evidence to support this charge and never made it myself.

I am quite sure that Mr. Clark's leaders had calculated on using the New York delegation to give him a majority vote in the convention and that they then expected to claim his nomination on the ground that he had a majority. One of his leaders had asked me while I was at the Chicago Convention whether I thought any candidate receiving a majority could be prevented from securing two thirds. I answered that I thought there was only one instance when the two thirds rule had ever prevented a majority candidate from receiving the nomination.

I expected the nomination of a majority candidate, not only because precedent favored it but I had never taken kindly to the two thirds rule. I believe that the rule should be changed so as to allow a majority to nominate, and have advocated the change, but I have coupled with it the abolishment of the unit rule, which gives the big states an unfair advantage in the convention. New York, for instance, with a delegation of ninety, can, under the unit rule, exercise a tremendous influence and do so in spite of the protests of nearly half the delegation. If those in control have forty-six delegates of the ninety with them, they can use the other forty-four to carry out their purposes in spite of any protest that the forty-four can make. It was because the New York delegation, under the control of Mr. Murphy, was used to give Mr. Clark a majority delegation that I was not willing to help to swell the vote to two thirds. I felt that during the campaign the party would be unable to deny that Wall Street had exercised a deciding influence in the naming of our candidate. I then entered the fight to prevent not Mr. Clark's nomination only but the nomination of any person by the New York delegation.

While the demonstration was still in progress I took my seat with the Nebraska delegation and from that time until the convention adjourned never left the hall during the sessions of the convention. One of the assistants of the sergeant at arms who was stationed in our part of the hall supplied me with water, keeping a large bottle under the platform, while my brother supplied me with sandwiches. My one thought was to save the Democratic Party from defeat at the polls. I believed then, and have believed ever since, that if the nomination of our candidate was brought about in such a way that the country would regard it as a triumph for Wall Street, he would be defeated no matter who he was.

Ex-President Roosevelt, defeated at Chicago, had not yet decided whether he would enter the field. I felt sure that he would become a candidate if he could charge that Wall Street had nominated both candidates and make his appeal to the progressives of both parties and I felt sure that in such a campaign he would have been successful. I think the result proved this to be true. Mr. Roosevelt took from the Republican Party more than half its vote, polling 4,119,582 votes as against 3,485,082 votes for Mr. Taft. Mr. Taft carried but two states in the electoral college, Utah and Vermont.

As the Democratic Party was more progressive than the Republican Party, what chances would we have had to win with any candidate not free from Wall Street domination? He would have been defeated if he had had to carry in the campaign the handicap of having secured his nomination by the aid of the New York delegation dominated by one man, Charles Murphy, who had back of him the influence of the financiers of Wall Street.

My interest was not in any candidate, but in the party. I was under no personal obligation to either of the candidates. Neither one had exerted himself in my behalf in the primary at which I was chosen delegate. Mr. Wilson had never supported me in my campaigns and Mr. Clark's support, while always given to me, was given to me as thousands of Democrats give their support. Being a candidate for Congress in each of my campaigns, he could not have opposed me without injury to himself, even if he had desired to do so. While, of course, his support was not perfunctory, because he believed in the things for which I stood, still it was never given to me at a sacrifice, and I had done fully as much for him as he ever had done for me. But I digress.

The vote of our delegation was cast solidly for Clark for thirteen ballots. A number of our delegates wanted to leave him as soon as New York went to his support, but I insisted that we should continue to support him, as I expected that New York would throw its vote to Underwood and thus leave Clark to secure his nomination—if he secured it—from the progressive delegates of the convention.

I felt sure from what I had heard that New York really preferred Underwood and would leave Clark at any time its influence could aid Underwood. After the thirteenth ballot the convention adjourned until Saturday morning. Realizing that to keep the promise I had made to the Nebraska Democracy when a candidate for delegate, namely, that I would have no part in turning over the party to Wall Street, and realizing that to carry out this promise it might become necessary to change from Clark* at any moment, I prepared a written statement to be read to the convention when I changed my vote, hoping all the time that it would not be necessary.

This statement was prepared before the convention opened on Saturday morning. I had kept it in my pocket ready for use and, as a further precaution, asked Chairman James to recognize me if I asked for recognition during roll call.

When I conferred with the delegates I found a number of them in rebellion against Clark. They were afraid to risk voting for him any longer. I still pleaded with them, but when the roll was called, half or a little more voted for Wilson, but I still cast my ballot for Clark. Senator

---

* Mr. Bryan's change from Clark to Wilson was soon after endorsed by the Nebraska State Democratic Convention, showing that he was right in his interpretation of the spirit of the instructions from his constituents.

Hitchcock, who advocated instructions for Harmon in the Nebraska primary, came to me and said he would have to demand a poll of the delegation. I replied that in case a poll was taken I would take the platform and explain my vote. I was willing to continue voting for Clark if the delegation was not polled, but expecting at any time that I might be compelled to change my vote, I was not willing to announce a vote for him that I might have to take back at any time. I decided, therefore, to make the change at that time if the poll was taken. Senator Hitchcock insisted upon the poll and when my name was called I went to the platform and read the explanation of the change which I had prepared. It will be found in the Appendix.

As might have been expected, this change caused a commotion in the convention. The Clark delegates, with four ex-governors among them, sat just in front of the platform. None of them questioned me, but two other delegates, one from Mississippi and one from West Virginia, did. One asked whether I intended to support the candidate. I answered that that was a hypothetical question and that such a question was never favored in a court of law because it was difficult to put into the question all the conditions that might enter into the decision, but that I would answer his question by saying that I expected to support the nominee, whoever he was. Another asked how I could support the candidate if I was opposed to his nomination. I answered that the questioner, being a lawyer, ought to know that an attorney could defend his client after the crime was committed, but that he was not allowed to join the client in committing the crime.

Early in the afternoon Senator Stone arose in his place in the Missouri delegation. Suspecting that he intended to make some motion relating to the two thirds rule, I immediately went to the front of the platform (our delegation, while on the front row, was some distance to the left of the speaker) in order to be ready to make an objec-

183

tion. He asked unanimous consent to move to suspend the rules and declare Mr. Clark the nominee of the convention, basing his argument on the fact that he had received a majority of the votes cast. Some one, I think from New Jersey, objected and the roll call proceeded.

A little later in the afternoon some of the supporters of Mr. Clark brought into the convention a banner on which was reproduced a sentence that I had used in eulogizing Mr. Clark when I spoke in his district in 1910. This caused an uproar as it was carried through the aisles. It was finally brought over to our delegation and caused such a burst of feeling from some of our delegates that I feared trouble might be precipitated. I immediately returned to the platform with the intention of explaining the time and the conditions under which the words were spoken and the reasons why I did not feel that an opinion expressed then required me to support Mr. Clark under the circumstances that had developed. While Speaker James was trying to secure order I stepped down from the platform to the Missouri delegates to inquire of its leaders whether the men carrying the banner were acting under their instructions. They assured me that they were not responsible for it. Finally Chairman James, acting wisely, I think, refused to recognize me, at the same time, as I recall it, directing that the banner be removed from the hall.

This was one of the exciting moments of the convention, because it stirred up much feeling. I think in the excitement blows were exchanged in two or three instances. I know that many of my friends feared for my personal safety. The Texas delegation of forty was, I afterwards learned, ready to lend assistance in case any attack was made upon me. It was the only time in my life when I was in danger of physical harm and, therefore, the only time when my physical courage was tested, if test it could be called. The thought of danger did not occur to me as I went among those who were highly excited.

184

When Saturday night came the issue was still undecided. Wilson had gained enough to make Clark's nomination improbable and Clark still held enough to make the selection of Wilson uncertain.

From the time the convention met there were many delegates who favored my nomination, some under instructions for Clark and some under instructions for Wilson. I had aided in the election of many of these delegates, the anti-Harmon delegates from Ohio being under special obligation for the trip that I made through that state. One of the Ohio delegates voted for me until I asked him to refrain, pointing out that it was unfair to me to make it seem that I had only one friend in the convention when others were restrained from voting for me out of regard for my wishes. When the convention seemed to be settling down into a deadlock there were many who urged my nomination as a solution of the situation. But I felt that it was not proper for me to consider the question as long as there was any chance for any of the candidates who had been encouraged to enter by my announcement that I would not be a candidate, and I felt, too, that the action I had been compelled to take out of a sense of duty to the party had alienated some of those whose support was necessary to an election. I told all who inquired that nothing but a situation which made the whole convention regard my nomination as necessary justified my considering the nomination and that there had been no time when circumstances presented such a situation or promised it.

While hostilities were suspended during the Sabbath the messages continued to pour in from over the country and these at last crushed the opposition to Wilson and compelled his nomination.

When the convention entered upon the nomination of candidates for Vice-President a delegate from the District of Columbia presented my name for Vice-President. I had not been consulted about the matter and am not sure that the nomination was made in good faith. I did not wait to inquire or to ascertain the sentiment of the delegates. I declined to be considered, embodying my reasons in a brief speech which will be found in the Appendix. When the names were being presented I made speeches seconding the nomination of two western men, Burke of North Dakota and Chamberlain of Oregon. I had no personal objection to Governor Marshall, but his support of Judge Parker for temporary chairman, his opposition to the initiative and referendum, and his attitude toward prohibition as shown in the campaign of 1908 seemed to me to raise issues that might endanger success of the party. While his views on the initiative and referendum and prohibition had not altered, these questions did not come before him during his term as Vice-President and I have admired the manner in which he presented the Democratic side of most of the big questions at issue. He made a very popular Vice-President.

CHAPTER XI

The Grape Juice Incident

I HAVE mentioned my aversion to swearing as due to my mother's teachings, my father concurring; and of my aversion to gambling taught by my father, my mother concurring. I am indebted to both for a third moral lesson in which they joined so heartily that I am not able to emphasize the influence of either over the influence of the other. They both abstained from the use of intoxicating liquor and impressed upon me at a very early age the evils that follow from its use. Even before I had any clear understanding of the temperance question I began signing the pledge. I have no way of knowing at what age I first signed—my recollection does not run back so far— I only know that I have been signing since I can remember. I met, a few years ago, a temperance lecturer who told me that I was among the signers at his meeting when he spoke there in 1872; I was then twelve, but it had by that time become a habit with me. The formative influence of these early habits is well illustrated in this case.

My wife was brought up in the same way and the antipathy toward the use of liquor as a beverage at any time and in any form was so great that she joined me in excluding it from public dinners when I was Secretary of State as we had excluded it from our table in private life. It may be better to speak of the "Grape Juice Dinner" here than to refer to it later in recording my experiences in that office.

When President-elect Wilson invited me to Trenton I surmised the purpose of the invitation was to invite me to become a member of his Cabinet and I discussed with my wife the matter of serving liquors before meeting with the President. We were not willing to violate our custom in this respect and to set such an example to others, and it was therefore understood that I should bring the matter to the attention of the President at the time in order that there might be no criticism later. After going over other matters connected with the office, I told him that there was one thing about which I felt concerned and that was whether he would regard the exclusion of intoxicating liquors from our table as an insurmountable objection to my assuming the duties of the office. He promptly responded that it was a matter upon which we could feel perfectly free to follow our own wishes. I said that we never had served it and as a matter of conscience did not wish to. The matter was never referred to again by the President in conversation with me.

Soon after I became Secretary of State we had occasion to entertain Ambassador Bryce at luncheon. In order to explain the absence of wine from the table I told him that Mrs. Bryan and I were departing from the official custom in this respect and that he was our first guest. He answered very cheerfully that he was a good person to begin on, as he did not use intoxicating liquors himself. He was preparing to leave Washington and not long after this we gave him a farewell luncheon to which all of the ambassadors were invited. Several Washington ladies were invited as luncheon companions for the ambassadors whose wives were not in the city. When Mrs. Bryan arranged the table she had a glass for grape juice, not that we thought of drawing a contrast between wine and grape juice, but because the glasses for plain and mineral water looked a little lonesome. At her suggestion, I explained to the guests very briefly the reason for our departure from the official custom, and stated that we hoped that our hospitality would be so cordial that the guests would not miss the wine. It was rather an embarrassing occasion to us, because we had no desire to emphasize our views on this subject and I felt quite relieved when the explanation was finished. To my surprise, the guests applauded very heartily and we had a delightful time together. I did not mention the incident to the newspapers and it was some days before anything was said about it. When the facts were published, I was called upon for a statement, and the statement gradually found its way throughout the world.

The foreign comments were numerous and for the most part unfriendly. Some friend who had gathered a collection of these comments sent me his file. About the only friendly reference among them was from a Canadian paper which remarked that, from the criticisms made by the newspapers on the absence of wine from our table, one might suppose that the luncheon had been a bartenders' reunion.

A few months afterward when a Republican ambassador was closing up his accounts at the department before retiring from the office, he called upon me and with evident emotion thanked me for my action at the luncheon, especially referring to the harm done young men by the bad example set by the use of liquors by men in high official position.

Within two years the war had aroused so much interest in the liquor question in foreign nations that a number of the crowned heads of Europe were lining up against intoxicating drinks. Then I received my reward. The papers began to cartoon me as driving a water wagon with kings crowding each other for a seat on the vehicle.

CHAPTER XII

THE CHILDREN

WE have been fortunate in our children and grand-children. The former are three in number, Ruth Baird, now Mrs. Reginald Owen, born October 2, 1885; William Jennings Bryan, Jr., born June 24, 1889; and Grace Dexter, now Mrs. Richard L. Hargreaves, born February 17, 1891.

Ruth came within a day of celebrating our first wedding anniversary. She was a precocious child and her parents and grandparents were kept busy expressing surprise at evidences of her early intelligence.

What a marvel a child is! It comes into the world with such perfection displayed in its mechanism, is so helpless, and yet so full of possibilities for good or for evil. It gives to one woman a sweet consciousness of motherhood and to one man a sense of responsibility otherwise never known before. Before its tiny hands can lift a featherweight, it has drawn two hearts closer together; its innocent prattle echoes through two lives and its influence upon its parents is almost as moulding as their influence upon it.

I think my wife never before looked so sweet as she did when she brought Ruth downstairs for the first time. The wrapper which she wore that day was long and flowing and she made me think of a Madonna. In fact, seeing a copy of Bodenhausen's painting of the Madonna a few weeks afterwards in an art gallery in Kansas City—the Madonna arrayed in a gown of almost the same tint as the gown my wife had worn—so impressed me by the resemblance that I took the picture home with me. It hung upon our walls until our son was married and desired to have it for his own home.

One of the distinct recollections of Ruth's babyhood was

190

the time when she was old enough to distinguish the different members of the family. Mrs. Bryan's father and I would often be sitting near the mother when the baby was being washed and dressed. When her night garments were removed she would hand them sometimes to the father and sometimes to the grandfather. It was an anxious moment when we were in suspense while she decided to which she would hand the garment. She was quite impartial, bestowing the favor on first one, then the other as if she thought favoritism to one might hurt the feelings of the other.

Ruth, when about three years old, delivered a prayer which we have always remembered as illustrating at that early age a keen sense of discrimination, as well as indicating a positive opinion. It was in the fall of 1888 and I was away from home campaigning. When it came time to go to bed she was irritated about some happening of the day and refused to say her usual prayer, which began, "Now I lay me down to sleep," and ended with, "God bless Papa, Mamma, Grandma, Grandpa, and all of Grandma Bryan's folks, Amen." Her mother tried persuasion along several lines, but in vain. Finally, thinking to appeal to her affections, she said, "Poor Papa is away on the train and might get hurt and his little girl will not say any prayer for him." This touched Ruth's heart. She went over to the bed, knelt down and said, "Dear Lord, take care of Papa—not Mamma nor Grandma nor anybody else, just Papa. Amen." It reminded me of Lincoln's letter to Horace Greeley in which he so specifically expressed his intentions and carefully negatived everything else.

Ruth early gave evidence of literary ability. She wrote stories which showed imagination. One day when eight or nine years old she came to her mother and asked whether it would be better to have the hero save the heroine from a fire or from drowning. Mrs. Bryan expressed a preference for a rescue from fire. In a little while Ruth had her story completed with a thrilling description of the rescue of a girl from a burning building.

It was about this time that she revealed her ambition and, at the same time, her doubts as to whether she would realize it. She was confined to her bed by an attack of measles. One morning when I took her breakfast to her room and sat by her while she ate it, I said, "Ruth, what would you like to do when you are grown?" She answered spiritedly, "I would like to write stories and books"—and then she added in a melancholy tone, "But I expect I'll get married and raise a family, like Mamma and Mrs. Schwind."

It was during this period, also, that she returned from the Sunday school one day very much disgusted and threatened not to go any more, giving as her excuse, "They don't teach righteousness; they just teach geography."

I may add here that Ruth always showed a discretion rather unusual for her years. In the campaign of 1896 when she was eleven she was, of course, often questioned by strangers. One day a man stopped her in the street and asked her whether she thought her father would be elected. She replied, "I think he will get a good many votes on D Street" (the street on which we lived), "but I do not know about the rest of the country."

After nine years in the Nebraska public school, two years at Monticello Seminary (Illinois), and two years in the State University of Nebraska, came Ruth's marriage the day following her eighteenth birthday anniversary, October 3, 1903. She had a son and a daughter by this first marriage.

In the autumn of 1907 she made her first venture on the lecture platform, filling engagements for the Extension Department of the State University of Nebraska and under other auspices.

Her second marriage occurred on the third of May, 1910. Reginald Altham Owen was a lieutenant in the Royal Engineers of the British Army at the time of their marriage.

IN THE GARDEN OF MAJOR AND MRS. OWEN

Photo. Underwood & Underwood

Left to right: Mrs. William P. Meeker; Major Reginald Owen, Mr. Bryan's son-in-law; Baby Helen Rudd Owen; Mrs. W. J. Bryan; Master Bryan Owen; Mrs. Reginald Owen, daughter of Mr. and Mrs. Bryan; William Jennings Bryan, and the ever-present "Trowser."

He served with distinction in the World War, throughout the entire Dardanelles Campaign and the three years of the Egypt and Palestine campaign. His health was so seriously impaired by his war service that he was retired from the service in 1924 after prolonged sick leave.

Major and Mrs. Owen's home since the conclusion of the war has been in Miami, Florida.

Ruth has during the past five years extended her lecture tours and achieved considerable success to which she has added some prominence in literary work. Her daughter Ruth, who was born September 28, 1904, grew from a bright child to a very attractive young woman. She was married June 20, 1923, to William Painter Meeker, of Baltimore, Maryland, and Miami, Florida, only son of our nearest neighbors in Miami. Their daughter Ruth, born June 30, 1924, is our only and much beloved great-grand-child.

Mrs. Owen's son, John Baird Bryan, was born November 16, 1905. He was a most interesting child and has developed talent for art and poetry, which he is disposed to cultivate. The two younger children of Major and Mrs. Owen are not yet old enough to give indication of their natural bent. Reginald Bryan, who was born in London April 14, 1913, gives evidence of a strong will, a quality of great value when well directed. Helen Rudd, born August 3, 1920, is a very precocious child with unusual poise and self-reliance.

William, our only son, was born on June 24, 1889. He was what is called "a regular fellow." He was one hundred per cent boy—never bad, but always mischievous. He could get into dirt more quickly after he was sent out washed and cleanly dressed, and into more different kinds of dirt than any boy I have ever known. This may be because I was never as well acquainted with another boy.

When Ruth was a baby she was a little thin—at least, not fat. William was quite a fat baby. Mrs. Bryan says that when Ruth was a child and rather thin I expressed a preference for thin children; but that when William came I thought he was just fat enough to look well.

Mrs. Bryan took care of the children herself. As the care of the children increased she turned over more of the domestic work to others in order that she might have entire charge of the children. She put them to bed and read to them until they went to sleep. Often after she had cleansed William of the dirt stains of the day and read him to sleep, she would lead me to the room that I might admire our young hopeful, exclaiming as she looked upon him with loving eyes, "Isn't he sweet when he is asleep?"

How a boy ever lives through the accidents of childhood is a mystery. William fell down the stairway and was insensible for several hours, but he was soon over it and ready to take another risk. One day his mother was badly frightened when she looked out and saw him working his way along the telephone wires some distance from the house. When we took him out with us on visits to friends, the conversation was often interrupted by a cry of alarm, some member of the family finding William up on the roof or in some other place of danger.

He had reached the age of eleven by the time of the second campaign in 1900. By that time he had become an excellent swimmer. I might add that Mrs. Bryan had taken upon herself the task of teaching all the children how to swim. Like all swimmers, he was fond of diving. During a few days' stay in Chicago the newspaper men, who take such an interest in every member of the family of the candidate, discovered his fondness for the water and gave a good deal of attention to his accomplishments, not diminishing in the least the sensational features. At one time he was described as hanging out of an upper window of a tall building and being rescued by General Wheeler.

A few years ago I discovered a photograph of William at this busy age. I had it framed and put on his mother's desk as a reminder of the anxiety she cheerfully endured during the superactive years of William's youth.

William was nearly seven at the time of the death of Mrs. Bryan's mother. His affection manifested itself in a bit of consolation that we have often looked back to with amusement. He went up to his mother when she was weeping and, putting his arms around her neck, said, "Mamma, when you feel sad, just think of me."

At another time when he was just recovering from a punishment for some misdemeanor, he sobbed out a warning to his mother, "If I died in the night, you would not feel so gay."

Like Ruth, he was studious enough to pass his examinations, but was not at the head of the class. I had hoped that he would early manifest an interest in public speaking as I had, but instead of showing an unusual interest in it, he manifested an aversion to speaking. Mrs. Bryan went over one day to the school to hear him speak a piece. When the teacher called on him to do his part, he sank down into his chair and clutched its arms. After his mother had waited for a few moments for her son to immortalize himself as a speaker, the teacher gave up in despair and said, "William will speak *next* Friday."

I was somewhat surprised, therefore, when my wife read me a letter from the superintendent of Culver Military School which he was attending, stating that William was studying public speaking. A few months afterwards, I met the great evangelist, Rev. J. Wilbur Chapman, and he told me that his son and mine were in the same elocution class; adding that he had promised his boy fifty dollars if he would surpass William in speaking. His boy replied that that was impossible, that not one of the boys could do better. This was the beginning of his efforts to express himself "on his feet." I found afterwards as I read his speeches and heard them that he had an analytical mind, logical arrangement of his arguments, persuasive delivery, and a sense of humor that enabled him to enliven his addresses.

Owing to the fact that his betrothed, Miss Helen Berger, with whom he fell in love when he was quite young and to whom he had been engaged for some years, found it necessary on account of her health to reside in Arizona, he was married before he finished school and continued his studies at the University of Arizona at Tucson, where he graduated. He afterwards became regent of the University by appointment by Governor Hunt and reappointed by Governor Campbell.

I was very much pleased to learn that he was made director of the Y.M.C.A. and a member of the Democratic Committee of Tucson the same week. I accepted it as an indication that he was interested in the two lines of work, religion and politics, which not only do not conflict but are entirely consistent.

After graduating he studied law at Georgetown Law School. He was elected president of his class, but in a few months he was compelled to return to Arizona on account of his wife's health and he resumed his law study there. After his admission to the bar he became assistant to the United States Attorney under United States Attorney John Flynn.

William was married in June 24, 1909, to Helen Virginia Berger, of Milwaukee, Wisconsin. They have three children —all daughters: Mary Scholes, born April 7, 1910, Helen Virginia, born August 13, 1911, and Elizabeth Baird, born December 31, 1914. They are as charming a trio as one could find, but three distinct types.

In 1920 William and his family removed to Los Angeles, California, which is their present residence.

[PUBLISHERS' NOTE. In publishing these unfinished Memoirs of Mr. Bryan, we are sure that no omission would

WILLIAM JENNINGS BRYAN, JR., AND FAMILY
Left to right: Helen, William Jennings Bryan, Jr., Mary, "Betty," and Mrs. Bryan.

ANOTHER FAMILY GROUP
The younger daughter of Mr. and Mrs. Bryan, Mrs. Richard L. Hargreaves, with her children, Bryan, Margaret, and Evelyn Mary Hargreaves.

THE CHILDREN

fill him with more regret than his failure to complete the chapter which tells of his children.

He was called from this task before he had written of his younger and much loved daughter Grace Dexter (Mrs. Richard L. Hargreaves of Berkeley Hills, California).

Herself born in the midst of a political campaign, Mrs. Hargreaves has always been deeply interested in politics. As a child she took part in all the children's parades with great zest and in later years followed her father's political work with keen interest and sympathy.

During Mr. Bryan's second term in Congress she was critically ill with pneumonia, which left her in a very weakened condition. She became a great anxiety to her parents, and several years of special care and sojourn in warm climates was required to restore her to strength.

She was educated at home by a governess and afterwards in the Lincoln, Nebraska, schools, and at Hollins Institute (Virginia).

She was married in June 7, 1911, to Richard Lewis Hargreaves, of Lincoln, Nebraska, and to them three children have been born: Margaret, born March 3, 1914; Bryan, born September 7, 1915; and Evelyn Mary, born October 16, 1920, the latter being the tenth and youngest of Mr. Bryan's grandchildren.]

CHAPTER XIII

FRIENDSHIPS

SO much is flippantly told about the fair-weather friends in politics who flock about the successful candidate and then desert him in times of trial, that I shall take this opportunity to record a few instances of heroes who came under my personal observation. I omit the names out of consideration for those who had been personally connected with the incidents and who may not regard them in the same spirit in which I regard them.

First I mention a Congressman and one of the Ways and Means Committee. He had retired from Congress in 1896 and resumed charge of a large mercantile business in the town in which he resided. He was an advocate of bimetallism when in Congress and took a large interest in my first Presidential campaign. He was one of the well-to-do men of his city and a director in the bank in which he kept his store account. Like most merchants, he enjoyed a credit in the bank and borrowed money from time to time to discount his bills.

In the midst of the campaign he was called before the directors of his own bank and informed that his interest in me was injuring the bank and then he was told that his notes could not be carried any longer if he continued to support my candidacy. He was put to a test to which I have never been subjected. There has never been a time since I was grown when my bread and butter depended upon the will or favor of any other person, and therefore never a time when I incurred any financial risk in exercising political independence. It was not so with the friend of whom I am speaking. He knew that he could not at that time secure loans elsewhere if the bank of which he was a director refused to accommodate him, but he did not hesitate for a moment.

He replied, "Gentlemen, you can bankrupt me, but you cannot take from me my right to vote as I please."

Of course, the directors dared not carry out their threat, but their bluff gave one friend a chance to show the mettle that was in him. Until he was called to his reward, I counted him as one of the inner circle of my friends.

Another illustration is taken from among my New York friends. I appreciate them the more because the coercion was there at its maximum and the support to be found in companionship at its minimum. As far back as 1893, the campaign of 1896 cast its shadow before it. I spoke at Cooper Union in the fall of that year, my subject being the unconditional repeal of the Sherman Law then before Congress. The hall was crowded and I learned a few days afterward the following incident relating to a man then and since prominent in the business world.

Not being able to find a seat, he was standing in the aisle near the door when an acquaintance on the platform spied him and invited him to a seat. A place on the platform did not necessarily indicate sympathy with the speaker, but one of the papers next morning gave a list of those on the platform and included the gentleman of whom I am speaking. I was about to say friend, but at the time of the incident I was not personally acquainted with him.

Upon reading the list this gentleman's banker sent for him and called his attention to the fact that he had been mentioned among those who sat on the platform. He explained the situation, assuring the banker that he was not there by pre-arrangement or for the purpose of being counted among those specially interested, but the explanation did not satisfy the banker and he notified this gentleman that they could not carry loans for those who gave the weight of their names to so disreputable a cause and insisted that he immediately pay a note of $25,000 which the bank held against him. Fortunately, he was able to do so without embarrassment and immediately complied with the request.

WILLIAM JENNINGS BRYAN

It is needless to say that the demand made a deep impression upon him and that that impression was not favorable to the bankers' side of the question. During the campaign of 1896 he took a prominent part, and Mrs. Bryan and I had the pleasure of being guests later in his beautiful home on the Hudson. From that time to this his sympathies have been with the masses on all the economic questions that have arisen.

A Massachusetts friend reported to me an experience through which he passed in the campaign of 1896. He was engaged in manufacturing upon a considerable scale and carried a credit of some $20,000 or more at his local bank. In the campaign of 1896 he was a Democrat and outspoken though not active in the support of the ticket. His banker sent for him and asked him whether he was supporting my candidacy. He answered that he expected to vote for me, but was not active beyond that. The banker informed him that they could not lend financial aid to those who were opposing the bank's policy and asked him to take up his notes. This he did and then went out and spoke for me during the rest of the campaign. He, too, has ever since that time continued his political activity.

A New York lawyer who had been a delegate to the Chicago Convention returned to the metropolis and entered the campaign. He was one of the delegates who had refused to join the New York financiers in support of the gold ticket. He was attorney for a bank, and the bank on reading of his attitude sent for him, withdrew all its cases from him and asked him to change his deposit to another bank. He complied with the request, opened his account in a bank not so illiberal in its politics and took an active part in the campaign until it closed.

This is the only case I know of where a bank compelled a depositor to withdraw his account. After the election was over the bank sent for the attorney, asked that the unpleasantness be forgotten and reëmployed him. In New Jersey

200

he afterward became a member of Congress and became quite conspicuous in public life.

I have a very delightful recollection of a conductor on one of the railroads running into Lincoln. "Pat" was the name by which he was known and it was spoken with affection by the multitude who knew him as a man of character—the kind of man who attaches his friends to him by hooks of steel. I became acquainted with Pat in my early trips through the first district even before I became a candidate for Congress. I had no more ardent supporter than he in my races for Congress and for the Senate.

In 1896, when so much pressure was brought by corporations upon their employees, Pat was called into the office and informed that the railroad was strongly in favor of Mr. McKinley's election and that they would expect him to give the benefit of his influence.

Did they intimidate him? Not for a moment. He replied: "Your salary pays for my services as conductor, but it does not include my citizenship. That is my own. I vote as I please." Pat continued to be a Democrat and he also continued to be a conductor.

In my own city one of the banks required a business man to agree to support the Republican candidate in order to continue a loan at the bank. He told of the instance himself. Upon my return from a trip around the world a dinner was given me. This merchant, whom we had known from the time I moved to Lincoln, asked whether he could secure a ticket, adding: "I have voted for Mr. Bryan at every election except one. I voted for him for Congress twice and for the Senate and would have voted for him in 1896 but for the fact that I owed a large amount to the —— bank. Just before the election Mr. ——, the president of the bank, refused to extend the loan unless I would agree to vote for McKinley. It would have meant bankruptcy if I had refused and so I promised to vote for McKinley and, having promised, I did so, but by 1900 I had so far reduced my indebtedness that I was independent and I voted for Mr. Bryan that year."

Shortly after the election I met on the train Mr. Yost, an Omaha business man who was president of the Lincoln Telephone Company. Introducing the subject himself, he said, "I have a friend of yours working for me at Lincoln."

Guessing whom he had in mind, I said, "Do you mean Mr. ——?"

"Yes," he replied. "I went down to Lincoln just before the election and told him that we were very much interested in Mr. McKinley's election and hoped he would do what he could to help him. He said, 'Mr. Yost, your company has been very good to me and I do not want to do anything that would injure it. If you think that my support of Mr. Bryan will hurt your company, I will resign.' After hearing his answer, what do you think I told him?"

"What?" I asked.

"I told him that if he did not vote for you we would discharge him."

I have often recalled this incident because it illustrates an important truth, namely, that a frank and firm defense of one's political rights is much better at all times than an evasion of the subject or the practice of deception.

In recording my political experiences I dwell with greatest pleasure upon the friendships formed in early years. I was in no position to reward men for what they did for me, so that their acts of kindness were wholly unselfish and were prompted by a devotion which I have come to regard as the most beautiful thing in American politics. We are too prone to explain service as selfish and kind acts as prompted by a hope of reward. The prevailing opinion of political support has been put into poetry in the description of those who "crook the pregnant hinges of the knee, where thrift may follow fawning." This may be an accurate description of some self-seeking politicians, but it is a slander upon the virtuous masses to suggest that what they do is done from other than the noblest spirit.

When George Hopkins, of Nemaha County, Nebraska, wins a place in my memory by taking me in a sulky some thirteen miles from Peru to Auburn after a night meeting and then appears regularly at every meeting held in this county for a quarter of a century and gives weeks of time to campaigning for me no matter to what office I aspire, it can only be accounted for by similarity of political ideals which made him feel that my campaigns were really his campaigns also.

When Will Glenn, of Knox County, takes me in a buggy fifty miles in a single day and night and puts me on a departing train a little before daybreak, it is proof of his heart interest in the issue at stake.

When a farmer in the center of the state gets out of bed in the middle of the night when we have lost our way, rides ten miles before us, and then when we come in sight of the lights of our destination, turns back, refusing compensation with the remark, spoken in a tone that indicated that even the offer hurt his feelings: "Do you think I would do this for money? I am a Bryan man," one catches something of the sentiment upon which campaigns are built and can better understand how it is possible for millions of people to coöperate without organization but actuated by a common impulse.

These incidents could be continued indefinitely; there has never been a time when in Nebraska or somewhere else in the United States I have not had occasion to be proud of the average man and his influence in politics. The names of the humble heroes in political battles of the United States is legion. Their names are unrecorded, but those whom they so faithfully support receive the glory. I cannot forget these soldiers upon whom the brunt of the battle falls.

As I look back over the years I see the face of one of the most loyal friends that any political leader ever had. His name was John Ahern, a big, brawny Irishman. He was nearly, if not quite, six feet four inches in height and broad in proportion. His face was round and no beard concealed the friendliness that beamed from every feature. I met him in 1888 when I made my first trip to Richardson County, Nebraska. He lived some twenty miles from Fall City, the county seat. Partly because his size made him a conspicious figure in the crowd and partly because of the devotion which he manifested, I came to look for him in the crowd whenever I spoke in his county. And I do not recall a meeting that he did not attend.

One night I went home with him and stayed all night. It is a rare treat to drop in upon one of these country friends, a treat in which I indulge myself whenever opportunity offers, but the opportunities have been all too few. Time and again at Chautauquas as I have looked into the faces of the old men for whom the front seats are generally reserved, I have picked out one of these American sovereigns, a well-informed voter whom an army could not terrorize and whom the federal treasury could not buy, and regretted that on account of the briefness of my stay I could not step up to him and say, "May I go and spend the night with you?" These are the common people, the people to whom the Bible pays the highest compliment it ever pays to any class when it says that the common people heard Christ gladly. It is by communion with such as these that one is assured of the impregnable strength of the nation and it is from such as these that one can learn the drift of the public sentiment and best predict with certainty the things to be.

But to return to Ahern. In the fall of 1894, when I was a candidate for the United States Senate, I made my usual trip to Richardson County and spoke to a great meeting in Fall City. When the crowd had dispersed Uncle John, as he was familiarly called, came up to encourage me by a grasp of his large warm hand and went with me to the hotel not far distant. We sat down and talked a little while about the political prospects and then prepared to start out to his country home. He hesitated for a moment and then, taking me by the arm, led me out of the hotel office and into the broad hallway to the farthest corner. Speaking in an undertone, he said:

"If we carry the legislature"—this was in 1888 before the popular election of senators—"I will come to Lincoln during the session. I do not know that I can do any good, but there may be some member whom I can influence.

"And then," lowering his voice, "if we can get you into the Senate you can take care of yourself."

I do not recall a more fatherly expression that that of this dear friend. He had done all he could for me in two Congressional campaigns and now he had a chance to aid in an election, which, if successful, would give me a six-year term in the Senate, and he felt that two terms in Congress and a term in the Senate ought to put me on such secure ground that I would be assured a permanent place in public life.

Sixteen years later, in 1910—sixteen years during which his unwavering devotion had expressed itself in three Presidential campaigns—the question of prohibition became an issue in Nebraska. I came out in support of county option, as is recorded in another chapter. Mr. Ahern was not only not a prohibitionist but he lacked something of being a teetotaler. I never saw him under the influence of liquor, but he drank with some regularity and possibly, when political excitement ran high, with some freedom. The newspapers soon reported my activity on the side of county option and one of the Democrats of Richardson County brought the matter to the attention of Ahern. The conversation was reported to me as follows:

"Uncle John, have you heard that Billy has come out for county option?"

"No," Uncle John answered in surprise.

"Well, he has," said his informant.

"Is that so?" replied Uncle John.

"What do you think of Billy now?" continued his informant.

"I am for him, wet or dry," responded my Irish friend. And he was.

Little differences like that did not disturb his friendship; it was built upon a more solid foundation.

A few years after this Mr. Ahern passed away, as I learned during a visit in Nebraska. By this time the demands of national politics kept me away from my home state most of the time. The only offset to the pleasure that comes from a large circle of friends is the frequency with which one is called upon to mourn when "from love's shining circle the gems drop away."

In 1916 the question of state prohibition became the dominant issue in Nebraska and I made a tour of the state in support of that movement. In the course of my travels I spoke at Shubert, the nearest Richardson County town to Mr. Ahern's farm. I spoke from an auto and told the group of listeners that I was more interested in prohibition than I ever was in my own candidacy and needed their support more than I had needed it in previous campaigns. When my speech was finished four men filed up to the auto, all over six feet in height, and informed me that they were sons of John Ahern. I greeted them as cordially as I had their father, and after telling them how much I missed his presence, asked them if they were with me in my fight for prohibition. They all answered very positively in the affirmative. I was greatly pleased to find that the sons had inherited from their father the friendship that had so long existed between the elder Ahern and myself.

My last campaign in Nebraska was made in the spring of 1920 when I was a candidate for delegate for Nebraska to the convention at San Francisco. In my tour from my old first district I passed Ahern's home and detoured a mile or so to visit the family. In a very few minutes the boys had come in from the field, and the children, including the oldest daughter, who was a cripple, assured me that they would be on hand to help make me a delegate.

Possibly the reader, if he has never been in politics, may feel that I have devoted too much space to one of my million and a half political friends, but I single him out as illustrative of a very large number from whom I have received so many manifestations of confidence and affection. It is to such as these that I owe the political opportunities which have come to me, opportunities without which it would have been impossible for me to be identified in a large way with great national problems—opportunities by the improvement of which I have been able to accomplish whatever may be placed to my account in the final reckoning.

Another friend lived in Dawson, in the same county, Richardson. He gave touching evidence of his devotion. Jerry Fenton was my friend and supporter from the time I entered politics in Nebraska until he died. During my Congressional campaigns my picture was used, as is customary, in the advertisement of meetings, and either in this way or by direct request Mr. Fenton secured my likeness and had it hung on the wall of his bedroom. My trip around the world was commenced in the fall of 1905, fifteen years after my first race for Congress. Mr. Fenton had supported me, therefore, in two Congressional campaigns, one senatorial and two Presidential campaigns. He, too, was always present at my meetings and was an influential factor in our party. When I returned in 1906 his family physician told me of an incident that I have remembered as one of the sweetest expressions of that affection which is not infrequent in political life. During my absence abroad I kept in touch with intimate friends through my paper, the *Commoner*, which published altogether more than forty letters written in various countries that I visited. While I was away Mr. Fenton fell ill, so ill that at times his life was despaired of. On one occasion he had a sinking spell which it was feared would speedily end in his death. After his priest had called and administered the sacraments of the Church, the patient, sustained by his faith, calmly awaited the end. During this period of suspense, while the members of the family stood by in helpless anxiety, Mr. Fenton called the doctor to the bedside and whispered to him, pointing to the wall, "When Mr. Bryan gets back tell him that his picture was before me to the last." One incident of such devotion outweighs a multitude of cruel and unjust criticisms.

PART II

AN EARLY PORTRAIT OF MRS. BRYAN

INTRODUCTION

MR. BRYAN'S time was so interrupted that further work was impossible. His records reach to his college days. I knew him first as a college boy, so it seems appropriate for me to begin at that point and carry on the story as I may.

I undertake this work with strong purpose. I certainly know my subject and have a hope that I may be able to write a book which people will like to read; a book which will show the more personal side of his life; a book by which his career may be interpreted.

CHAPTER I

A Picture of the Times

THOUGH a young civilization is freed from the burden of custom and of precedent, an older community has the advantage which comes of permanence. A man born in a stabilized environment has a well-defined background which may be traced with clearness and accuracy. Stratford-on-Avon still gives a setting for Shakespeare. The Scottish Highlands revive again the poems and personality of Burns. One sees from the bridge of the Arno the dim figures of Beatrice and Dante. London jealously guards streets and buildings where lurk the shades of Chaucer, Johnson, Dickens, and a long procession of statesmen and scholars.

In the older part of America time has given in a less degree some permanence of background. Our New England States have not a few spots hallowed by memories of our early scholars, and near the old North Church one can almost hear again the hoof-beats of the ride of Paul Revere.

In the newer part of our country such conditions do not obtain. Landmarks of fifty years ago are gone. The trail of the pioneer has given place to paved highways; the log-built home has vanished to be replaced by structures of steel and cement; the time of Lincoln can no longer be read in the context (if one may use that expression) and the student must reconstruct the environment by research. Even to one born sixty-five years ago in the Middle West, the background grows dim, for almost within the life of a generation a vast region has been completely changed.

When my grandfather, Colonel Darius Dexter, and his two brothers, left the village of Dexterville, now a suburb of Jamestown, New York, for the great West in 1838, they built a sort of raft boat, and with their families and household goods, voyaged up the Great Lakes and down Lake Michigan to the present site of Chicago. Mother, then a child of ten, has told me that only a warehouse, standing on piles above the swamp, and three or four small houses, foreshadowed the presence of an immense city. The fertile plains of central Illinois enticed my grandfather, and thither he went and here he lived and died. My paternal grandfather, coming with his children the following year from near Easton, Pennsylvania—where the first of his family had settled in 1628—located in the same community.

This chapter is not intended to produce for inspection a leaf from my family tree, and I only mention this early migration to prove that I am not unfamiliar with the development of the West.

Illinois, assuming the responsibilities of statehood in 1818, held within her wide plains a wealth as great as any gold mine; a soil of such depth and richness that it seems inexhaustible, and fortunate are they whose ancestors bought and kept these acres.

While Illinois was receiving many settlers, and little towns began to dot the watercourses, railroads were not numerous, and the stage coach was the usual means of travel.

As I was born in 1861, my very early recollections may help to place the times. My father, second generation from the pioneer in Illinois, did a general merchandise and commission business, which, at its height, included dry goods, groceries, china and glassware, cooking utensils, boots and shoes, farming implements, hardware, a harness shop, and a millinery store filled with wonderful bonnets. I recall snow-covered ground, horses with frost-encircled nostrils and steaming coats, dragging creaking sleds, on which were piled high the neatly scraped and stiffly frozen carcasses of hogs. These were brought by the farmers to my father's pork house. We did not know about packing plants in those days, and the Swifts and Armours had not yet shown the inefficiency and wastefulness of the small concern. In this long, low building the bricklayers, carpenters, and others of the community who could not carry on their work in cold weather, found winter employment. Here the hogs were prepared for the city market. Lard was rendered in two huge kettles, side meat was salted, pickled pork, sausage, and other by-products were made ready, and once or twice I peered into the door of a brick building—mysterious and awesome—where I dimly saw long rows of hams hanging from the rafters and taking color from the smoke of hickory wood smouldering in heaps upon the earthen floor. I recall long rows of wagons loaded with these finished products and with many sacks of wheat, slowly rumbling along to the Illinois River, eight miles distant. The stern-wheel river steamer, into which this produce was loaded, chugged away down the Illinois and into the Mississippi, until it reached St. Louis, even then a city of importance. Along the river banks stretched the levees, paved with rough stone, where rows of steamers docked. There were no cranes or derricks in those days and the produce was unloaded by negro deckhands, droning their monotonous songs, and hurrying up and down the gangplanks like busy ants. The wholesale produce houses faced the river at that time and there was no great river bridge.

Belonging to this period, though perhaps five or six years earlier, is a story my father told me of the campaign methods of Douglas. During the famous Lincoln-Douglas debates, so I was told, whenever the stage coach stopped to change horses or to take on or deliver mail, Douglas would descend with his pipe filled and beg a coal to light his tobacco. This opened the way for friendly chat and banter. When he took his place again, the coal and tobacco were thrown away and the pipe returned to his pocket, where it rested until the next station was reached, when it was refilled and the request repeated. This was one of our family stories, and often when Mr. Bryan and I were driving, I have said: "Why are you stopping here? Are you going to light your pipe?" And he would reply, "Yes, I believe I'll look in and see if he has a coal."

While the Mississippi Valley States were growing steadily in population and in everything which makes for comfortable living, the farther West was untouched. Illinois was admitted to statehood in 1818; Iowa in 1846; while the next state in line, Nebraska, did not gain this distinction until 1867, a half century between Illinois and Nebraska. The act which constituted Nebraska a distinct territory and which opened her lands to settlement, was passed in 1854, but in 1861 there were less than 30,000 people in the state.

The natural barrier was the Missouri River; on the eastern bank a busy population and on the western bank the Indian and the buffalo, with here and there a trail winding toward the Western coast.

It may seem unnecessary to remind Americans of the fact that the West was peopled by the East. Immigrants, when settling in colonies, have made here and there spots of foreign influence, but for the most part the foreign element sank into the life of communities already organized and controlled by our own citizens. Not only was the West peopled by the East, but in this migration the East lost many of her best citizens. Men of energy, of education, of broad outlook, saw the possibilities in the West and joined the ranks of those who were bent upon the task of subduing a new land.

With men of vision and of education in the lead, the young civilization did not neglect the founding of churches and schools. Illinois College was the first to be established in that state, followed soon by other colleges, by state universities and young ladies' boarding schools. In Lincoln, Nebraska, almost the first act of the new capital was the founding of the State University, which has grown to be a great educational center. From the beginning the West was not only developing the material resources of the country, but was looking to the intellectual and spiritual development of her citizens. While I bore no conspicuous part, I count myself fortunate to have been born in the Mississippi Valley, and regard as a privilege my small part in this wonderful development, which has sometimes been called the "heart of our government."

I have spoken chiefly of Illinois and Nebraska, the two states which I know best, but which I hope may be regarded as typical.

The economic and political conditions surrounding western people in approximately the year 1860 may be briefly summarized in the words "unrest and discontent," with the question of debt underneath. The West was in debt and in debt to the East. The money had been used to improve their land and they were depending upon an increase in land values, upon good prices for their products and upon sufficient loanable capital to meet their obligations. None of these were forthcoming. Money grew "tight"; the farmers could not pay their interest; failures were frequent, and everyone was searching for a panacea.

The Civil War had brought industrial problems and the age-long question of the relations between capital and labor was stirring in the public mind. The railroads were at once a blessing and a curse to this generation, and were so important to the development of the country that anxious-eyed settlers were eager to have the roads upon any terms. This was particularly true of the more Western states where watercourses are fewer and where distances are so tremendous that transportation seemed impossible without the aid of the iron horse.

In this environment a dark-eyed little boy opened his eyes upon the world March 19, 1860. The political problems which existed in the United States thirty years later when, in 1890, William Jennings Bryan stood for Congress in Nebraska, are worthy of attention.

WILLIAM JENNINGS BRYAN

To even a casual reader of history, it is evident that conditions had not improved. The whole country had felt the stringency of money conditions, and a movement was in evidence which showed that the average citizen had less confidence in the masters of finance and was inclined to seek his own remedies. This independence took the form in the New England States of the Grange with its demand for the issuance of greenbacks by the Federal Government as opposed to paper money issued by the banks. In the West this independence was shown in the formation of the Farmers' Alliance and the Populist Party, both of which were recruited from progressive Republican ranks.

The Populist Party, while not often in office, held the balance of power in Nebraska for many years. This period, too, witnessed great activity in the development of natural resources. The achievements of American railroad builders, promoters, miners, traders, manufacturers, and financiers between 1864 and 1890 exceeded their work of the whole preceding century—another evidence of restlessness. The cotton mills of New England were disturbed by the awakening of the South. The Southern states had reached the very sensible conclusion that it was better to build mills where the cotton grows than to send it to New England. One could hear at every crossroad discussions on monopolies and combinations in restraint of trade because of the aggressions of the trusts, and the expression "tainted money" as applied to church contributions, came into common use.

Chief among the elements of discontent was the bitterness the people felt toward the railroads. It is difficult to justify the tremendous concessions given to the railroads in the Western states. I quote briefly from "The Menace of Privilege," by Henry George, Jr.:

"Besides a continuous strip of land from one to four hundred feet wide for a right of way, with additional land for sidings, stations, yards and the like, the Federal

218

A PICTURE OF THE TIMES

Government granted all alternate sections (a section is a square mile in United States land measurement) in a belt of land a number of miles in width running on each side of the right-of-way strip. The grant to the Southern Pacific, for instance, consisted of a belt of land 60 miles wide in California, and 100 miles wide in the Territories (now States). The grant to the Northern Pacific consisted of alternate sections in a belt of land 120 miles wide, running from the western boundary of Minnesota to Puget Sound and the Columbia River

"Besides land, the Federal, State, and municipal governments made enormous grants of money and bonds for the stimulation of railroad building, mainly in the West. The five Pacific roads received from the Federal Government alone United States bonds amounting to $64,000,000."

The settler, who had been most anxious to secure the building of a railroad, found he had invited in a relentless and apparently unmanageable power. The railroads sometimes ran the track far enough away from the old town to ruin it—the old town representing so much hard work and sacrifice on the part of the settler. The railroad selected a site and laid out the new town, having sold the lots beforehand to Eastern investors who were willing to resell these lots to the community at a neat profit. The original town had to be abandoned. As we who lived in the North never quite understood what the people suffered under "The March of General Sherman to the Sea," so the individual in the East cannot realize what was endured by the individual in the West during this period. Such incidents as these were not infrequent.

Grain elevators for the storage of wheat would be erected at intervals along the track by men who were secretly in league with the railroad officials. The farmer cut and threshed his wheat which he planned to ship. He found the

219

freight rates had gone up and he could not afford to ship. He could not afford to hold the wheat; he had no place to store it; he needed money. At this point the owner of the elevator made an offer, lower than it should have been, but which, under the circumstances, the farmer could not refuse. The wheat was bought by the elevator man and stored in the elevator. This process was repeated until the elevator held all the wheat of that community. A little later the freight rates suddenly came down; the wheat was shipped, and the elevator man and the railroad officials shared the profits, while the inhabitants stood by in impotent rage.

I can add here a personal experience. When we went round the world, we sent back from Japan some heavy freight, a stone lantern, some bronze lions, etc. The goods were billed to Kansas City, and when we paid the account, our enterprising railroad had charged us considerably more to bring the boxes from Kansas City to Lincoln, Nebraska, then we paid from Yokohama, Japan, to Kansas City.

It is not surprising that the West urged railroad regulation.

There was, too, a frequent source of anger in the "long and short haul," that delicate bit of railroad mechanism the functioning of which was past understanding. People would see their coal hauled through their own town to a town beyond them. They would have to pay freight charges to the distant point and then back again to their own place. One town (usually the one owned by the railroads) was built up, and another ruined through discrimination in freight rates.

In this connection I might add that in 1910 Mr. Bryan advocated an enlargement of the powers of the Interstate Commerce Commission. This was the only body which was authorized to cope with the "long and short haul." In spite of tremendous opposition and outcry, the powers of the Commission were enlarged and the "long and short haul" is now more staid in its movements, and is called upon to show cause for its action, such as competing water rates.

While it is the duty of every citizen in a republic to understand political questions, there is an undercurrent of delightful possibilities in these studies. Think of the racy reading we shall have when some scholar decides to write a thesis on railroad methods in 1900, and think of the pleasing symposium which might be contributed by old gentlemen who remember these times!

I have tried to paint a picture of these times—although with clumsy fingers and inadequate colors—in order to show that the subject of this biography found his political issues ready for him. The issues were here when he was born. When we removed from Illinois in 1887, to Nebraska, we entered a younger civilization in which people were even more harassed by conditions and more determined to find a solution.

Mr. Bryan came upon this stage endowed by nature and by training for his work. He saw the problems. He recognized the needs and became the voice of an unorganized multitude which was seeking a leader.

CHAPTER II

Student Days

I FIRST made the acquaintance of Mr. Bryan in the autumn of 1879 in Jacksonville, Illinois. I had heard from my maiden aunt rumors of a splendid young man named Bryan, but I did not meet the gentleman until he appeared at a reception at the boarding school which I had entered that year. A group of college boys entered the parlors and passed the receiving line. From an adjoining room I watched this row of students. I am sorry not to chronicle a case of love at first sight, but one boy among the number attracted my notice and I asked my companion, "Who is the tall fellow with dark hair and eyes?" and when she replied, "Will Bryan," I knew he must be the youth of whom I had been hearing. Our families had known of each other through mutual friends, but had never met.

Years ago I wrote a short biography of Mr. Bryan, and as my early impressions were probably more vivid at that time, I turn to this book for a description of his appearance:

"His face was pale and thin; a pair of keen, dark eyes looked out from beneath heavy brows; his nose was prominent—too large to look well, I thought; a broad, thin-lipped mouth and a square chin, completed the contour of his face. He was neat, though not fastidious in dress, and stood firmly and with dignity. I noted particularly his hair and his smile. The former, black in color, fine in quality, and parted with distressing straightness; the latter, expansive and expressive. In later years this smile has been the subject of considerable comment, but the well-rounded cheeks of Mr. Bryan now check its onward march, and no one has seen the real breadth of the smile who did not see

THE HOUSE WHERE WILLIAM JENNINGS BRYAN WAS BORN,
MARCH 19, 1860   *Photo. Brown Bros.*

THE BRYAN FARMHOUSE NEAR SALEM, ILLINOIS
Where William Jennings Bryan spent his boyhood.

"FAIRVIEW," THE HOME OF MR. AND MRS. BRYAN AT LINCOLN,
NEBRASKA   *Photo. Brown Bros.*

it in the early days. Upon one occasion, a heartless observer was heard to remark, 'That man can whisper in his own ear,' but this was a cruel exaggeration.''

While I was completing my inspection of the young men, Mr. Bryan was brought to me and formally presented. I learned later that he had chosen me among all the girls present and had inquired my name.

For exercise, the schoolgirls were in the habit of walking around the square upon which the academy stood, and it was natural that Mr. Bryan, who lived with relatives just across the street, should often find it necessary to walk toward town at the same hour we were taking our promenade. I grew to expect him and could see his smile the whole length of the square. Mr. Bryan in an earlier chapter has given many details of this period and there is not a great deal to be added. My chief source of material is found in his letters, extending over our four years of engagement, for we were betrothed the following spring. We owe much to Mrs. Jones, our old friend, with whom he lived, who sang his praises in season and out of season to me, and was equally industrious in praising me to him. Dear Mrs. Jones, with her quaint primness and stiff little side curls, was the soul of goodness and entered upon the dangerous business of matchmaking without fear, and we have had no reason to question her judgment.

Another factor in bringing us together was the presence of my mother at a local sanitarium during the winter of 1879 and 1880. I went to visit her often and Mr. Bryan asked permission to call upon me there, which was granted and from there we sometimes took an afternoon drive. These drives, although taken with my mother's consent, were very wrong from the viewpoint of the head of our school, who was so horrified upon the discovery of our meetings that he punished me by not allowing me to remain at the school through commencement. After I had passed my examinations, I went home. But, as was then arranged, I returned the following term and won the first honors of my class.

I dreaded to leave school a few days early, dreaded to tell my father, and dreaded what he might think of Mr. Bryan, whom I was beginning to regard as a most admirable and mature man. The morning I left Jacksonville, the irate principal put me on the train for my thirty-mile journey, not knowing that a young man was concealed in the baggage car. When the train was under way, Mr. Bryan came and joined me, and we planned for him to make an early visit to my home and for him to ask my father's consent to our engagement at that time. Father was what is known as a gentleman of the old school, tall, dignified, and very reserved. But to my surprise and great relief, he had no fault to find with this young man, and the pleasant relations then established continued without a break until my father's death.

While I have never regarded Mr. Bryan as a great letter writer—a little too absent-minded, a little too didactic— glimpses of his character may be gathered from the following extracts:

UPON A WITHERED BOUQUET

"May 12, 1880.

". . . Beauty, how changing! That lovely bouquet whose beauty charmed while its fragrance enchanted, is falling a victim to the cruel tooth of time. Its form still remains, but its freshness has gone forever. Yet why should we wonder? Like the flowers we have grown, and like them we also must decay. Yes, its beauty is gone, but the memory of her who gave it still lives, and like the dew, refreshes by its presence. Those who rejoice in the memory of noble actions and heroic deeds look back. Those who live only in the present are concerned neither with the past nor the future. There is still another class of people who anticipate events.

To those the writer belongs. The first object which now meets his eye is commencement week."

Upon Receiving a Letter
"May 12, 1880.

". . . You know well both how to sadden and how to gladden as the first page of your kind letter proved:

" 'W. J. B.', how icy! I went home and built a fire, sharpened my skates, and then took up your letter again. Imagine the change in temperature, if you can. Behold the new address!"

Upon Receiving a Prize
"October 17, 1880.

". . . The prize is won—at least, received. That is the second, and I do not feel as I thought I would. I prayed that humility might be given with success. My prayer is answered, for I cannot feel that I am anything more than I was before, and as I look over the possibilities of life, I can honestly ask in the language of Lincoln's favorite hymn, 'Why should the spirit of mortal be proud?' If one obtains the highest position to which an American can aspire, he can return thanks to God, for He gives both talents and favorable circumstances, and commands that both should be used. What honor then if one does all that he possibly can! He only does his duty."

Upon Reading a Life of Lincoln
"April 3, 1881.

". . . Have been reading 'The Life of Abe Lincoln.' It is quite interesting. He was ambitious and is the most humble statesman we have ever had. He had an eloquence which seemed born of inspiration. He spoke the truth and with it won the hearts of his hearers. As a lawyer he was a perfect model. He only wished justice for his clients and always got it. He was scrupulously honest, once walking three miles to return six and a half cents he had taken by mistake. He is a good character for study."

UPON A GOLD THIMBLE

"December 3, 1883.

". . . How much did you say a gold thimble costs, and what size do you wear? If I have the money, I will get you one for Christmas. That statement 'if I have the money' does not sound very well, but I do not hide even my poverty from you." [He always earned the money with which he bought gifts for me.]

"So you have learned to make waffles. I am so fond of them."

ON SHAVING HIS MUSTACHE

"April 17, 1881.

". . . How do you think I look without my mustache? As I shaved off that long-petted and delicately fondled evidence of manhood, I was deeply impressed with that awful truth that it is easier to destroy than to create. The result of weeks of patient, weary watching gone in a moment. Did I say gone? No, not gone, for the remains of that capillaceous production still live and will bear to future ages testimony of the beauty they bestowed as well as the care and trouble which they gave."

ON THE PRINCIPAL OF MY BOARDING SCHOOL

"March 27, 1881.

". . . I cannot blame you for being angry. It is difficult to control one's temper *always*. It is a life work to become able to govern oneself. Two or three times since I have been here at school I have been angry," [he had been in school for six years at that time] "but I am always sorry for it as soon as it is over.

". . . You must not let such prevarications on the professor's part give you a dislike for the religion which he professes. He is not, I think, a perfect example, but the religion which he pretends to live up to, is perfect. Look at Christ instead of B."

THOUGHTS ON PUBLIC OFFICE

Referring to himself, Mr. Bryan writes, under date of May 17, 1880:

". . . But since he belongs to you, perhaps he should not speak lightly of your possessions. He has no past except that spent with you, upon which he delights to look. He has taken four prizes in college, but who could not with his surroundings? Of his dear, honored father you have read. All that son could say of mother, he can say of his. His future I cannot tell. Law will be his profession; his aim, to mete out justice to every creature, whether he be rich or poor, bond or free. His great desire is to honor God and please mankind. He does not desire to be wealthy, believing that money fails to bring happiness as soon as it is made the object of pursuit. Yet by willing labor he hopes and expects to be able to provide for himself and one more. Do not laugh when he tells you that he desires to stand with Webster and Clay. Noble aims make noble men, and his father, who still lives to aid him, often said that one could by diligence, make himself just what he wished to be, and that our duty was to make ourselves worthy of any office within the gift of the people. Such are his parents and such his aspiration."

TRIBUTE TO MEMORY

"Chicago, November 30, 1882.
(Thanksgiving Day)
". . . Oh, memory, God given garden of the soul, where flowers once planted will forever bloom. May

we scatter on thy sacred soil only seeds of kindness, truth, and love. Seeds watered by the dews of Heaven which may blossom and bear fruit through eternal years."

FIRST JURY SERVICE

"Chicago, January 29, 1882.

". . . I notified you last week of my success, or rather, misfortune. I was a little surprised at being elected on the first ballot; came near missing the oratorship by being put on as debater. I preferred to be orator and could not be both. Trumbull and Kagy were with me and helped me to the position for which I think I am best fitted. My subject for oration is 'Vigilance.' I have been deeply moved by the lethargy of our people. The perpetuity of a nation I think depends more upon the character of its people than upon the principles which underlie its government, and observing the inaction of our people, the carelessness with which they elect their representatives and neglect the administration of justice, I am wrought up to such a pitch that I cannot hold in. There are reports of recent jury packing in this city and they only indicate how criminally negligent and selfish we as a people are becoming.

"And just here let me relate a novel incident. I had been writing on my oration and had reached the corruption of the jury system, attributing it to the fact that our better class of citizens would excuse themselves from serving the public because their private affairs were so pressing. Feeling tired, I went over to the gymnasium, and after I had refreshed myself, was starting away when I was met by a man with a small open notebook in his hand. He was a constable looking for a juror to try a case before a justice of the peace near by. He told me his business and wanted me to go with him.

"Remembering that my oration was unfinished, I tried to excuse myself, but he said he wanted to get some good, honest man and was unwilling to let me go. I told him that I was studying law and I believed lawyers were excused.

" 'Not until they are admitted to practice,' he said.

"Then I remembered the point I was trying to make in my oration, and the preciousness of consistency occurred to me in a new light, and this, together with the assurance that the law allowed jurors 50 cents for serving, overcame my objection. I went and did my best to prove to the world that the jury system which Blackstone says 'is the bulwark of English liberties' is also the palladium of our safety.

"The facts of the case in brief were as follows:

"A policeman received word that certain parties were stealing potatoes from John Murphy. The policeman went to the men and claimed to have a search warrant, but did not read it. He asked them to go to a justice near by and settle the matter. They all started, but soon the men with the potatoes whipped up their horses and tried to get away. This aroused the policeman's suspicions and he arrested them and took them to a justice, where the matter was examined into and the parties released. The arrest, however, made one of the parties angry and he appeared as a prosecuting witness in a case of assault and battery. It was claimed that the arrest was without authority and hence became an assault. After the witnesses were examined, the lawyers rose to tell us our duty. One told us that the policeman had no right to make the arrest, and that by fining him, we would teach him that he should regard the rights of free men and their immunity from arrest on groundless suspicions. The other explained to us the discretionary power of officers of the law; how they were compelled to act on the spur of the moment lest the criminals should escape; how they watched while we slept, and having to deal so often with the lower classes, they were necessarily suspicious and liable to error, even when most conscientious in the discharge of their duty.

"The jury was then sent out to agree upon a verdict, and as the papers were handed to me, some one suggested that I act as foreman. On the first ballot four voted not guilty and two guilty. We who were for acquittal were young men, and the two who voted guilty were about forty years old. After about three minutes' discussion, we signed our verdict which read 'that the jury finds the defendant not guilty,' signed, etc. Then it was announced that in people's cases where the verdict is for the defendant, the jurors receive no pay!'"

LAST LETTER BEFORE MARRIAGE

"Jacksonville, September 28, 1884.

". . . Your ring is bought and engraved with the strange device 'Won, 1880. One, 1884.' I think my 'regulation black' will be all that could be desired. If you can boast of wearing the finest wedding dress ever worn there, I think I may be the first to wear a swallow tail. . . ."

"Professor T. [president of the college] yesterday informed me that he and his wife had received their invitation and that he was preparing himself for the ring ceremony. I am practicing on 'and with all my worldly goods I thee endow' so as to make it duly impressive. If you dare laugh when I say that, I won't kiss you when he tells me to salute my bride.

". . . I trust no angry words will ever pass between us and nothing must ever be allowed to shake our confidence in each other. If we keep no secrets from each other, we cannot wander far from the right path."

The first official document signed by Mr. Bryan in the first office he ever held, that of notary public. (His deposition before himself declaring his love for Mary E. Baird. Dated May 21, 1883.)

CHAPTER III

Our First Decade Together

THE next three years after the wedding day were spent in our little home on College Hill, Jacksonville, Illinois. This home had been built before our marriage and contained a suite of rooms for my parents, who needed my care and who made their home with us until their death.

Very early in our married life Mr. Bryan and I discussed together the best use to make of our leisure hours. Young friends had asked us to join the tennis and social clubs, but after considering the matter carefully, we decided to study instead. Mr. Bryan read a great many books, chiefly on the tariff, railroad problems, political economy, and the science of government. When the family wished to give him a little present, we bought a book along these lines. I joined a German Conversation club, took a course in early English in Illinois College, and worked at night on the same course of law which Mr. Bryan had pursued in Chicago—a busy and a happy time.

Mr. Bryan's law practice grew slowly but steadily and each year we added to our savings. Mr. Bryan's ideals as a lawyer are well illustrated by his answer to a letter of a young attorney who had asked him for advice. He said:

"Remember that a lawyer is an officer of the court and, as such, is sworn to assist the court in the administration of justice. That being true, no lawyer can afford to make an argument he does not believe to be sound, or try to mislead either the judge or jury. It is better to refuse a case that you believe to be unjust than to risk, for any amount of compensation, the strain upon your morals involved in the attempt to deceive the court or jury. One who repeatedly attempts to prove that 'black is white' in time becomes color blind and cannot himself distinguish between right and wrong.

"Besides this effect upon himself, he must consider the effect upon the court and also his reputation, which will have an effect upon the jury. If a judge has been deceived by a lawyer, he spends his time watching for deceptions when the lawyer is speaking before him. There is nothing so valuable to a lawyer as the confidence of the judge and jury in his integrity. When a lawyer has secured for his client all that the client is entitled to, he has done all that the law requires, all that any honest client would desire, and all that an honest lawyer would do."

Mr. Bryan has dwelt on the causes which led us to remove to the West in June, 1887—leaving one school center for another. We had both in Jacksonville, Illinois, and in Lincoln, Nebraska, delightful association with college faculties, and found the new friends quite as satisfying as the old ones.

During our first years in Lincoln we were instrumental in the organization of the Sorosis Club for women and the Round Table for men. These clubs are particularly valuable because they discuss only current questions and keep the members in touch with the times. Both those organizations, now more than thirty-five years old, are vigorous and influential in the life of the city.

After two and a half years of diligent work accomplished in addition to the care of my parents and my baby girl, I passed the examination and was admitted to the bar in Lincoln, in 1887, being the only woman in the class and ranking third in a class of seventeen.

Mr. Bryan had an increasing reputation as a speaker and during these years we went to many public gatherings. I hold the theory that if a wife does not show an interest in her husband's work and does not go with him when he asks her, the time may come when he will cease to ask her. I pass this idea on to young wives for whatever it may be worth.

One seventeenth day of March we went to a St. Patrick's Day celebration in Lincoln where Mr. Bryan was to speak, and he greatly enjoyed an incident of the evening. I feel sure he would want this story to find place here.

The meeting was presided over by the rather pompous Nebraska governor against whom Mr. Bryan had made fifty speeches during the previous autumn. In Mr. Bryan's words:

"I was a little nervous when I saw the Governor in the chair, for I felt he might be annoyed because of the fifty speeches I had made against him.

"The program was a varied one—an instrumental selection, a declamation, a song, etc. The Governor rose and read from the list prepared for him, 'The next number is by Mr. W. J. Bryan.' As I stepped forward the Governor advanced and extended his hand. It ran through my mind that he was a kind old fellow to forgive my opposition. Then the Governor drew me toward him and said in a hoarse whisper, 'Do you speak or sing?' He did not know I had spoken against him and had not even heard of me. The sudden revulsion of feeling was almost too much for me. I could hardly control my laughter and began to speak with great effort. I have always regarded this as one of the best jokes which Fate has played upon me."

I find also one of his early post-prandial efforts which shows so clearly his views on the separation of Church and State, that I venture to reproduce it:

"Mr. Chairman, Ladies and Gentlemen: It is rather by accident than by design that this sentiment has fallen

234

to me. Had not my law partner been called unexpectedly from the State he would have responded with more propriety and more ability to 'The Law and the Gospel.'

"These are important words; each covers a wide field by itself and together they include all government. There is not between them, as some suppose, a wide gulf fixed. Many have commenced with us only to be called to a higher sphere, and a few ministers have come to us when they were convinced that they had answered to another's call.

"In the earlier days the prophet was also the lawgiver. He who wore the priestly robe held in his hands the scales of justice. But times are changed. For the good of the State and for the welfare of the Church, the moral and the civil law have been separated. Today we owe a double allegiance, and 'render unto Cæsar the things that are Cæsar's, and unto God the things that are God's.' Their governments are concentric circles and can never interfere. Between what religion commands and what the law compels there is, and ever must be, a wide margin, as there is also between what religion forbids and what the law prohibits. In many things we are left to obey or disobey the instructions of the Divine Ruler, answerable to Him only for our conduct. The Gospel deals with the secret purposes of the heart as well as with the outward life, while the civil law must content itself with restraining the arm outstretched for another's hurt or with punishing the actor after the injury is done.

"Next to the ministry I know of no more noble profession than the law. The object aimed at is justice, equal and exact, and if it does not reach that end at once it is because the stream is diverted by selfishness or checked by ignorance. Its principles ennoble and its practice elevates. If you point to the pettifogger,

I will answer that he is as much out of place in the temple of justice as is the hypocrite in the house of God. You will find the 'book on tricks' in the library of the legal bankrupt—nowhere else. In no business in life do honesty, truthfulness, and uprightness of conduct pay a larger dividend upon the investment than in the law. He is not only blind to his highest welfare and to his greatest good, but also treading upon dangerous ground, who fancies that mendacity, loquacity, and pertinacity are the only accomplishments of a successful lawyer.

"You cannot judge a man's life by the success of a moment, by the victory of an hour, or even by the results of a year. You must view his life as a whole. You must stand where you can see the man as he treads the entire path that leads from the cradle to the grave —now crossing the plain, now climbing the steeps, now passing through pleasant fields, now wending his way with difficulty between rugged rocks—tempted, tried, tested, triumphant. The completed life of every lawyer, either by its success or failure, emphasizes the words of Solomon—'The path of the just is as the shining light, that shineth more and more unto the perfect day.'

"By practicing upon the highest plane the lawyer may not win the greatest wealth, but he wins that which wealth cannot purchase and is content to know and feel that 'a good name is rather to be chosen than great riches, and loving favour rather than silver and gold.'

"There are pioneers of the Gospel whose names you speak with reverence, Calvin, Knox, the Wesleys and Asbury, besides many still living, and you love them not without cause. There are those in our profession whom we delight to honor. Justinian and Coke, Blackstone and Jay, Marshall and Kent, Story and Lincoln, men who have stood in the thickest of the fight, have met every temptation peculiar to our profession, and yet maintained their integrity.

"It is a fact to which we point with no little pride, that with a history of an hundred years no member of the Supreme Court of the United States has ever been charged with corrupt action, although untold millions have been involved in the litigation before the court. Nor do I recall any member of the Supreme Court of any State who has been convicted of misusing his office.

" 'The Law and the Gospel.' Great in their honored names, great in their history, great in their influence. To a certain extent they supplement each other. The law asks of the Gospel counsel, not commands. The Gospel goes far beyond the reach of law, for while the law must cease to operate when its subject dies, the Gospel crosses the dark river of death and lightens up the world which lies beyond the tomb. The law is negative, the Gospel positive; the laws say, 'do not unto others that which you would not have others do unto you,' while the Gospel declares that we should 'do to others that which we would that others should do unto us.'

" 'The Law and the Gospel.' They form an exception to the rule that in union there is strength, for each is strongest when alone. And I believe that the greatest prosperity of the State and greatest growth of the Church will be found when the law and the Gospel walk, not hand in hand, but side by side."

December, 1891, found us en route to Washington, where Mr. Bryan took up his duties as Congressman. Our children then numbered three, the youngest being nine months old, and we broke our journey by a few days in Jacksonville, Illinois. Dr. Jones, our host, owned a particularly fine microscope with many carefully prepared slides. Under his supervision our daughter Ruth, age six, was standing on a chair squinting down the barrels of the microscope when her brother came in, watched her a moment, and said, "Sister, get down from there; I want to smell that too." Honesty compels me to admit that our children were not always infallible.

Even at that remote date the hotel and apartment owners of Washington had declared against children, and Mr. Bryan had a long search to find a home for us. At one time we regarded the drowning of our entire family as a necessary prelude to establishing ourselves. We saw race suicide from a new angle, and experienced great relief when we had secured pleasant quarters opposite the National Library on Capitol Hill. Our good friends, the Brides, gave us, their first lodgers, a home for four years.

In the House of Representatives the organization of Committees occupied first attention, and among these the Committee on Ways and Means is regarded as most important.

During the rivalry between Congressman William M. Springer, whom we had known in Illinois, and Speaker Charles F. Crisp, of Georgia, for the Chairmanship of this committee, Mr. Bryan supported Springer with that tenacity which he always showed in a fight. When Springer won and the smoke of battle cleared, Mr. Bryan was given a place on this important committee. I have been told that no other new member has been thus honored. This gave him a standing at once and prepared the way for his Congressional work. His first extended speech, March 16, 1892, was in support of the Wilson Tariff Bill. Here Mr. Bryan received the reward of his patient study in our first home. He knew his subject and was able to take the lead because of that knowledge. I was exceedingly anxious about this first speech in Congress and sat in the gallery of the House of Representatives with my hand clasping the arm of the seat so tensely that my glove was split across the palm. That he affected his listeners was shown by a conversation which I heard in the gallery.

Soon after Mr. Bryan began to speak a lady came in and said to a earlier arrival, "Who is speaking?"

The first lady replied, "A young man from Nebraska who is said to consider himself a great orator."

When his speech was nearing its close, a third lady entered and asked the first one the same question, "Who is speaking?"

Her changed reply was, "Congressman Bryan of Nebraska, and he has been making a wonderful speech."

In his second term Mr. Bryan took up the matter of monetary legislation and favored free coinage of silver. His speech, August 15, 1893, upon this subject, attracted great attention, and again his charm of speech was aided by his thorough knowledge of the subject. He spoke in January, 1894, upon the income tax, boldly standing for a most unpopular measure. The full text of these speeches cannot be given here, but may be found in supplementary volumes.

After four years in Congress he became a candidate for the United States Senate, but the landslide of 1894 gave the Republicans a great majority in the Legislature and Thurston was elected. The following extract from a letter was written to friends after the Senatorial defeat:

"The Legislature is Republican, and a Republican Senator will now be elected to represent Nebraska. This may be mortifying to the numerous chairmen who have introduced me to audiences as 'the next Senator from Nebraska,' but it illustrates the uncertainty of prophecies.

"I appreciate more than words can express the cordial good will and the loyal support of the friends to whom I am indebted for the political honors which I have received. I am especially grateful to those who bear without humiliation the name of the common people, for they have been my friends when others have deserted me. I appreciate also the kind words of many who have been restrained by party ties from giving me their votes. I have been a hired man for four years, and, now that the campaign is closed, I may be pardoned for saying that as a public servant I have performed my duty to the best of my ability, and am not ashamed of the record made.

"I stepped from private life into national politics at the bidding of my countrymen; at their bidding I again take my place in the ranks and resume without sorrow the work from which they called me. It is the glory of our institutions that public officials exercise authority by the consent of the governed rather than by divine or hereditary right. Paraphrasing the language of Job, each public servant can say of departing honors: The people gave and the people have taken away, blessed be the name of the people.

"Speaking of my own experience in politics, I may again borrow an idea from the great sufferer and say: What, shall we receive good at the hands of the people, and shall we not receive evil? I have received good even beyond my deserts, and I accept defeat without complaint. I ask my friends not to cherish resentment against any one who may have contributed to the result.

.   .   .   .

"The friends of these reforms have fought a good fight; they have kept the faith, and they will not have finished their course until the reforms are accomplished. Let us be grateful for the progress made, and 'with malice toward none and charity for all' begin the work of the next campaign."

CHAPTER IV

Growth of Oratorical Power

MUCH valuable time has been spent in discussing whether or not an acquired trait may be transmitted to descendants. As one moves along in life, he grows less and less sure of a conclusion. One instance clearly supports one side of the controversy—only to be flatly contradicted by a later instance.

Therefore I do not attempt to say how far a certain slender, dark-eyed boy was influenced by the fact that his father had a great interest in oratory and was himself a forceful speaker. Judge Bryan took his son with him to court, and the boy from his seat on the steps of the platform, listened to the arguments of the counsel and to the decisions of the bench.

The first recorded efforts of declamation show that at the age of seven or eight he committed to memory his geography lesson, and then was placed on a little table where he declaimed the same.

Looking through our letters, I find light upon the feeling which he had for his father.

"Our church has no pastor, so we had a kind of prayer meeting in the forenoon on Sunday. I spoke. Afterwards Mr. Chance (Jakie's father) said: 'While our young brother was speaking, I thought of his good old father. How he used to encourage us by repeating the promises of the Bible, and my heart went up in silent prayer that the mantle of Elijah might fall on Elisha, and then I prayed that he might become a shining light and that his influence might be felt far and wide for good.' I tell you, I could not help weeping, nor was I alone, for I felt so un-

16

worthy to take my father's place." (Letter dated August 29, 1880.)

"Later in reading over an address delivered by father to the grand jury as he left the bench after a term of twelve years service as circuit judge, I find this, which you will pardon me for quoting. 'I have not grown rich from the spoils of office. During the whole term of twelve years I have received not more than a living. I have nevertheless succeeded reasonably well in the affairs of life and have of the world's goods a reasonable competency, but it has not come to me from office. It has been the result of rigid economy, long and patient professional labor, and the sweat of the face in agricultural pursuits, aided and supported by Heaven's greatest bestowment—an affectionate, confiding, and prudential companion—and finally, gentlemen of the jury, I add that the experience of public life has tended to confirm in me the convictions of my early education —that the more we conform our lives and actions, both in private and public relations, to the demands of honor, truth, sincerity, justice, and Christianity, the greater will be our happiness and prosperity, and the better we shall enjoy this present world, and the broader will be our foundation for the enjoyment of the world to come.'

"Such is the example set me by my venerated father. I have been reading several of his speeches today."

Mr. Bryan gives a list of the prizes he took in college under the caption "The Lure of the College Prize." If one refers to this list, it is quite apparent that failure did not discourage him. He entered the next contest with his best effort. Some samples of his youthful style may be of interest. The reader will note that he began to run true to type at an early age. Below appears a speech, "A Defense of Democracy," which was written for delivery in chapel,

A PRIZE WINNING ORATOR
An early portrait of Wm. Jennings Bryan

January, 1880. He was evidently smarting under the defeat of Hancock.

"It was the custom in ancient warfare, when the battle was over, to follow the vanquished and put each individual enemy to the sword. Advanced civilization, however, denounces the practice as barbarous in the extreme, and hails with joy the dawn of a brighter period, when charity, instead of revenge, will characterize the conduct of victors toward the conquered.

"The result of the last Presidential election has caused those who hoped for a more enlightened age, to despair, and has deferred for some years at least, the day when true bravery will appear in the conflict, rather than in despoiling the slain. Since the wires flashed the startling news of our defeat; since that pompous funeral demonstration, when, with beating of drums and sounds of mingled shouts and rejoicings, one of America's greatest generals was laid to rest in his political grave; since 'requiescat in pace' was written over the silent tomb of 'The Superb,' pure in character, and great by name and nature; we have been the object upon which the *cruel* mercies of a party, driven to desperation before the election, have been exercised.

"But such a devotion to their cause does not prove its righteousness; on the contrary, a devotion which overreaches its bounds, more often defeats than promotes its object. We, who have exhibited a patience of twenty years duration" (the speaker was twenty years old at this time) "can well afford to wait until the Republican party finds its death from suicide; but *duty* calls upon us to defend by word and act the principles which we believe.

"Before advancing to the statement of principles, it is necessary to free ourselves from the charge of slander. It has been urged from this platform by those

243

flushed with unexpected victory, that the Democratic leaders and even the stump speakers, as they are contemptuously called, have been guilty of making false accusations against the good and the great. How fortune changes the fate of man! Success finds an eraser of crimes, for which party managers had sought in vain; and the noise of triumph too often drowns the voice that cries out against corruption in high places. Let it be remembered by our accusers that all the charges made against Mr. Garfield were found among the records of their own investigations. Do they distrust them? An unfortunate reflection upon their party! All the charges we have made remain upon the records, and there they will remain forever. They accuse us of slander. Let them prove, not by witty evasions, not by ridicule, but by facts that the charges are false; then, and not till then, will those who expose corruption, deserve the names, 'vile slanderers and calumniators.'

"They tell us we are dead. *In memoriam* has appeared in every Republican journal throughout the land. How they long to plant the cypress over our final resting place! But, gentlemen, they sing their solemn dirges too soon. The Democrats may have been slaughtered, but like the oxen of the sun, which the companions of Ulysses butchered, the hides crawl after their tormentors.

"But what are the principles for adherence to which we are so denounced? Look at the word democracy itself, 'the rule of the people.' That is the fundamental idea of the party, and a government by the people is the form which we desire. Contrast this with the form proposed by Hamilton, that aristocrat who has been represented, during the last campaign, as the embodiment of sagacity, wisdom, and statesmanship. His plan was that the president should hold office for life, or during good behavior, and that the governors of the

244

states should be appointed by him. He feared and distrusted the people, chose for his model the English government, and once declared that Cæsar, who had the courage to take and destroy the power of the people, was the greatest man who had ever lived. Against Hamilton and the followers of Hamilton the Democratic party has raised and will forever raise, its voice.

"We want no one-man power. The people are equal before the law and are *supreme*. They waked this new world from its sleep of ages; they drove the savage red man toward the setting sun and turned his fertile hunting grounds into fields of waving grain; they made the mountain torrents turn the mighty mill wheels; back and forth, the busy shuttles flew to do their bidding. Armed with the strength of conscious right, they freed themselves from English oppression. France trembled before them, and Mexico acknowledges their power. A civil war has been put down by their arms. Their history covers an hundred years of unparalleled progress; why should we distrust them now or take from them the power they have so nobly used?

"Again, we believe in the superiority of civil law to military rule. Hancock, acting upon this principle, won the admiration of all who were not blinded by party zeal or sectional hatred. We believe in a free press and free speech—twin guardians of liberty.

"We believe in the entire separation of Church and State for the benefit of both. Read, by the light of the fagot and the torch, the history of the bloody deeds perpetrated during those long years when Church and State joined forces and crushed opposition by the heel of power. Hear, in the agonizing cries of martyred heroes, as they come with mournful cadence from the darkness of the middle ages, that solemn voice warning us against the dangers of so terrible a union. We stand upon the Constitution. The general government has powers delegated to it, and the powers not delegated to it are reserved to the states and to the people. Thus reads the Constitution. Who can doubt the wisdom of the provision?

"We believe in free schools, fostered and protected. Are you proud of the school laws of Illinois? They were made before the Republican party was born, and will still live when weeping willows shade the sod which hides its lifeless form. Education is necessary to self-government. The schoolhouse is the dearest friend of a free people. Intellectual and moral development is the only safeguard against corruption. God speed the day when education shall banish bigotry from every mind, when the man of learning will stoop to help the man less fortunate and confess himself superior only in his ability to do greater good.

"These are some of the principles which the Democratic party cherishes, and these are the pillars upon which our government stands. Behold these massive columns fashioned by the hands of those who built more wisely than they knew, as, unimpaired, they continue to give stability and permanence to the grand structure that rises above them. Is the party dead? No, it still lives; and standing, Samson-like with its arms around these mighty columns, it will die only when this governmental fabric shall fall, involving parties, freedom, and human hopes in one common ruin."

While others of this period will be reproduced in his collection of speeches to be published later, I venture to add a few paragraphs from one of the orations which he prepared during his school life. This oration we found in an old purple-backed notebook written in a cramped, boyish hand.

"We may not, my fellow classmates, be able to declare like a Whitefield or a Beecher, the 'glad tidings of great joy.' We may not, as did Washington and Lincoln, receive the nation's highest honor. We may not equal in eloquence Webster, Calhoun, and Clay. The Muses may not lead us to those lofty heights of poetry and song which Bryant and Longfellow were able to reach. Our names may not be written with those of Choate and Prentiss as the champion defenders of justice, yet in our humble calling, whatever it may be, we can stand in the protection of our country's trust. * * *

> " 'To some we find the
> Ploughshare's annual toil assigned;
> Some at the sounding anvil glow;
> Some the swift sliding shuttle throw;
> Some, studious of the wind and tide,
> From pole to pole our commerce guide;
> While some, with genius more refined,
> With head and tongue assist mankind.'

"No class of man can cease from labor. There is a place for all, there is a work for all. No drones are needed in the human hive. The idle are not only unnecessary, but dangerous to society. * * *

"Nature has given the material. Man must shape it. It is possible to grow in size, but strength comes only with exercise. No one can become strong in body without much patient, and we may say, continued labor, for no sooner does he relax his efforts than the receding tide bears him back whence he started. Intelligence is necessary to direct physical force, and the training of the mind, like that of the body, is accomplished slowly and steadily. Success, glory, and honor have been placed as the reward of the diligent; defeat, misery, and shame are the lot of the idle.

"We value that most which has cost us most of toil. Gold is more precious than silver because it is more difficult to procure. Marble brings a higher price when polished than in the crude state because labor is necessary to bring it to perfection. Natural talent does not remove the necessity for labor. Even the flame of genius burns more brightly when fanned by busy hands. Indeed, it would cease to exist if not employed.

" 'The lamp of genius, though by nature lit,
    If not protected, pruned and fed with care,
        Soon dies, or runs to waste with fitful glare.' * * *

"We are so bound together in the relationship of life that each one exerts an influence upon those about him, and is in turn affected by their actions. Nor is influence ended by the confines of the tomb. History is made up of the words and deeds of men. We must employ our every talent and quicken our every energy, or yield our places to others more willing to toil than ourselves. Cities have been built; magnificent structures speak of the powers of man; moving palaces plough the ocean; the iron horse speeds over the prairies, hills, and valleys; nations and continents converse through whispering wires; colleges and universities of learning are scattered through the land; wise men are rising to take the lead in law, in science, and in the ministry. * * *
"An infinity of the unknown lies before us. It stands open and invitingly to all."

An epoch in his career as a speaker came at the age of twenty-seven, shortly after we went to Nebraska. He had spoken in a town in the western part of the state, came home on a night train, and arrived at daybreak. I was sleeping when he came in, and he awakened me. Sitting on the edge of the bed, he began: "Mary, I have had a strange experience. Last night I found that I had power over the audience. I could move them as I chose. I have more than usual power as a speaker. I know it. God grant I may use it wisely." And as it was his custom all through life to carry to his Heavenly Father any new development, he prayed.

This was the beginning of that power which was his— explain it as you like. I speak positively of his power, for I have seen proofs. For years I attended political meetings. Social functions might be crowded out, but political meetings went on forever, and from the platform I saw it all. If conditions were favorable, his mood was transmitted to his listeners. He smiled, and the smile rippled away over his audience; he frowned, and so did they; he grew tense with emotion, they bent forward and sat upon the very edge of the seats.

Nor was the power over an audience shown only in these moods. An unusual instance may be cited at a meeting in the summer following the campaign of 1896. Mr. Bryan spoke in a little Utah mining town. The surrounding mountains were so high that the valley in early afternoon was already in shadow. He spoke from the second-story balcony of the railway station to a great audience of miners with mine lamps on their caps. Mr. Bryan had just suffered a defeat. He was speaking to them after an unsuccessful struggle. But his youth and his deep earnestness rang to his audience on every clear note of his voice. While he was speaking, the shadows had deepened. It was twilight when he closed his speech with the statement that "all his life, whether in victory or defeat, he would fight the battles of the common people. His life was pledged to their cause through all the years to come."

With his closing phrase, there came the moment when applause conventionally follows, but none came. There was a deep silence, and one miner after another took off his cap, until that great crowd was standing with bared and bowed heads. His mood of consecration had carried to them.

After a tense pause such a roar of cheers filled the valley as sent echoes rattling back from the hills; a clamor of applause.

When Mr. Bryan and our little girl and I came down to enter our carriage, the miners crowded forward to shake his hand, but again the crowd had grown still, and so full of emotion were they that they could scarcely speak their words of gratitude and affection, and those who could not reach his hand, put out their hands to touch him.

A phase of his oratory which is not well known is his debating. In his campaigns for Congress formal challenges to debate were sent to his opponents and accepted. These debates were held in the larger towns of the district and attended by thousands.

He used the same plan in debate which he used in the discussion of any issue, namely, to study both sides of the question. He was quite as familiar with the arguments he expected to combat as with those he expected to advance.

These debates interested me more than any form of discussion. Knowing both sides, Mr. Bryan was able to set little traps for his opponents. When he had the opening speech, he would deliberately seem to leave open a loop-hole; the enemy would seize upon the weakness only to find a danger lurking within, for his closing speech would clamp down the argument like the teeth of a steel trap.

The neatness of his work may be shown in the closing speech of his first Congressional campaign, the last of a series of debates with Mr. Connell.

"Mr. Connell: We now bring to a close this series of debates which was arranged by our committees. I am glad that we have been able to conduct these discussions in a courteous and friendly manner. If I have in any way offended you in word or deed I offer apology and express regret and as freely forgive. I desire to present to you in remembrance of these pleasant meet-ings this little volume, because it contains 'Gray's Elegy,' in perusing which I trust you will find as much pleasure and profit as I have. It is one of the most beautiful and touching tributes to humble life that literature contains. Grand in its sentiment and sub-lime in its simplicity, we may both find in it a solace in victory or defeat. If success should crown your efforts in this campaign, and it should be your lot 'Th' applause of list'ning senates to command,' and I am left

> " 'A youth to fortune and to fame unknown,'

forget not us who in the common walks of life perform our part, but in the hour of your triumph recall the lines:

> " 'Let not ambition mock their useful toil,
>   Their homely joys and destiny obscure;
> Nor grandeur hear, with a disdainful smile,
>   The short and simple annals of the poor.'

"If, on the other hand, by the verdict of my country-men, I shall be made your successor, let it not be said of you:

> " 'And melancholy marked him for her own,'

but find sweet consolation in the thought:

> " 'Full many a gem of purest ray serene,
>   The dark unfathomed caves of ocean bear;
> Full many a flower is born to blush unseen,
>   And waste its sweetness on the desert air.'

"But whether the palm of victory is given to you or to me, let us remember those of whom the poet says:

WILLIAM JENNINGS BRYAN

" 'Far from the madding crowd's ignoble strife,
Their sober wishes never learn'd to stray;
Along the cool sequester'd vale of life
They kept the noiseless tenor of their way.'

"These are the ones most likely to be forgotten by the government. When the poor and the weak cry out for relief they, too, often hear no answer but 'the echo of their cry,' while the rich, the strong, the powerful are given an attentive ear. For this reason is class legislation dangerous and deadly; it takes from those least able to lose and gives to those who are least in need. The safety of our farmers and our laborers is not in special legislation, but in equal and just laws that bear alike on every man. The great masses of our people are interested, not in getting their hands into other people's pockets, but in keeping the hands of other people out of their pockets.

"Let me in parting express the hope that you and I may be instrumental in bringing our government back to better laws which will give equal treatment without regard to creed or condition. I bid you a friendly farewell."

From writing and committing speeches to memory, Mr. Bryan passed to speaking from notes and wrote nothing unless the speech was of official importance.

In any story of his oratorical equipment, his voice must find a place. A wife may be considered an incompetent witness and on this point I confess enthusiasm.

Among the losses the world has suffered by Mr. Bryan's going, the stilling of his voice is to me most irreparable. I speak now of his voice, not of what he said. When he had attained sufficient skill to dispense with manuscripts and really speak, the beauty of his voice was revealed. There was in it a reverberating quality—vibratory hardly expresses it. Upon occasions when he was especially moved I have heard his tones ring out with bell-like clearness and resound far beyond the circle of his hearers. As years passed, this quality grew less, but never was entirely lost. Few voices have ever equaled his in carrying power. Many instances might be cited. I mention one.

During the winter of 1898–99 Mr. Bryan spoke in Corpus Christi, Texas. I was tired and did not go to the meeting. I was reading in my upstairs room when I heard some one speak. I went to the open window and found that Mr. Bryan was talking. I listened several minutes, hearing every word quite clearly. Next morning I asked how far the meeting had been from the house and found that it was three long blocks distant.

The skill with which he used his voice was natural, no forcing or straining. When in school he had a few lessons in so-called elocution, but not enough to change his methods. His intonation and emphasis were excellent and his gestures simple and effective. His speeches were free from any stumbling or hesitating for words. His words flowed along like the steady current of a stream and always fitted the subject. Although a good Greek and Latin scholar, and appreciating the finer shades of meaning, he used the simple words and the more colloquial expressions. Uneducated people caught his meaning and understood as clearly as the learned.

Among debates, the one I remember best is the closing debate of his second Congressional campaign. To begin with, I felt more interest in this than in any other campaign, presidential not excepted. It seemed to me most necessary that he should win, as he was not sufficiently established in national affairs to withstand a defeat.

The district had been gerrymandered and was more hopelessly Republican than ever. Lincoln, then a town of sixty thousand, furnished the opposing candidate. He was a judge and had lived there longer than we. Interest became so intense that when the time came for the last debate no place could be found large enough for the crowd except the ball park—a huge place with a semicircle of bleachers facing east and a platform built for speakers in the space in front.

That year the tariff was the main question. Anticipating this campaign the winter before, when in Old Mexico, Mr. Bryan and I had made a tour of the hardware shops of Mexico City, and as we had suspected, we found American cutlery selling for much less there than it sold for in the United States, some articles costing fifty per cent less. This fact seemed to prove to the friends of tariff reduction that the tariff wall enabled the manufacturers to charge the American consumer any price he chose, and then dump the surplus on the foreign market, and still make money on a twenty-five to fifty per cent reduction. We bought several articles—particularly pocketknives and butcher knives of different sizes—put them into a neat handbag, and Mr. Bryan produced his wares at the first debate. The effect was good. People saw the point, with the result that our opponent shortly appeared with cutlery too—although to Democratic ears his arguments were not convincing.

The night of the debate found everything in readiness. Bleachers were filled with eager people; arc lights turned night into day; ice water was put on a table for the speakers. Thomas Stinson Allen (stanch Democrat and Chairman of the Congressional Campaign) was concealed under the platform with a large floral pillow mounted upon a standard. Stretching diagonally across the pillow was the word "Eloquence." This floral piece was to be presented to Mr. Bryan at the close of the evening.

The two debaters arrived, each with his handbag of cutlery. Mr. Bryan had the opening speech and was getting under way when the wind freshened a bit, and from the southeast advanced the vanguard of a dust storm. A low-hung brownish cloud swept through the park, enveloped everything, and passed on. At intervals cloud after cloud came and went. At times we could not see the speakers or the platform. Sometimes shouts were in order and we shouted, swallowing our quota of dust without a murmur. Did anyone leave? As far as I know, not one.

Mr. Bryan spoke with his usual fire, and his opponent advanced to the fray in good form except that he was at times a little confused. When he rounded a period with "Germany and the other islands of the sea," the Democrats jeered exultingly.

And, after refuting Mr. Bryan's statements on wire nails, when he wished to enlarge the field and was evidently trying to mention "wire bed springs," he said, "And wire-wire-wire bed *quilts!*" The delight of the great unwashed (a most appropriate expression for a dust storm) knew no bounds. The loyal Republicans stood firm for their man and cheered again and again.

The last speech by Mr. Bryan was the usual summing up of arguments with clearness, rapidity, and rapier-like thrusts. The close was a scene of cheers and counter cheers, clapping, stamping, whistling, confusion and clamoring, but no riotous disorder. There may have been one or two policemen present, but I cannot now recall one. Democrats, so long in the minority and rejoicing that they now had some one to voice their feeling, hurried to the platform, crowding the aisles, to shake hands with their defender.

After several minutes a voice issued from under the platform: "Say, make room there! Let me out!" And then emerged our good T. S. Allen with the floral tribute. The psychological moment had passed. Few people saw the word "Eloquence," but we carried the piece home with the accompanying thought that even if they had not seen the word, they had felt the power.

As I am making a picture of that time, I venture to finish the story.

Election came the following Tuesday. The vote was

so close that the result was in doubt. Outlying counties must settle the matter. Wednesday found both head-quarters crowded. A telegram came which elected the Republican by 116 votes—out marched the Republicans, and with hurrahs and horns celebrated the victory, while gloom settled upon the other headquarters. Perhaps before they had finished their march, the returns came from another county electing the Democrat by 54 votes. The Republicans slunk back and the Democrats marched proudly out and a new set of hurrahs arose. No one could settle down to work. This swinging back and forth continued all day Wednesday and all night. I went down town Thursday and men came to speak to me, so hoarse they could only whisper; all showed lack of sleep, but were resolute. Men took turns at night guarding the ballot boxes.

On Wednesday noon more than a hundred women were to give a parting luncheon to a friend who was leaving Lincoln. I was to toast the guest. That morning things looked dark for us. The Republicans seemed to have it. I knew the wife of our opponent would be there, and the majority of the women were Republicans. I felt at first I could not go—am afraid I cried a little—but my pride led me to dry my eyes, dress as nicely as I could, and go to congratulate our enemy. I had a little speech ready. The successful candidate's wife was there, surrounded by friends, all happy and smiling.

Shortly after I came I was called from the room. Word had been telephoned up from headquarters that later returns gave the election to Mr. Bryan by 75 votes. What a load off my heart! I could smile too. The Republicans, not having the latest news, were jubilant and so was I. I did not make my speech of congratulation.

On Thursday it was decided that an official count must be taken, and Friday afternoon the result made Mr. Bryan the winner by 140 majority.

Perhaps I have given too much space to this campaign, but it may be justified by the hope that this book may live, and that readers fifty years hence may find interest in a picture of the time when people took a personal interest in their policies and in their candidates.

The great Ecumenical Conference was held in Edinburgh in May, 1911. Perhaps a more distinguished body of clergy never was assembled, leaders in mission work coming from all over the world. Mr. Bryan was in England and cabled me to meet him in Edinburgh. I had not intended making this journey and seemed to be needed at home, but decided to go. I was rather proud of the fact that I went, attended the conference, motored about in Scotland, returned, and reached Fairview, our Nebraska home, in exactly four weeks.

So many notable people were present at the Conference that the mornings were given over to speeches limited to three minutes. I was interested to watch what the different people were able to accomplish in so short a time, and was particularly proud of the American delegates. These eliminated all introductions and preliminaries, and beginning, "I wish to say, first—second—third," and in three minutes had stated their position quite fully. Some could not condense and wasted time on nonessentials. Of course I was pleased when Mr. Bryan was asked to take an evening service and make an address in the great Cathedral, and the following Sunday was asked to speak in the leading church in Glasgow, which he did.

We went to the Cathedral—that solemn pile whose walls have echoed the voices of so many prominent divines. The edifice was crowded. We were met in the vestry by several clergymen, and Mr. Bryan went to the pulpit while I sat in one of the front seats with those who had joined us. Dr. James Stalker, known the world over for his clear ideas on theology, sat beside me. Because I had read two or three of his books, his name meant something to me. He was

WILLIAM JENNINGS BRYAN

evidently not quite sure about Mr. Bryan and looked him over indifferently. Mr. Bryan's subject was "The Fruits of the Tree." He had put the address in shape while crossing the ocean. He read his text from the last chapter of Revelation, second verse: "In the midst of the street of it, and on either side of the river, was there the tree of life, which bare twelve manner of fruits, and yielded her fruit every month; and the leaves of the tree were for the healing of the nations," and remarked that his subject naturally divided itself into twelve heads. A chill ran down my spine. Twelve! Even the driest and most hardened seldom went beyond *sixthly*. It was a question whether an audience even of Scots would tolerate a *twelfthly*.

But I had no reason to be anxious. Mr. Bryan began to discuss the "twelve manner of fruits," the interest grew, and a rumbling sound, deep and inarticulate, rose from Dr. Stalker, which proved to be his first, "Hear, hear!" Shortly another, more clear and emphatic, "Hear, hear!" Then he hastily exchanged his spectacles for a pair of more distant vision and gazed at the speaker. Soon he augmented his applause by stamping with his cane, and until the end of the speech, no old political friend could have been more enthusiastic.

His attitude was typical. If prejudice existed in the audience, it disappeared. Indifference was changed to interest; suspicion gave place to confidence, and a critical spirit became one of hearty approval.

The same eloquence which had held his hearers in the dust storm echoed through the Cathedral and the concourse of critical scholars paid him the highest honor.

When he became an older man he received many letters from young speakers asking for advice and suggestions. Below is his reply.

"Webster, the great orator, said of eloquence that it must exist 'in the man, in the subject, and in the occasion.' And then he proceeded to elaborate the statement, showing that it was a combination of high purpose, firm resolve, and dauntless spirit, speaking from every feature and reaching the heart of the hearer. There are two things absolutely essential to eloquence. First, the speaker must know what he is talking about, and, second, he must mean what he says. Nothing can take the place of knowledge of the subject and earnestness. To these other things can be added, such as clearness of statement, felicity of expression, aptness in illustration, beauty in ornamentation and grace in delivery.

"Eloquence is heart speaking to heart. There is no mistaking the cry of terror or the shout of joy, and so there is no misunderstanding the sincere message that passes from heart to heart.

"The young man who would fit himself for real influence in the forum must himself feel deeply upon the subjects which he discusses, and he cannot feel deeply without being in full sympathy with those whom he addresses. He must also be able to give them information which they do not possess or to state what they know more forcibly than they can state it themselves.

"The young man ambitious to stand as the representative of his people—not as an official nominally speaking for them, but as a man actually voicing their aspirations and giving utterance to their hopes—such a young man is advised to read the address entitled, 'The People in Art, Government and Religion,' delivered by George Bancroft at Williams College in 1835. (It will be found in Volume VII of Modern Eloquence, known as Reed's Collection of Speeches.) This oration is one of the greatest tributes ever paid to the common people, and it will furnish not only thought, but inspiration to young men. It defends not only the rights of the people, but the capacity of the people for self-government, and declares not that 'the people can make right,' but that 'the people can discern right.' This admirable address is referred to because of the sound advice that it gives to young men, advice that is pertinent in this connection.

"Bancroft says: 'Let the young aspirants after glory scatter seeds of truth broadcast on the wide bosom of humanity, in the deep fertile soil of the public mind. There it will strike root and spring up and bear a hundred-fold and bloom for ages and ripen fruit through remote generations.'

"The difference between a demagogue and a statesman is that the former advocates what he thinks will be popular, regardless of the effect that it may ultimately have upon the people to whom he appeals; the statesman advocates what he believes to be the best for the country regardless of the immediate effect which it may have upon himself. One is willing to sacrifice the permanent interests of others to advance his own temporary interests, while the other is willing to sacrifice his own temporary interests to advance the public welfare. While the conduct of the statesman may seem unselfish, and is unselfish in the usual acceptation of that term, yet it is really an enlightened selfishness, for no man, when he takes a broad view of his own interests, can afford to accept an advantage which comes to him at the expense of his country. The statesman is building upon a firmer foundation than the demagogue, and in the end will find a more substantial reward for his self-denial than the demagogue will be able to secure for himself.

"It has been said that the orator, more than anyone else, needs information upon all subjects, for questions that are no longer matters of controversy can be used as matters of argument, and no one can speak so well of the future as he who is well acquainted with the past.

GROWTH OF ORATORICAL POWER

"A knowledge of human nature is necessary to the orator. Pope has said that the proper study of mankind is man, and in the study of man the heart is the most interesting as well as the most important subject of investigation. He who would succeed in public speaking must understand that a sense of justice is to be found in every heart, and that that sense of justice is the safest foundation upon which to build a government. Bancroft, in the address above referred to, declares that popular government is the strongest government in the world, because 'discarding the implements of terror, it dares to rule by moral force and has its citadel in the heart.'

"Moral courage is indispensable to the orator. A man cannot speak eloquently while he is running from the enemy; neither can he inspire courage if his knees smite each other, and there is a tremor in his voice. Courage rests upon conviction; a man has no convictions to speak of, who is not willing to endure suffering in support of them.

"The orator must have faith—faith in God, faith in the righteousness of his cause, and faith in the ultimate triumph of the truth. Believing that right makes might, believing that every word spoken for truth and every act done in behalf of truth contributes to the final victory, he does his duty, more anxious to help the cause which he espouses than to enjoy the fruits of victory.

"And, finally, let the ambitious young man understand that he is in duty bound to discard everything which in the least weakens his strength, and under obligation to do everything that in any degree increases his power to do good. Good habits, therefore, are always important, and may become vitally so. He can well afford to leave liquor to those who desire to tickle the throat or to please the appetite; it will be no help to him in his effort to advance the welfare of his fellows. He can even afford to put into books what others put into tobacco. The volumes purchased will adorn his shelves for a lifetime, while smoke from a cigar is soon lost to sight forever. He does not need to swear; logic is more convincing than oaths. Let him feed his body with food convenient for it, remembering that food is only useful in so far as it strengthens man for his work; let him train his mind to search for the truth, remembering that his power to discern the truth will increase with the effort to find it. Let him keep his heart diligently, for 'out of it are the issues of life.' Let him recognize service as the measure of greatness, and estimate life by its outgo rather than by its income. Let him to himself be true, 'and it follows as the night the day, he cannot then be false to any man.' "

CHAPTER V

PRIVATE LIFE OF A CANDIDATE

MR. BRYAN in his Memoirs has dealt at length with the Chicago Convention and the circumstances which led up to his nomination for the Presidency in 1896. But while his record ceases with the fact of his nomination, and while history records the balloting which gave the election to his opponent, William McKinley, the following November, nothing is recorded on that peculiar subject, the private life of a candidate, if, indeed, a candidate can be said to possess a private life.

Up to the time of his first nomination a few pages will suffice to record the outline of our busy, quiet days.

In our new home in Nebraska and in Washington, during Mr. Bryan's years as Congressman, we lived serenely. The care of my father, who, by that time, had become totally blind, and of my mother, an invalid, and of my three young children, together with my close participation in all of Mr. Bryan's legal and political work, filled my years. Mr. Bryan had applied himself unremittingly, and though we were progressing steadily up the ladder which ambitious youth may ascend, the first nomination found Mr. Bryan and me, at thirty-six and thirty-five years of age, a very serious, quietly prosperous, closely congenial couple.

Upon our small household suddenly shone the white light which is said to beat upon the throne. Our very house had altered its appearance when we returned home to it from the Chicago Convention. Streamers of bunting festooned it from porch to eaves; small boys sat in rows along the roof; the crowd which filled the front yard overflowed into the house; flowers and smilax decorated the crowded rooms. It was a symbolic atmosphere. The public had invaded our lives.

WILLIAM JENNINGS BRYAN

There must be certain features which are common to the lives of all Presidential candidates. I think Mr. Bryan's conscientious desire to reply personally to every correspondent and to admit the inquiring reporter into every recess of his life, may have intensified some of these features in his case. The mail poured in upon us and inundated our little home. Letters of congratulation, commendation, and abuse; inquiries on every known and unknown subject, and much advice generously bestowed by the public. It is indeed a humble citizen who cannot advise a political leader. While it is recognized that technical training is necessary to produce a doctor, a lawyer, or a clergyman, a multitude will rise up, apparently without study or even thought, to shower advice upon a political candidate. But while giving the candidate advice upon his own business, the public do not fail to ask his counsel upon their most intimate concerns. The candidate is asked to advise on domestic relations, to furnish material for debates and essays, and to give his judgment on innumerable manuscripts of varying length. Some manuscripts, which would have required from a week to a month of careful study, were submitted during a busy campaign, and the senders would indignantly protest if the candidate did not give their efforts his mature consideration.

The demands for autographs were not so difficult to satisfy, even though these were numerous. Occasionally their form was varied to include writing the autograph on a sofa pillow, a tablecloth, or a piece of material to be later embroidered and incorporated in that sort of bed covering so fittingly termed a "crazy quilt." Often such sofa pillow tops or table covers would be lost in the mails, and we would receive a series of abusive and threatening letters demanding their return.

Then there were the prophets and the seers who had predicted Mr. Bryan's nomination by the position of the stars, or tea leaves, or sand, or other mysterious methods, and having predicted his nomination, offered also to forecast the election. There were thousands who had had dreams and visions of prophetic content. One man, I remember, wrote a letter telling Mr. Bryan that he had seen in a dream Mr. Bryan's election. He offered furthermore, if the candidate should request it, to dream again and find out what the statistical majority would be. The number of our prophets in America is surprising and bewildering.

It is natural that a public man should be the storm center for requests of benevolence and charity, and that the petitions for aid should run the entire gamut from the request from a total stranger for a pink silk dress or a bicycle, to a petition for a new church building—requests equally beyond the means of a young lawyer struggling to adjust his finances to the new demands.

Great numbers of churches augmented their finances in 1896 by doll and handkerchief sales: "We hope you will dress a doll for us. It will not mean much to you," they would write, to the harassed wife of the candidate, who had in the same mail received several identical requests. We bought and dispatched dolls by the dozen and handkerchiefs by the gross. There were a number of devices for raising church funds which required time and science as well as benevolence. There were cards to which had been attached a little pair of overalls, with the request that the victim measure his own waist and then place in the little breeches pocket one penny for each inch of his girth. In other similar devices the candidate was penalized for each pound of his weight or each inch of his stature. Many churches and schools issued cookbooks compiled from the favorite recipes of well-known people, and I paid for the honor of a place among their number by broadcasting my culinary methods through the pages of these volumes.

But while we were struggling to satisfy the demands made upon us, we were in our turn receiving gifts. A stuffed alligator of tremendous size, so long that its tail protruded its scaly length from the back of the express wagon, and also from every room in our house where we tried to place it, and four live eagles of prodigious size and strength, were among the largest gifts. After trying in vain to place the alligator in the house, we were obliged to lodge him in our back yard until the University Museum came to our aid and housed him amongst its treasures.

I recently found amongst our papers a small notebook in which we recorded, as they arrived, the gifts received at our home during the first Presidential campaign. This book awakens vivid memories of those days, when waves of friendly delegations inundated our garden and, receding, left in their wake demolished flower beds and shattered trellises. Here follow a few items from our notebook:

> One set of harness.
> One pair of suspenders.
> One cane.
> One band wagon.
> One mule.
> One silk bed quilt.
> A large watermelon in a gilded laundry basket (this was enthusiastically received by the children).
> One dog.
> Four volumes of Thomas Jefferson's works.
> One ostrich egg.
> One cane.
> One picture frame made from cigar boxes.
> One frosted cake.
> One silver plate with presentation inscription.
> One cane.
> One cane.
> One cane.

As canes were, perhaps, our most frequent gift, some of these deserve very special mention. It takes ingenuity to make a walking stick from the vertebræ of a fish, or from petrified wood, or from the horns of the antelope. And we must add to this list a cane made from macerated newspaper editorials. This strange material was then pressed into the shape of a cane and lacquered on the outside. There were canes made of bone with loaded heads; made of the pith of the cactus plant; of rattan, and of rings of pressed leather; canes of bogwood from Ireland; canes made of hickory from Andrew Jackson's birthplace, and of cherry, presumably from George Washington's cherry tree; canes with silver heads, decorated with a daisy with sixteen silver petals and one gold, and in some cases canes with gold heads, voted by church fairs to the most popular candidate. I remember one of these canes, the head of which represented an eagle whose eyes were made of diamonds, until after a large public reception, when we found that his eyes had mysteriously disappeared.

Then there were the natural phenomena; fungi with the strange resemblance to the candidate, and the egg with the curious conformation of shell which suggested his initials, etc.

The term "sixteen to one" took hold upon the popular imagination, and we would receive a potato with sixteen sprouts to one potato; an ancient Phœnician vase with sixteen handles to one vase. I recall seeing in a political parade an ingenious development of the idea of bimetallism. Borne high on a standard was a huge replica of the silver dollar (the dollar at that time contained 53 cents in silver bullion). High upon the standard was the inscription "In God we trust for the other forty-seven cents."

In no subsequent campaign has Mr. Bryan received such quantities of mascots as in the campaign of 1896. I cannot vouch for the fact that this explains his tremendous popular vote in that campaign, but for want of a more suitable place, I may as well set it down at this point.

Mr. Bryan received the largest Democratic vote ever

cast in the history of the country up to that time and exceeded by 946,007 the vote of Cleveland, who had been elected four years before. His vote in 1896 exceeded by 1,425,014 the Democratic vote cast for Parker eight years later, and his vote in 1908 exceeded by 116,984 the vote of Wilson, elected four years later.

If there be virtue in the hind foot of a rabbit procured under the most favorable circumstances, Mr. Bryan should have won this election. It is difficult to imagine that his opponent was more adequately supplied with rabbits' feet; plain, furry little feet, feet mounted in every ingenious form; horseshoes, plain, gilded, wrapped in tinfoil and in ribbon, came to us with such frequency that they are not included in the notebook record.

The bizarre election bets also seem to have become less frequent in succeeding campaigns, but in 1896 there were large numbers of men who had been so certain of a Democratic victory that they wagered recklessly, and after election found themselves pledged to abstain from shaving for the term of their natural life, to hauling their Republican friends around the town in a wheelbarrow, to rolling a peanut interminable distances, or riding a donkey from New York to San Francisco. I recall the day when the last-named individual called at our house in Lincoln in the course of his donkey pilgrimage. He was maintaining himself by selling photographs of his beast and its trappings and patent medicines. We felt in a sense personally responsible for his weary journey.

Several men wrote to Mr. Bryan and indignantly demanded reimbursement for the loss of money and time occasioned by their election bets. One man, I recall, wrote and told us that he had lost in an election bet on Mr. Bryan the money which he had intended to use to mend his roof. "My house is leaking badly," he wrote. "Please send the money at once." Another man said that he had bet his cow on the election and wrung the heart of the candidate by a story of his children left without milk by this reversal of fortune.

If these seem unusual demands upon the purse of a candidate, we had even more tenuous claims to consider. During a trip into the far West, Mr. Bryan's approach to a city had been heralded by a volley of loud explosions. On our return to Nebraska Mr. Bryan received a bill for $87.00, as nearly as I can recall it, the amount computed by a chicken raiser as the sum he had lost when the eggs which he had placed in an incubator had been prevented from hatching by the concussion of the gunpowder.

The kindness and good will which was represented in the gifts and other evidences of friendliness received by Mr. Bryan during a campaign warmed his heart and amply compensated him for incidents which were trying and discouraging. The mementoes of the early political days were always treasured by him and are now treasured by his family.

One of the most valued gifts, and one which bespeaks unmistakably the faith and devotion of the sender, is the photograph of a namesake baby. In 1896 our daughter Ruth made the namesake babies her particular charge and pride. When a letter was received telling of a new little "William Jennings," or another little "Bryan," Ruth claimed him proudly and recorded his arrival. Those were special days when we received the three photographs of three sets of triplets having been given respectively the names "William," "Jennings," and "Bryan." One mother wrote a letter saying she had heard that Mr. Bryan's family treasured the liknesses of the namesake babies, but that her baby had not lived long and they had no photograph of the little boy to whom they had given the name of "Bryan," but she enclosed in her letter two pieces of cloth, one from the baby's christening dress and one from his shroud, and asked that these be kept along with the pictures of the living babies who bore Mr. Bryan's name, and there they have remained during the years.

CHAPTER VI

Soldier and Editor

WHEN, after a vigorous campaign for the Presidency, Mr. Bryan received news, on November 5, 1896, that his opponent had been elected, his first act was to send the following telegram:

> Lincoln, Nebraska
> November 5
>
> Honorable William McKinley,
> Canton, Ohio
> Senator Jones has just informed me that the returns indicate your election, and I hasten to extend my congratulations. We have submitted the issue to the American people and their will is law.
>
> W. J. Bryan.

President-elect McKinley wired the following response:

> Canton, Ohio
> November 6
>
> Honorable W. J. Bryan
> Lincoln, Nebraska
> I acknowledge the receipt of your courteous message of congratulation with thanks and beg you will receive my best wishes for your health and happiness.
>
> William McKinley.

This exchange of courtesies received much comment at the time, but Mr. Bryan, in his book, "The First Battle," wrote of it:

> "Our contest aroused no personal feeling on the part of either. I have no doubt that had I been elected, he would as promptly have sent his congratulations."

270

WILLIAM J. BRYAN.
LINCOLN NEBRASKA

April 25 — 1898

Hon William McKinley
President

My Dear Sir —
I hereby place my services at your command during the war with Spain and assure you of my willingness to perform to the best of my ability any duty to which you, as the commander in chief of the army and navy, may see fit to assign me.
Respectfully. Yours
W. J. Bryan

Letter from Mr. Bryan to President McKinley volunteering his personal services in the Spanish-American War.

WILLIAM JENNINGS BRYAN

In 1894, after Mr. Bryan's defeat for the United States Senate, he became chief of the editorial staff of the Omaha *World-Herald*, which position he held until his first nomination for the Presidency, and he contributed various political articles to the *World-Herald* and other newspapers after he had given up his position as editor-in-chief; but in 1898 circumstances arose which directed Mr. Bryan's life for a while into unforeseen paths. America had become involved

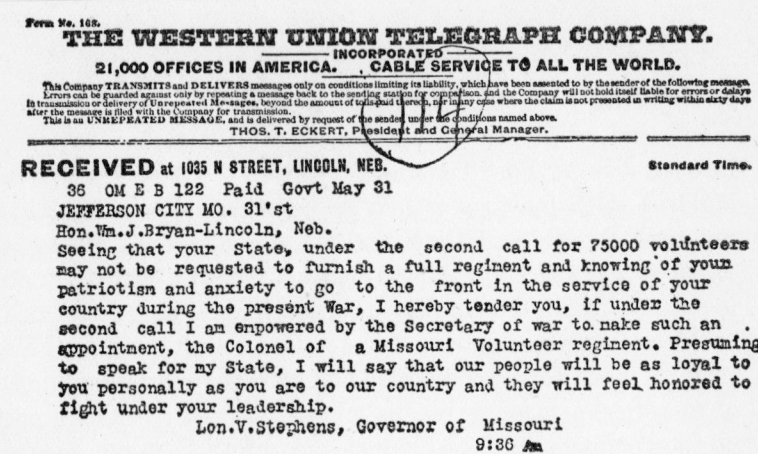

in the war with Spain and on April 25, 1898, Mr. Bryan sent to President McKinley the offer of his services in any capacity. Mr. Bryan had been authorized by the Governor of Nebraska to take all necessary steps looking to the speedy formation of a provisional regiment, and in less than a week from the announcement of his intention, Mr. Bryan received applications from over thirty organizations for a place in his command. From these he selected twelve, recognizing each of the six Congressional districts of his State. The Governor of Missouri had telegraphed, asking Mr. Bryan to serve as colonel of a Missouri regiment, but Mr. Bryan replied in the following telegram:

SOLDIER AND EDITOR

Honorable Lon V. Stephens

Jefferson City, Missouri

I am deeply indebted to you for the great honor you do me. I should be pleased to be associated in any capacity with the Missouri volunteers, but it is quite certain that all or a considerable portion of my regiment will be accepted, and I feel that my first duty is to the Nebraska boys.

W. J. BRYAN.

On July 13, 1898, the Third Nebraska Volunteer Regiment, under Colonel William Jennings Bryan, was mustered into service at Fort Omaha, Nebraska. I had taken the children with me to see their father take command of his regiment for the first time, and we watched as he rode out on *Governor*, his shiny black Kentucky horse, which we all loved as one of the family, into the hollow square formed by his waiting regiment. As he gave his first order and his sword flashed for a moment in the sun, the motionless lines of men began to move at his command, and we felt proud of the regiment and its colonel—so proud that our hearts were pounding anxiously. Memories of those days are so vivid and the intervening time has passed so swiftly, it is difficult to realize that a stretch of years lies between the present and those tense days. We could not know when we sewed the insignia of rank on Colonel Bryan's uniform overcoat and found the tears blurring our stitches that the regiment which he raised would be stationed for months in Florida, awaiting its turn to cross the channel to active service, and that the grim enemy he would face was fever in a southern camp.

I found a yellowed newspaper clipping with date of twenty-seven years ago, which gives recognition to the soldiers who waited.

WILLIAM JENNINGS BRYAN

LET US NOT FORGET THE HEROES WHO ARE READY FOR THE FRONT

While we cry aloud the praises
  Of the heroes at the front;
Tell of deeds of valiant soldiers
  Who have borne the battle's brunt.

While we love to speak of Dewey,
  And of Sampson, and of Schley;
And we cheer the name of Hobson,
  Who was not afraid to die.

While with pride we speak of Shafter,
  And of Wheeler, and of Miles,
Who have fought so well for country
  In the proud Castilian Isles.

Then there's William Jennings Bryan,
  Just as eager now is he
For the Cuban Independence
  As that silver should be free!

While we cheer the distant soldiers,
  Who have borne the battle's brunt,
Let us not forget the heroes
  Who are ready for the front.

J. FRED DE BERRY.

To W. V. Allen, Senator from Nebraska, Mr. Bryan sent the following telegram, lest the well-intentioned efforts of friends might make request for preferential treatment of his regiment:

COLONEL WILLIAM JENNINGS BRYAN AND THE THIRD NEBRASKA VOLUNTEERS
A regiment recruited and commanded by him during the Spanish American War.